IMAGES of America

ADIRONDACK PEOPLE AND PLACES

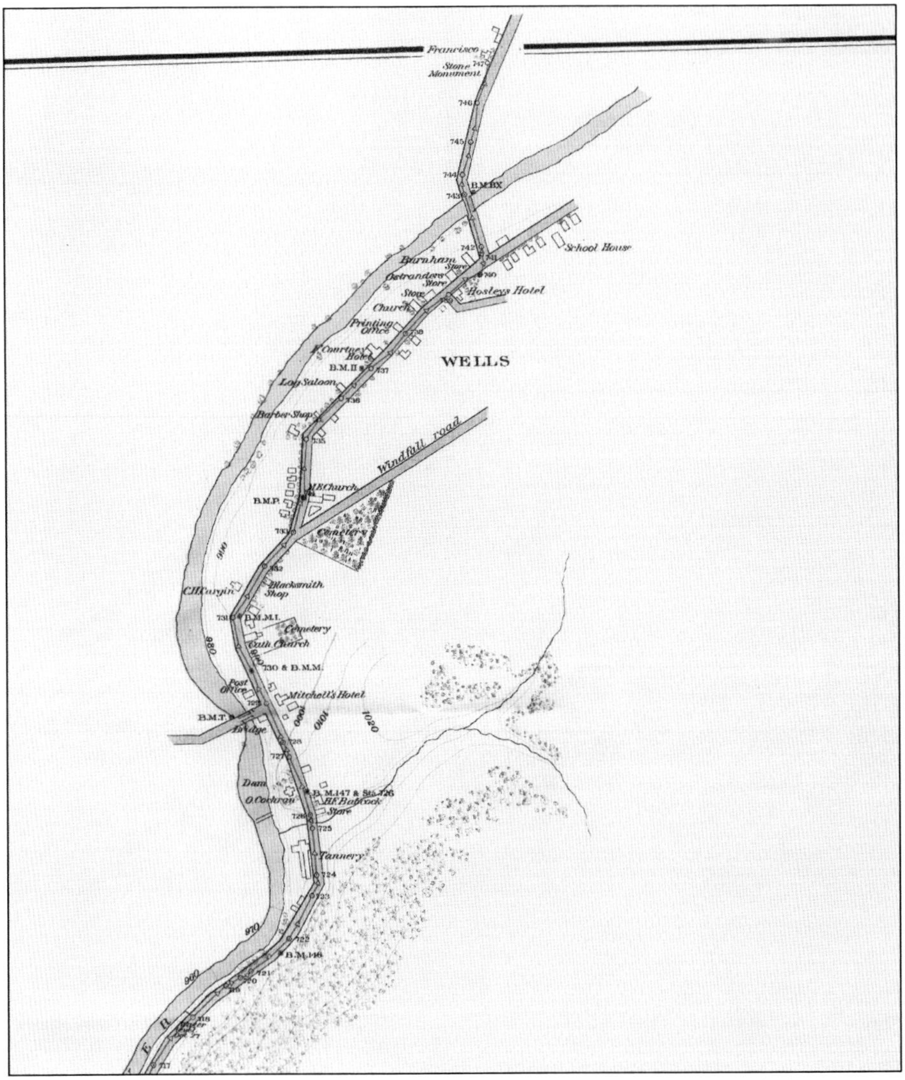

Near the end of the 19th century, it became evident that the growing Adirondack region needed a better survey and some accurate maps. Verplanck Colvin became superintendent of the New York State Land Survey and then spent a good quarter of a century surveying and making maps of the Adirondacks. His map section includes the highway between Northville and Wells, today's Route 30. Also known as the Adirondack Trail Byway, Route 30 is a historic highway with several interesting associated stories, including the "Benson Werewolf," the "Ghost of Lost Georgia," the "'Sick' Draft Dodgers," the "Indian Abduction," the "Hope Love Triangle," the "Jello 'Airport' Failure," the "Abandoned Gauging Station," and the "First New York State Campsite." (Author's collection.)

ON THE COVER: Boardinghouses played an important role in the Adirondacks for those who wanted to pursue a summer vacation out of the hot, smoky cities. Year after year, families could return to enjoy the same accommodations in the mountainous Adirondacks. Originally based on the products of the forests, the economy was largely tourist driven by the 20th century. Tourism continues to be the major industry in the Adirondacks today. (Author's collection.)

IMAGES
of America

ADIRONDACK PEOPLE AND PLACES

Donald R. Williams

ARCADIA
PUBLISHING

ISBN 978-0-7385-9169-8

Published by Arcadia Publishing
Charleston, South Carolina

Printed in the United States of America

Library of Congress Control Number: 2011941841

For all general information, please contact Arcadia Publishing:
Telephone 843-853-2070
Fax 843-853-0044
E-mail sales@arcadiapublishing.com
For customer service and orders:
Toll-Free 1-888-313-2665

Visit us on the Internet at www.arcadiapublishing.com

Dedicated to those Adirondack guides of yesteryear that opened the Adirondack country, and to all those who continue to attract visitors to one of America's most unique regions.

CONTENTS

ACKNOWLEDGMENTS

Those who record the history and lore of New York State's Adirondack region are blessed with one of the most extensive collections of regional literature in our nation, dating back to Thomas Jefferson's *Lake George* in 1791. Vintage magazines found the Adirondacks a popular subject, including the *Ladies Repository*, *Appletons' Journal*, and *Harper's Bazaar*. Travel guides by S.R. Stoddard and the Delaware and Hudson Railway, among others, collected detailed Adirondack information. Oral history was collected by Adirondack authors and published in Adirondack magazines and books. Historians amassed Adirondack stories in nonfiction volumes. Newspapers printed detailed Adirondack events. Surviving ephemera, realia, and tools also added to the wealth of information on the forested mountain-and-lake region of New York State. Talented photographers provided an unsurpassed pictorial record of the majestic mountains, sparkling waterways, rustic summer camps, lumber camps, tanneries, hunting lodges, animals, hotels, hamlets, beaches, and winter sports centers. Let us here, then, record a big thank-you to all those who helped to preserve the Adirondack story. All images in this volume appear courtesy of the author.

Introduction

English iron industry businessman Izaak Walton retired in 1643 at the age of 50 to write the definitive work on fishing. *The Compleat Angler* (using an old, variant spelling of *complete*) came to be known as "the bible of fishermen." The American version of Walton's book included the story of the America's first modern sporting club—a fishing club established at Piseco in the Adirondacks in 1840.

The sixth book in the Images of America Adirondack series, *Adirondack People and Places* somewhat completes the Adirondack story. Combined with the other five books, the series can be thought of as the "Compleat Adirondacks." A wide range of photographs and stories add to vivid bits of information that relate the story of that place called "Adirondack." The story of New York's Adirondack Mountains is told through a historical past, diverse people, unique places, unlimited pursuits, and interesting pastimes. To know the rich history of the Adirondack Region of New York State is to know the compleat Adirondacks.

Today, New York State's Adirondack Mountains are completely surrounded by the six-million-plus-acre Adirondack State Park. Within the Blue Line (the original boundary drawn on the map), the people of the state of New York own about 44 percent—known as the Adirondack Forest Preserve, state-owned lands established by the New York legislature on May 15, 1885. The 1894 Article 14 of the state constitution protects the lands within this preserve—lands that are "forever wild."

The "little people" who eked out a living on tough farmland and the densely forested wilds made much of Adirondack history. Surrounded by shining lakes, bubbling streams, wooded glades, and grottoes, they found joy and contentment. Each season had its challenges and offerings.

Early mapmakers summarily neglected the dense wilderness of the Adirondacks. Their vagueness helped to preserve the remote and open land for some two centuries. The land is called Couchsachrage Country, or "beaver-hunting ground," on the early maps. The 1775 British Colony map simply notes that the lands in this area "by reason of mountain swamps and drowned lands, are impassable and uninhabited." Guy Johnson's 1771 map records, "The boundary of New York, not being closed this part of the Country, shall belong to the Mohawks." The map in *New York State Education Leaflet No. 7* by state archeologist William Ritche notes the Adirondacks as "uninhabited."

Other maps called the Adirondack region "parts but little known," "not yet surveyed," "not only uninhabited but even unknown," and "a wild barren tract covered with almost impenetrable bogs." Nelson Greene provided a warning for the early farmers of the Mohawk Valley, referring to the lands north of Johnstown to the St. Lawrence as "clothed with dreary forests with a soil that forbids cultivation." Thus, the maps formed a protective shield around the vast wilderness that limited man's intrusion for some time.

A word should be said about Prof. Ebenezer Emmons; his exploration led to the opening up of the Adirondack country. Our western frontier was explored and on its way to being settled when

Emmons made his historic assent to the top of the Adirondacks in 1837. During the previous year, Emmons, a professor at Williams College, had been appointed geologist-in-chief of the Second District of the Geological Survey of New York. The high peaks of Essex County fell within his district. The amazing Professor Emmons—a botanist, geologist, mineralogist, chemist, and physicist—was the ideal leader for the exploration of the Adirondacks.

Along with the economic and scientific promise of the region, the professor made his contribution to the future growth of the region through vivid descriptions of its scenic beauty. He also gave the "Great Wilderness" the name that remains today. "The cluster of mountains in the neighborhood of the Upper Hudson and Ausable rivers, I proposed to call the Adirondack Group, a name by which a well-known tribe of Indians who once hunted here may be commemorated," writes Professor Emmons, in *New York State Assembly Document No.* 99 in 1837.

Some 25 years later, another scientist of equal ability and drive made his mark on the Adirondacks. Verplanck Colvin, superintendent of the Adirondack Survey, arrived on the scene to make his contribution. His work, unsurpassed by any other, speaks for itself. He drove himself and his staff beyond human endurance in conditions that would have defeated a lesser man. Colvin wrote about his concern for the forested lands and made a major contribution in their preservation.

Once the Adirondacks were explored and surveyed, the influx of settlers began in earnest. Those connected with the woodland industries were the first to move in. Hunters and trappers arrived in droves. The wealthy camp owners built their large Adirondack estates and employed hundreds. Adirondack guiding became a reputable vocation, and guides were in great demand.

In 1869, the Reverend William Henry Harrison Murray wrote a small book called *Adventures in the Wilderness*. His glowing descriptions of the Adirondacks caused a rush to "adventure" in the wilderness. Many believe that this clergyman's eloquent descriptions, from the facilities available to those miraculous cures in the pine-scented air, seemed to be exaggerated—causing disappointment and disillusion. Whatever the reason, the rush to visit the Adirondacks was on, and there was no turning back.

Over the years, the Adirondack Mountains of New York State have fulfilled many purposes for those who have been attracted to the region's depths. Its forested hillsides and waterways have provided inspiration and rejuvenation for some and livelihood for others. Settlers, sportsmen, loggers, artists, writers, campers, hikers, camp builders, and outdoor enthusiasts have beaten a path to the Adirondacks. They have found their places, pursued their dreams, and enjoyed happy pastimes among the trees and lakes in the shadows of the high peaks. Today, the Adirondacks continue to inspire artists, stimulate writers, invite visitors, satisfy sportsmen, and pose a never-ending challenge to preserve them for future generations.

One

THE PAST

The Adirondack region has been the subject of geological and historical research and speculation for hundreds of years. Geologists theorize that over millions of years, the Adirondack region was subjected to heaving and buckling, erosion, and icy glaciations, eventually creating the Adirondacks visitors enjoy today. Some of the oldest mountains in the world, the Adirondacks have had their ups and downs.

To this land of mountains, waterways, and forests came Native Americans and hermits, trappers and hunters, anglers and hikers, and, eventually, those who built their log cabins and settled the wild country. Pioneers came to log trees, mine minerals, serve the wealthy camp owners, and work in the tanneries. The next wave of settlers was attracted by the opportunity to make a living off the tourists who came to enjoy the recreational offerings, the pure mountain air and water, and the health-giving features found in New York's great park. Sanitariums (often for patients with mental illnesses), sanitoriums (for those with comsumptive illnessses), and hotels spread throughout the mountains and employed hundreds. Summer camps expanded. Artists and writers came to be inspired. Winter sports attracted players and spectators. It was during these growing years that the Adirondack Forest Preserve and the Adirondack Park were created.

Two major industries were born in the Adirondacks: outdoor guiding and guide-boat building. Guides were necessary to keep visitors safe and to help them learn the ways of the wild. Special boats were needed to traverse the mountain streams and lakes. As a result, a craft was developed that was light, versatile, and durable enough to carry a full load of passengers and gear.

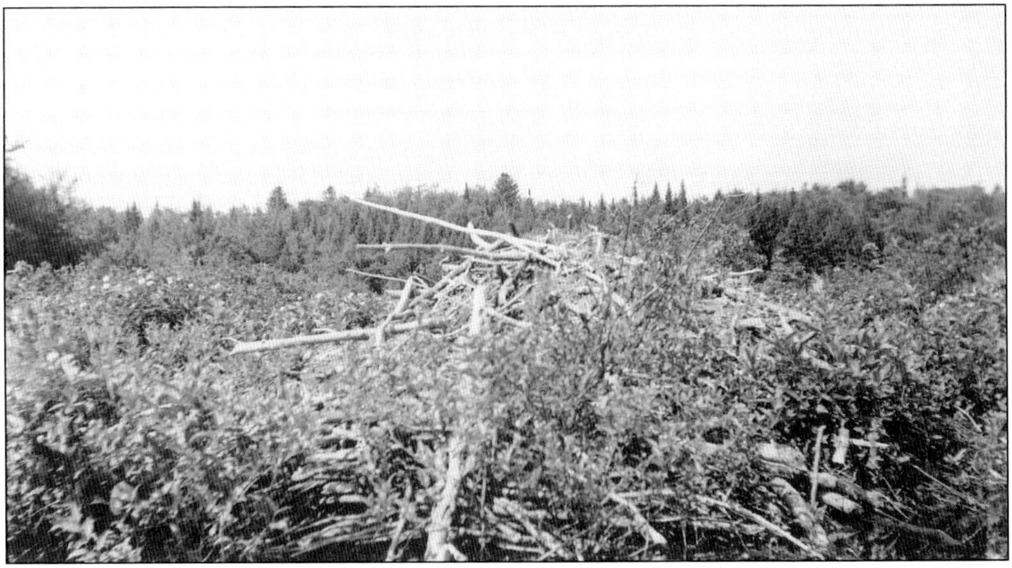

The Adirondacks were once known as Couchsachrage Country, or beaver-hunting ground. Beaver hides, used to make hats, coats, and castoreum for medicinal purposes were in great demand on the European market. The beaver became as valuable as gold, and the Native Americans, English, French, and Dutch competed for the lucrative beaver trade. Wars were fought over the New World lands. Trappers fought over traplines. Beaver dams and houses, such as the one shown here on Cherry Creek near Speculator, created water impoundments throughout the mountainous Adirondacks. The impoundments provided a rich habitat for fish, waterfowl, and other animals, meeting the needs of the growing beaver population. The original Adirondack beaver was much larger than today's reintroduced population.

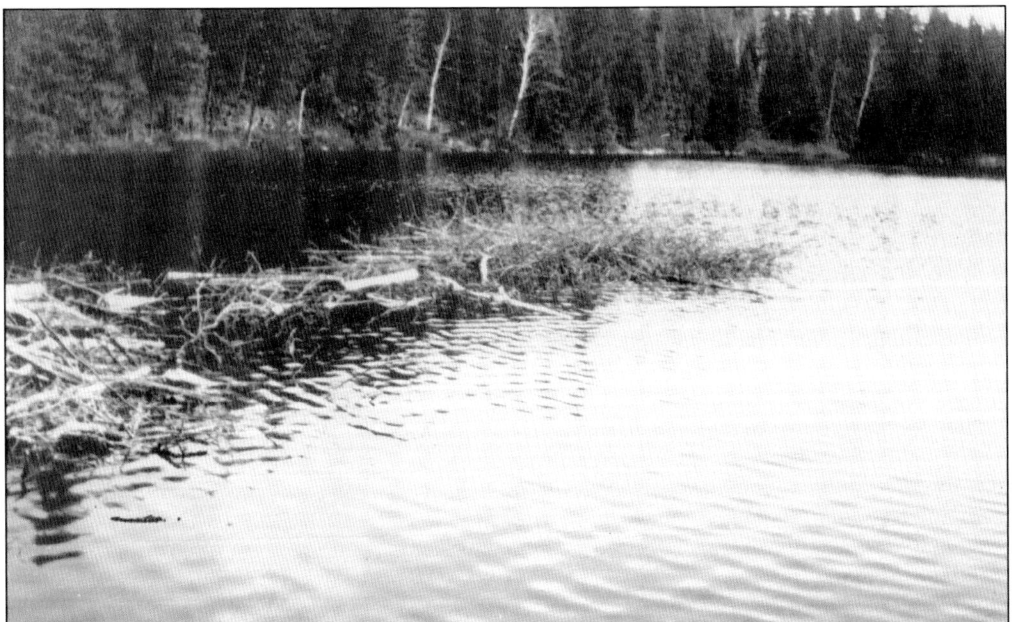

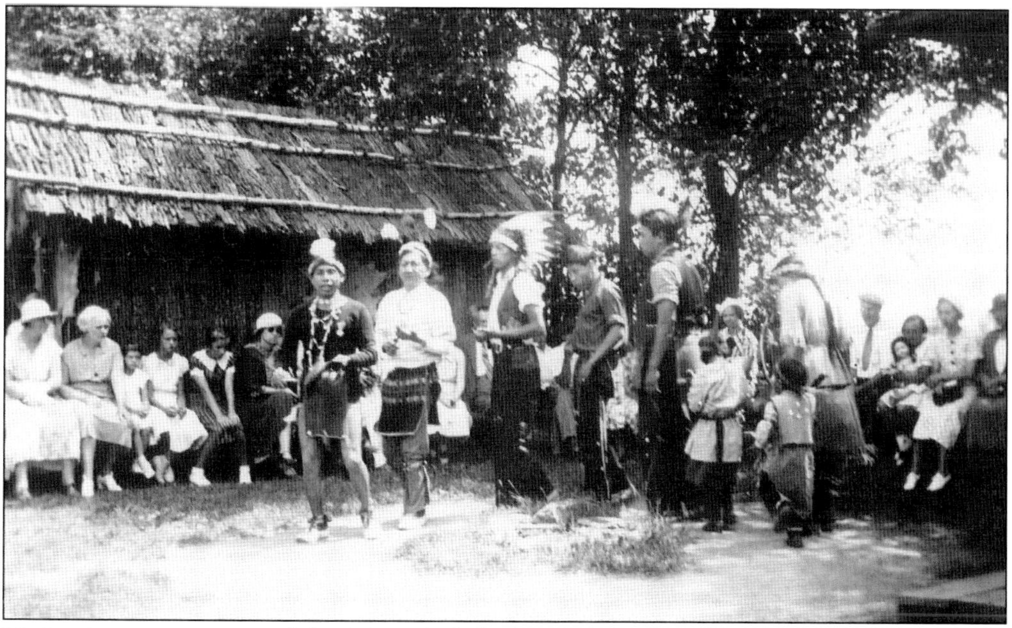

Native Americans traversed the Adirondacks before the American Revolution, and Indian trails were used for transportation routes during wartime. The Adirondacks were their hunting and fishing grounds; Native Americans never established a settlement in the mountainous country. Evidence exists that Native Americans summered in the Adirondacks to take advantage of the game and to make tools and weapons. An arrowhead-making shale bed is located on the Sacandaga River. Some of the first individual Adirondack settlers were Native Americans, including Sabael Benedict near Indian Lake and Peter Sabattis of Long Lake. Peter's son Mitchell receives some credit for the development of the Adirondack guide boat. Native Americans often worked as Adirondack guides, and some moved from town to town making and selling pack baskets. Today, many Native Americans gather each year at the New York State Fair.

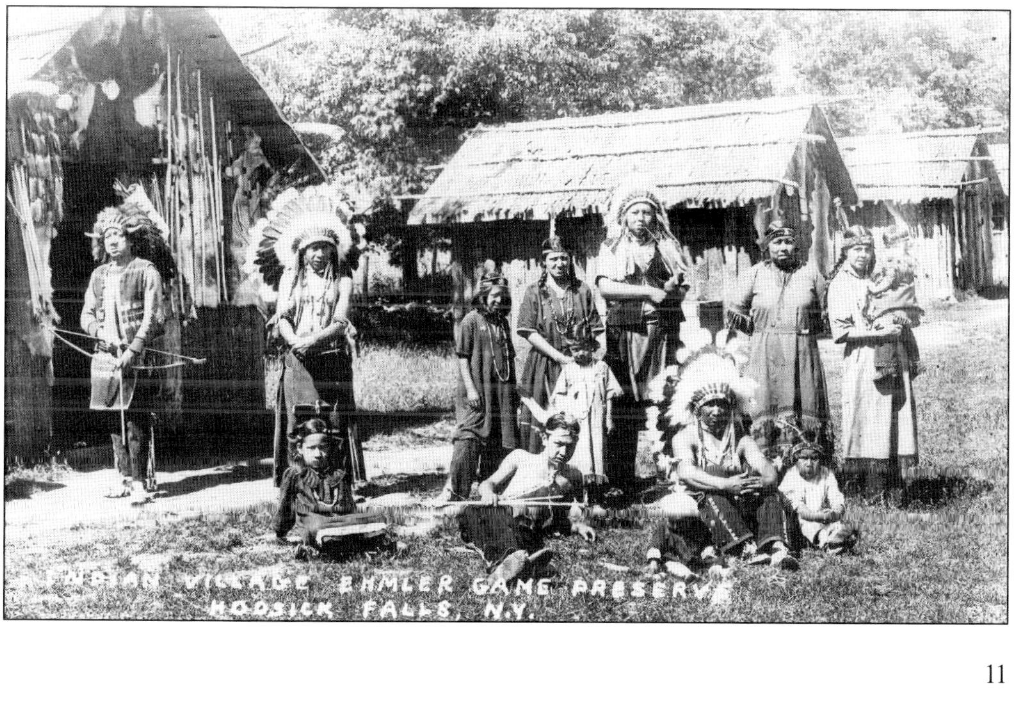

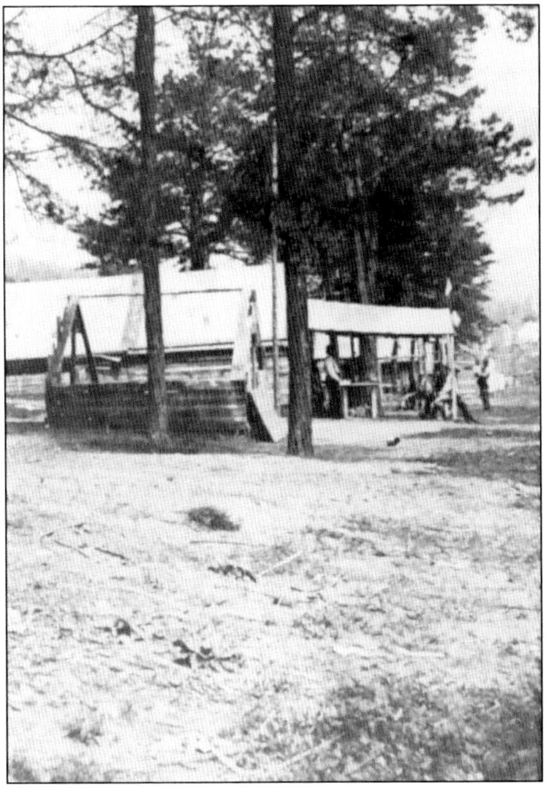

Tourists visited a permanent Indian encampment at Lake George for several years. The nearby town of Horicon, incorporated in 1838, may have been named for the Horikan Indians. Lake George was once known as Horicon, a name promoted by the author James Fenimore Cooper. In the same vicinity, Brant Lake may have been named after Joseph Brant, a Native American friend of Sir William Johnson.

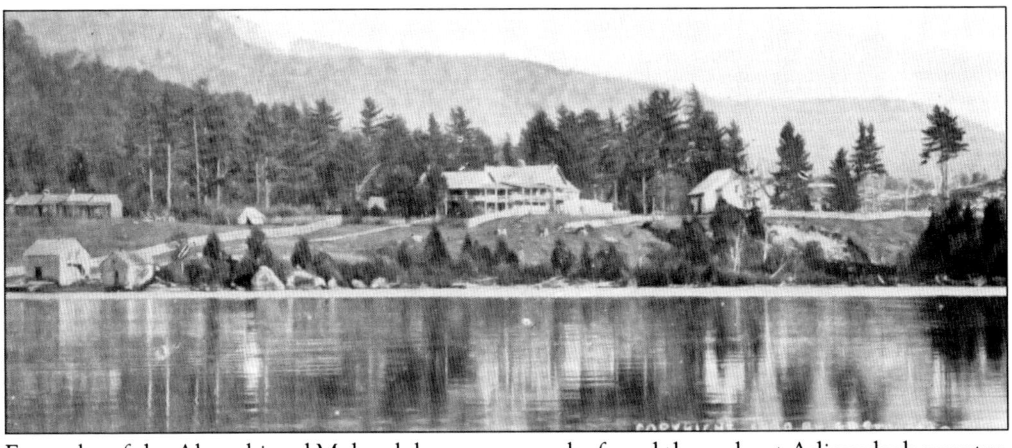

Examples of the Abenaki and Mohawk languages can be found throughout Adirondack country. Many place-names are of Indian origin or related to Indian history. One of the most obvious is a place known as Indian Carry. Portages, where boat and gear traveled overland between waterways, are known as carries in the Adirondacks. Indian Carry appears in the early guidebooks. Rustic Lodge is at the south end of Upper Saranac Lake.

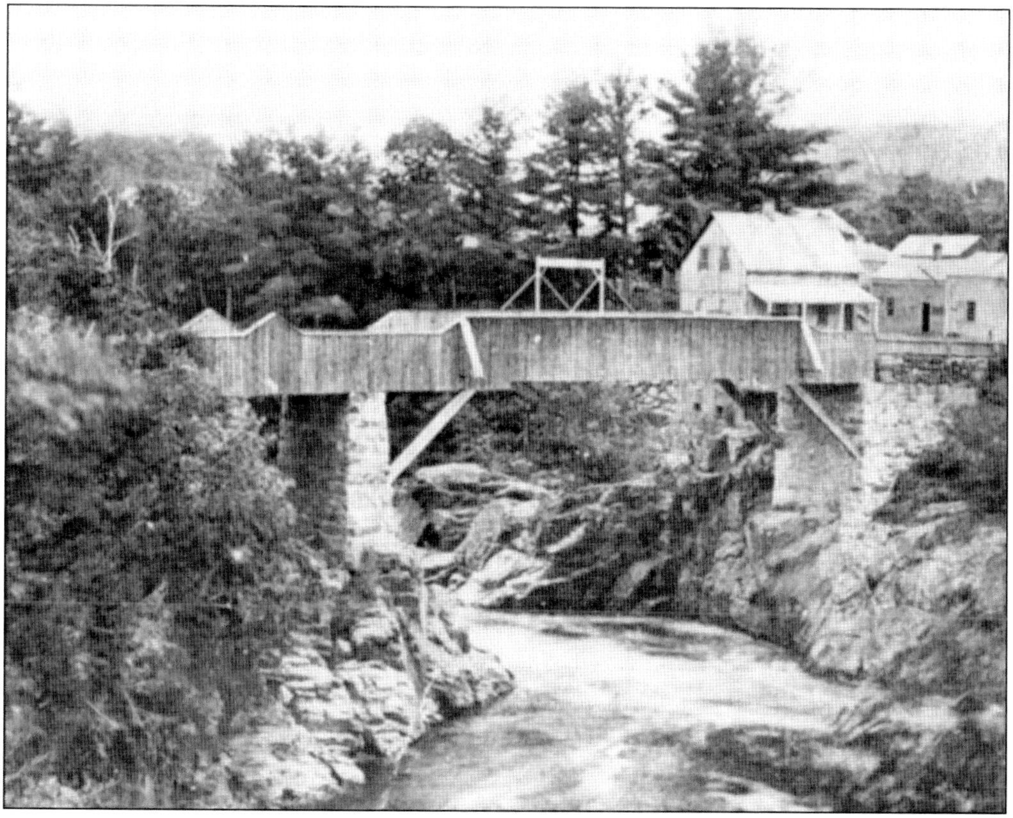

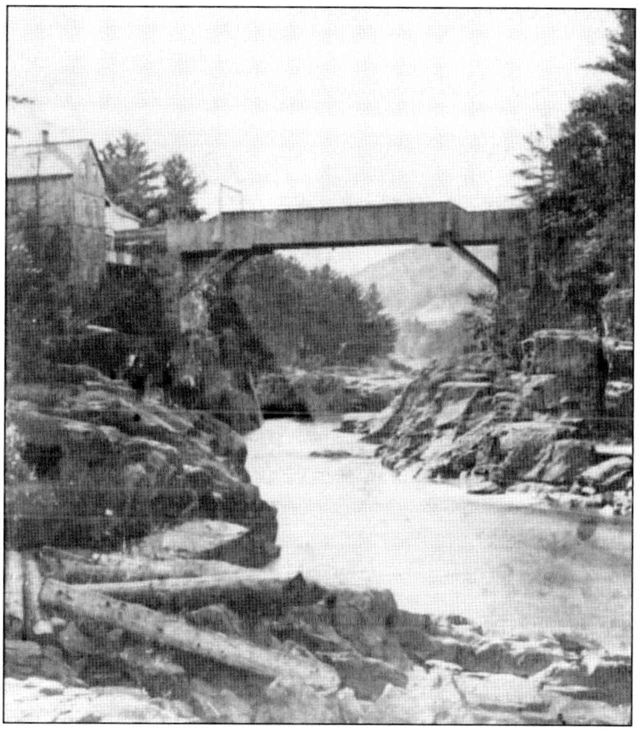

The bridge crossing the rapids on the Hudson River at Luzerne connected the two parts of the growing lumber town. Ebenezer and Edward Jessup were the first lumbermen to make their homes in Luzerne before the outbreak of the American Revolution. They were the first in the Adirondacks to use the technique known as "timber rafting" or "timber floating" to move logs down the Sacandaga, Schroon, and Hudson Rivers in the 1770s. The Jessups were not the only ones to see that money was to be made in supplying a growing nation with lumber. Lumbering got off to a good start in the Adirondacks in the 1700s.

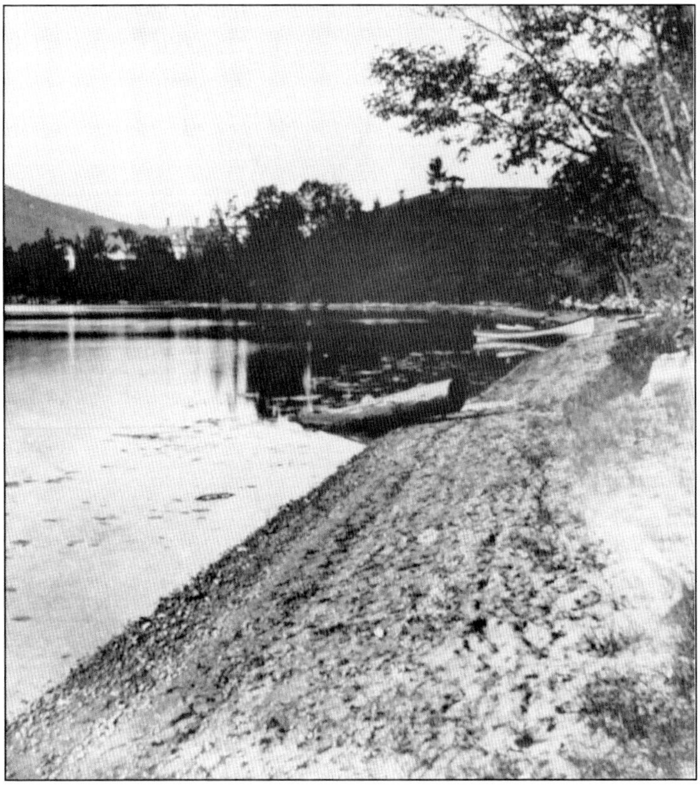

Luzerne, located on the Hudson River and Lake Luzerne, became one of the earliest communities in the Adirondacks. Early lumbermen occupied the area, and by 1797 a settlement developed. By 1815, Jeremiah Rockwell operated a sawmill there (often a major contributor to a growing hamlet). The 1920s guidebooks published by the Delaware and Hudson call for "a vacation in this historic place."

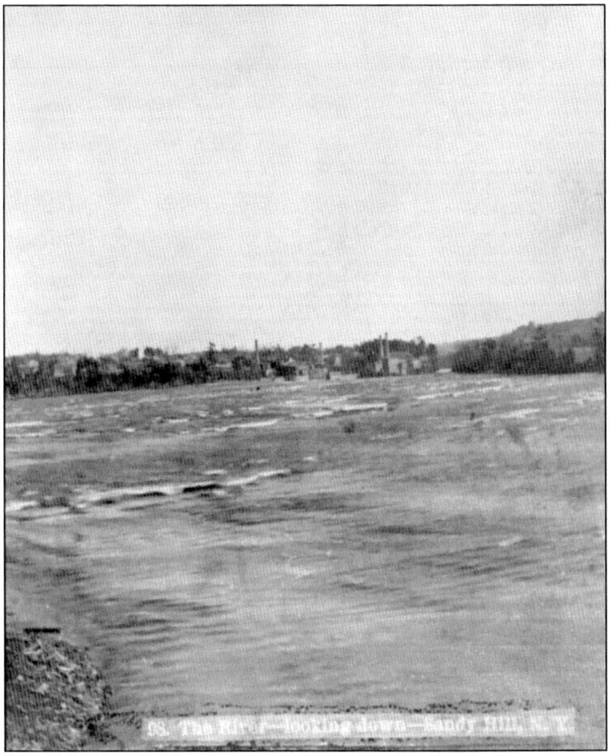

In this photograph, logs float down the Hudson River at Sandy Hill. The first distinctive Adirondack lumbering had begun along the upper Hudson and its tributaries in 1813, sending the logs to Fort Edward, Sandy Hill, and Glens Falls. Logs were not only needed for lumber, the giant white pines of the Adirondacks were also in demand for ships' masts. Spruce became a major crop, as it was used for pulp to make paper.

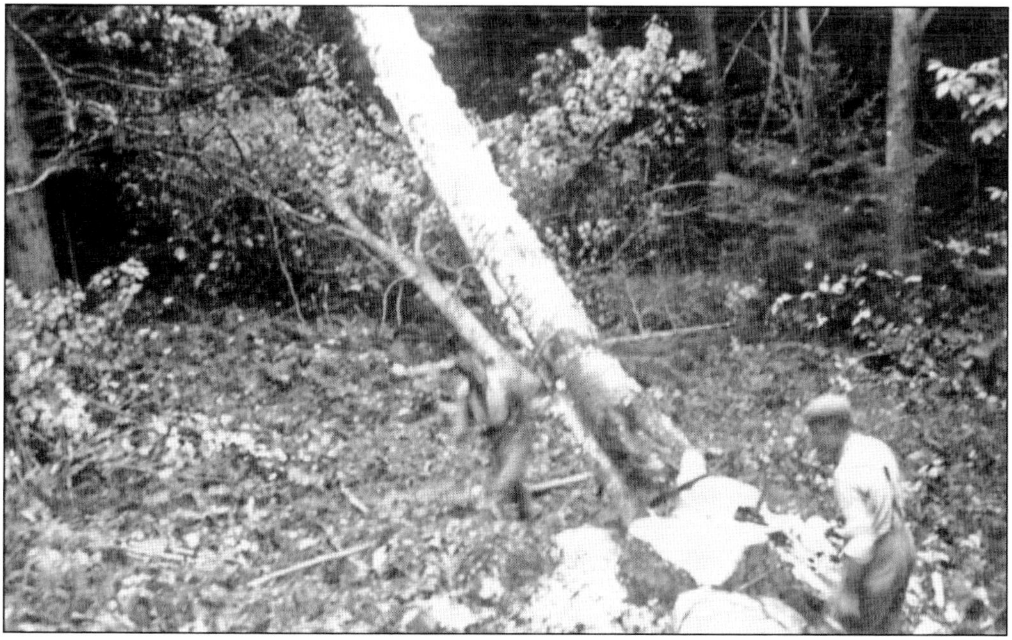

Beginning in 1813, logging became a major industry in the Adirondacks. Here, a two-man crosscut saw is used to fell the tree and size it to the 13-foot standard for market. Yelling "timber" and watching for "widow-makers" (hung-up branches) were part of making a very dangerous job a little safer. Oddly, logs of the Adirondack forests were standardized at 13 feet when the rest of the country was at 16 feet. At that time, loggers were also cutting "two-log trees," which were 19 inches in diameter at the small end. Logging remained a major industry in the Adirondacks for over 75 years.

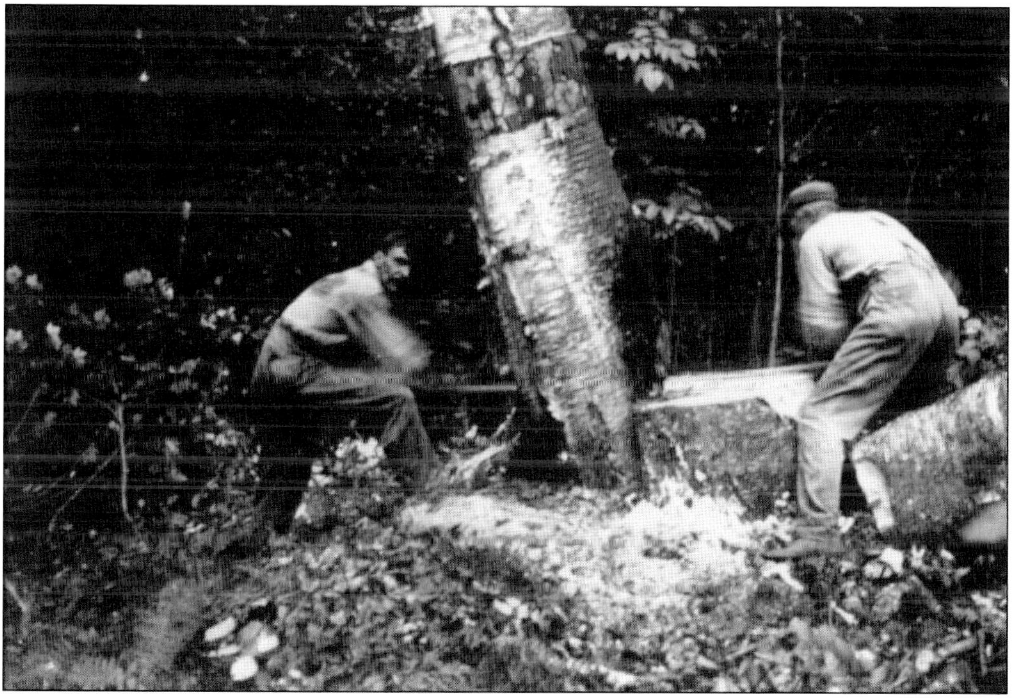

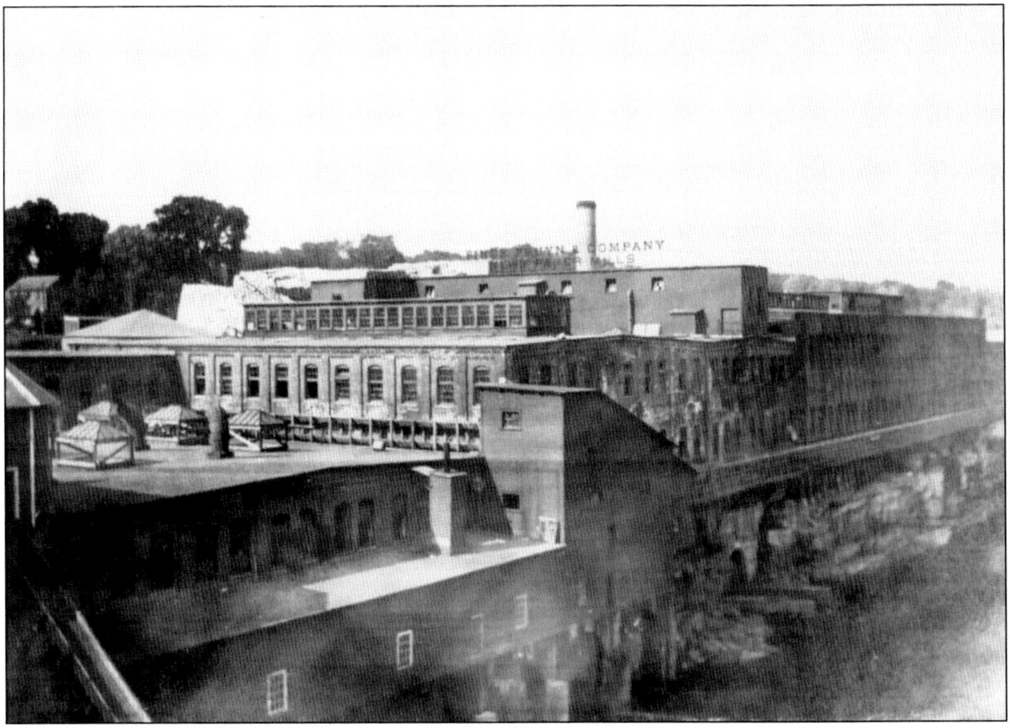

Founded by James Finch and Samuel Pruyn in 1865, Finch-Pruyn and Company was the first major logging company to practice good forest management in the Adirondacks. In 1910, the company hired a professional forester to ensure environmentally sound practices. It was also the last to drive logs on the Adirondack rivers, continuing the practice into 1950.

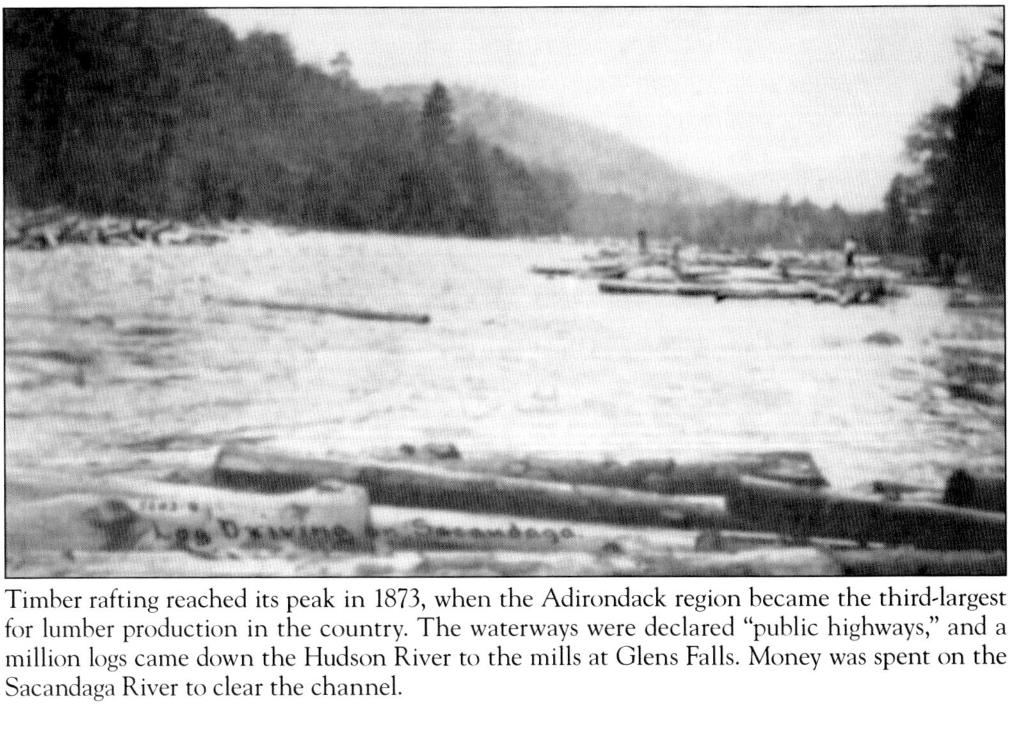

Timber rafting reached its peak in 1873, when the Adirondack region became the third-largest for lumber production in the country. The waterways were declared "public highways," and a million logs came down the Hudson River to the mills at Glens Falls. Money was spent on the Sacandaga River to clear the channel.

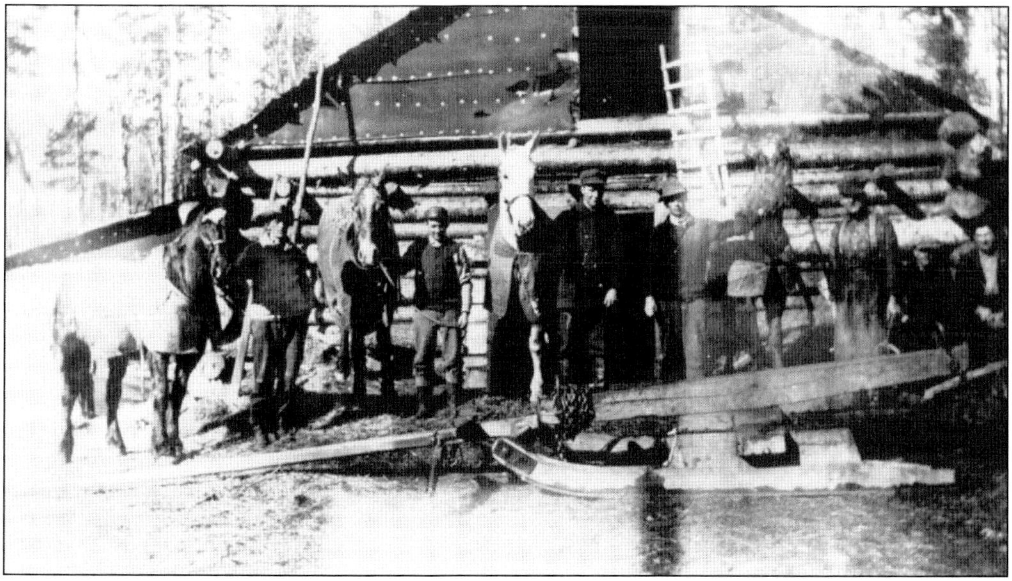

Once lumbermen decided it was easier and cheaper to move logs via existing waterways, they had to find a way to get them out of the woods and onto the riverbanks. Before the winter logging season, front men were hired to go through the Adirondack settlements, where they made arrangements for teams of horses. Once cutting began, horses showed up in large numbers to draw the logs to streams, rivers, and lakes so that they could be sent to the mills in the spring. The sledge in front of the men lifted one end of the logs, making it easier to drag them over snow, rocks, and mud.

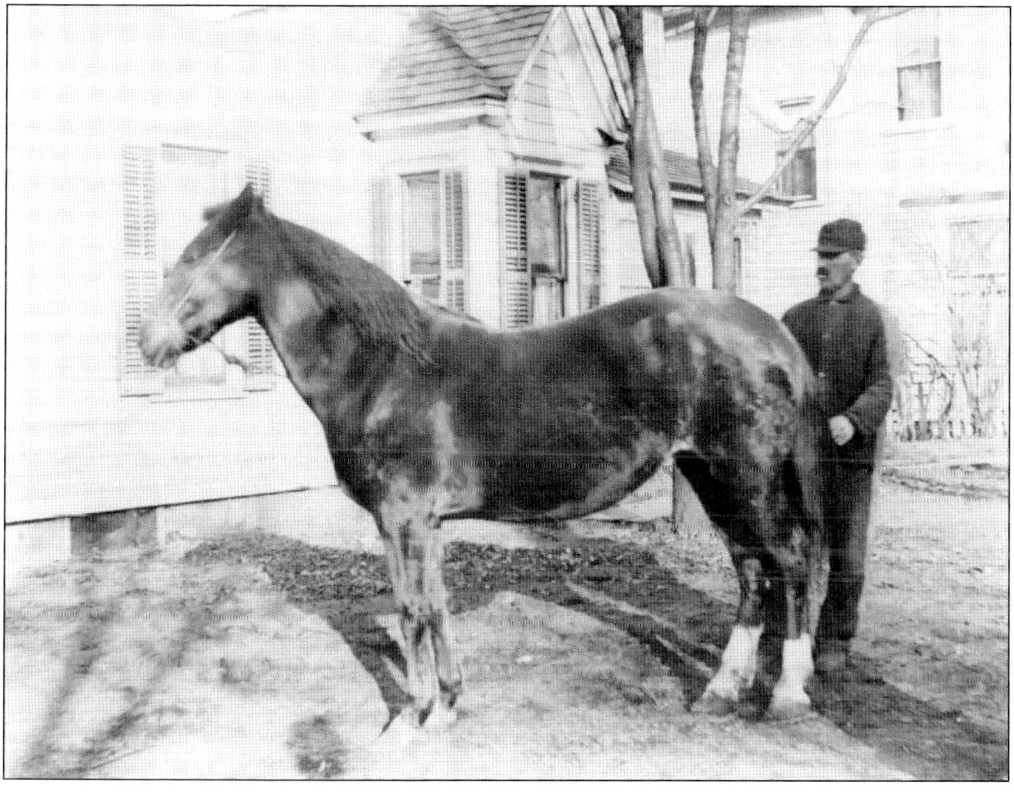

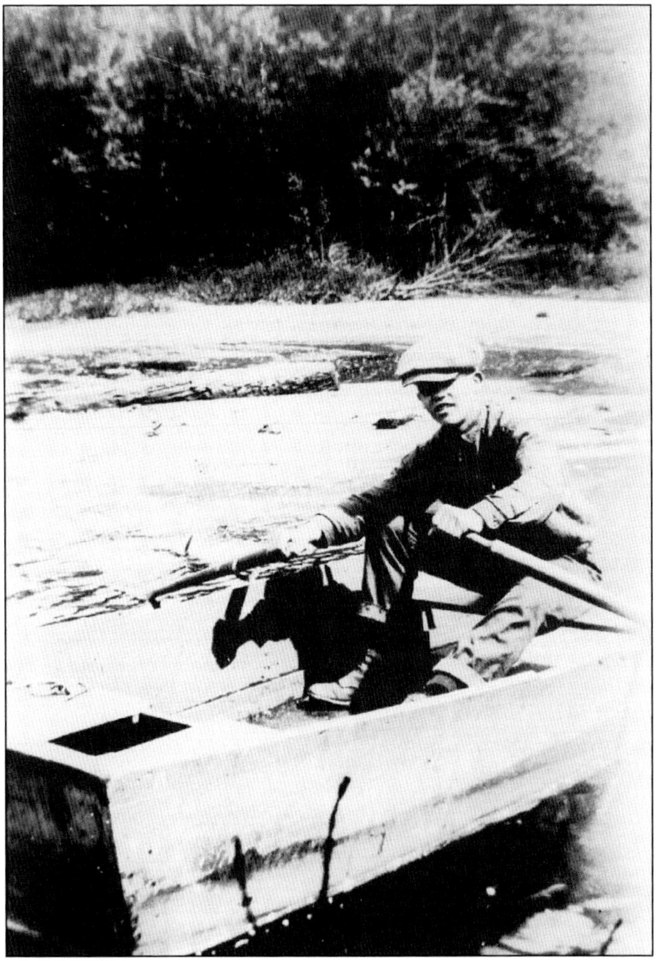

Some of the bravest people in timber rafting were those who kept the logs moving with the peaveys and pike poles and those who chased down the logs in wooden boats. Called "jam boats," the heavy crafts were rowed out to loosen trapped logs and rescue river drivers.

When some 60 logging companies shared the rivers, lakes, and streams, an important part of logging became keeping track of ownership. When the logs arrived at mills such as Northville or Glens Falls, they had to be counted. Beginning in 1804, marking or branding of logs became standard practice. One by one, legislation was passed requiring the branding of logs on certain rivers. Brand marks were registered with the town clerks.

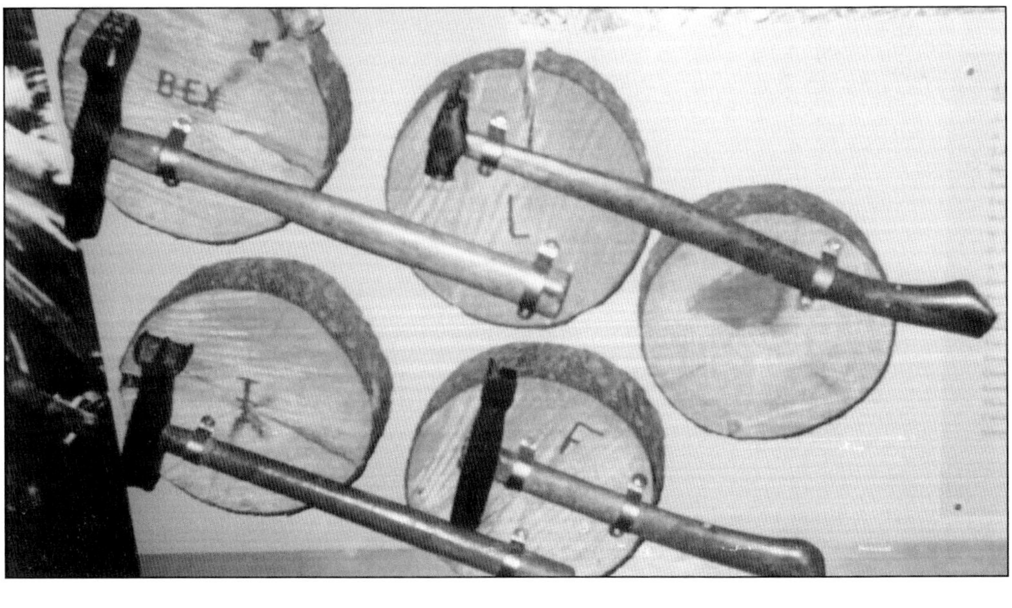

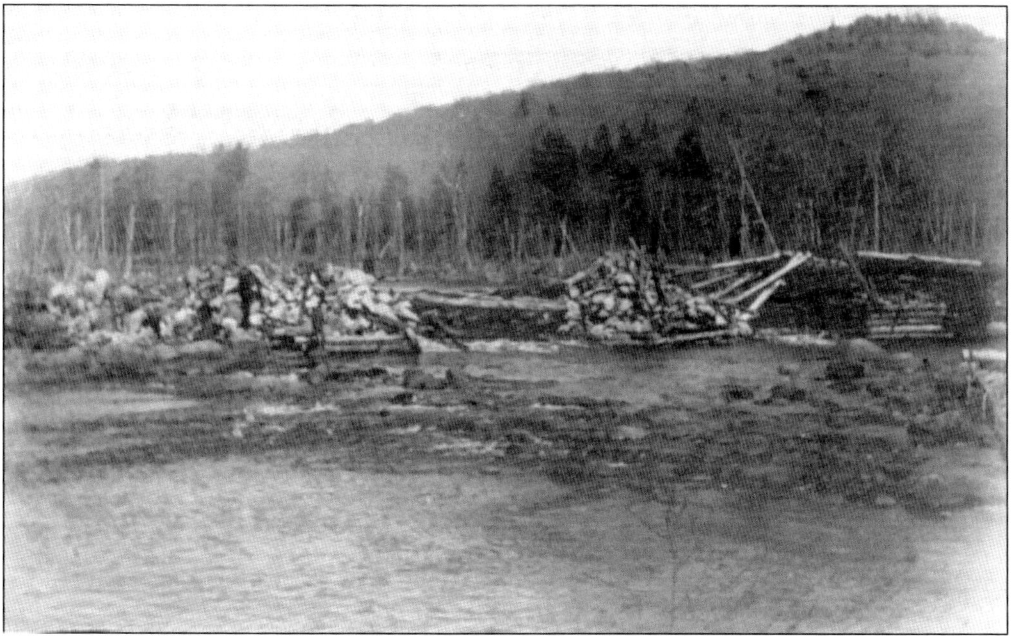

Remnants of logging dams and sluices are still found in Adirondack country. Most Adirondack waters were dammed up for logging and transportation before settlers moved in. Water had to be deep enough to easily move hundreds of logs each cutting season. Major dams are found on most of the larger lakes, and hundreds of smaller dams are scattered throughout the mountains. Logs were pushed into the waters in the springtime, the dams and sluices were opened, and the logs had a cheap ride to market. Timber rafting may have been the easiest part of transporting the logs. During the winter months, icy conditions were a problem, and roads out of the mountains had to be made by compacting the snow.

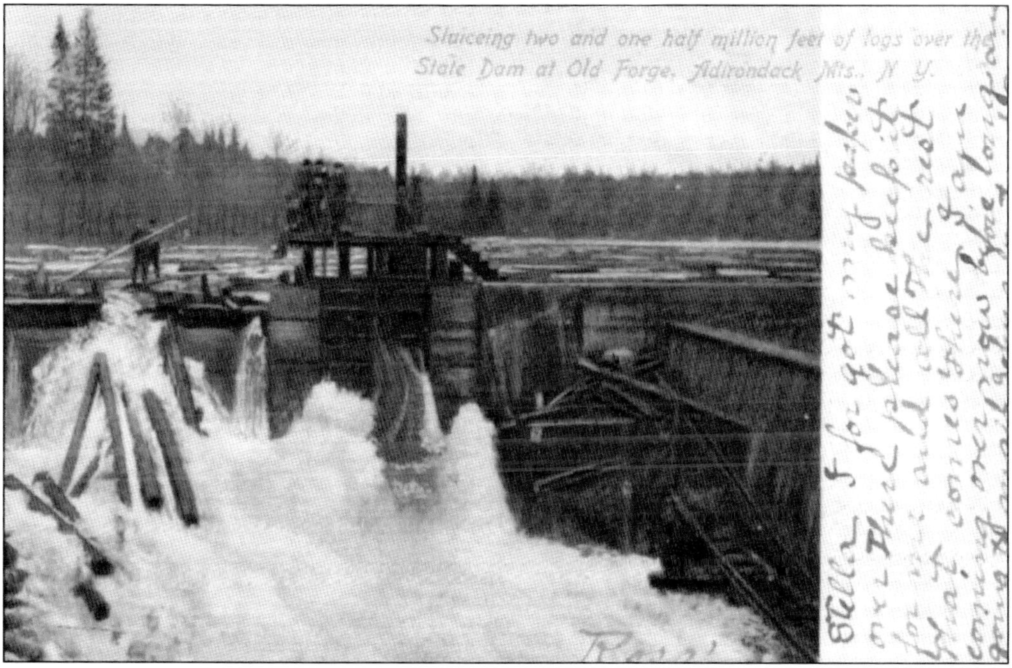

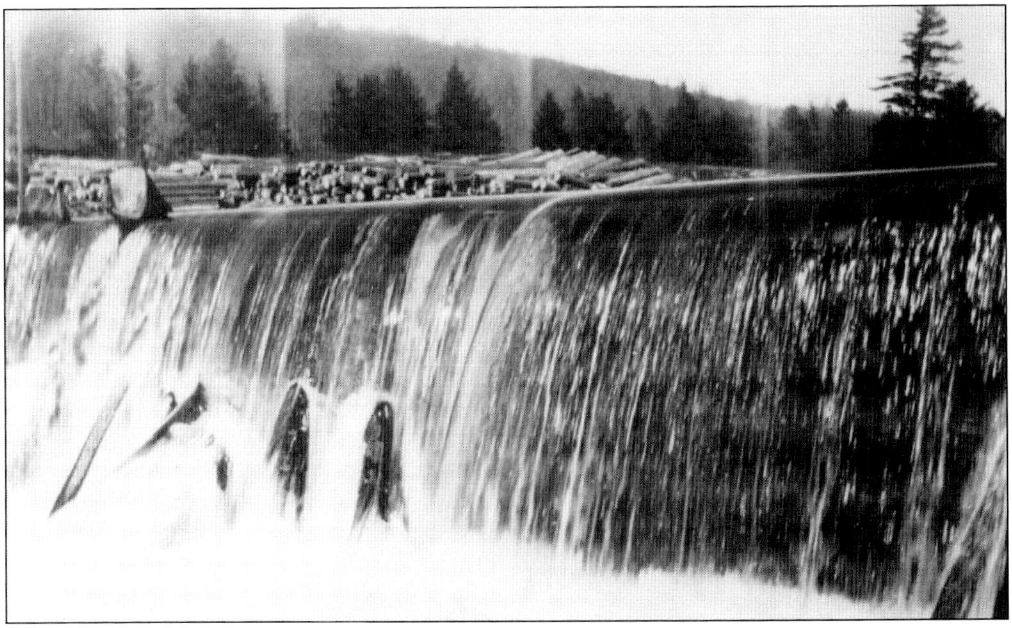

During the days of timber rafting, it was common to see logs piled on the banks of the rivers and lakes in the springtime. Note the logs in the photograph stacked above the dam and waiting to be sent to market. Lumberjacks spent the winter getting the logs to the banks of the waterways, and they then faced the challenging task of timber rafting. Logs often got hung up on the shores, jams were dangerous, and, in some cases, it took two seasons to get the logs the entire way to the mill. It was quite a sight to see those once stately trees floating in Adirondack waters.

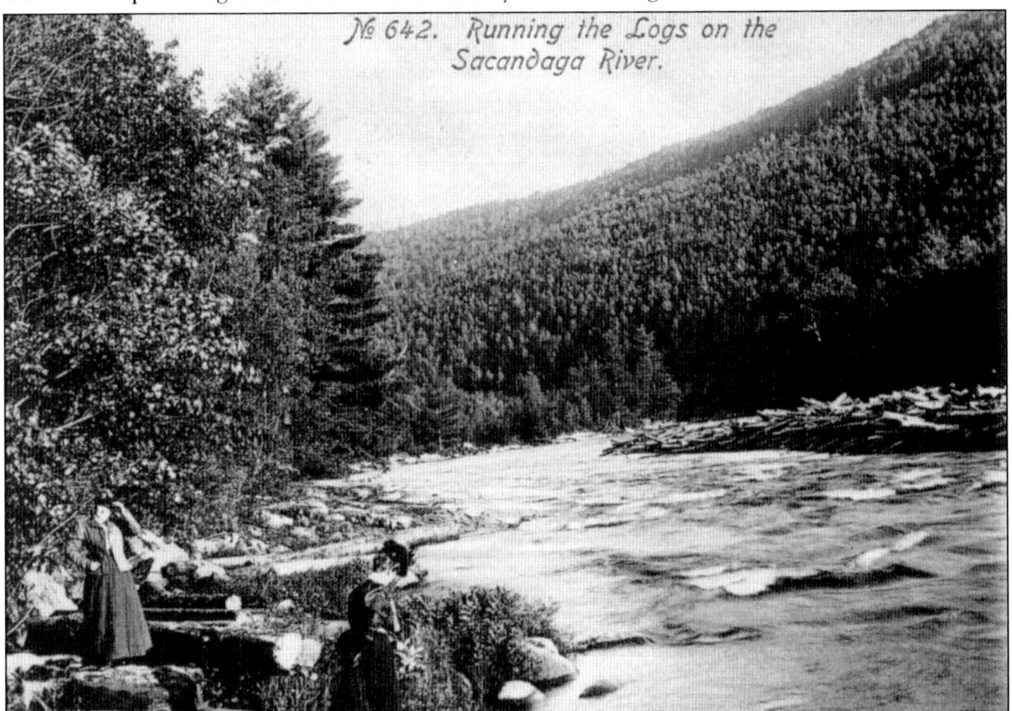

Up the Hudson River west of Glens Fall, the seven-foot Palmer Falls cascades over the rocks. The falls were once owned by the International Paper Company (IPC) to power its Corinth plant. Ira Haskins built the first sawmill near the falls in 1804, and it was the site of an IPC mill by 1898. The pulp and paper mill at Palmer Falls was the oldest operating paper mill in New York State. Part of International Paper's ground wood specialty papers, the mill closed in 2002. When there was a demand for pulp and paper, thousands of softwood logs cut to four-foot lengths were floated to the mill. Timber rafting made it possible for lumbermen to go deeper and deeper into the Adirondack woodlands.

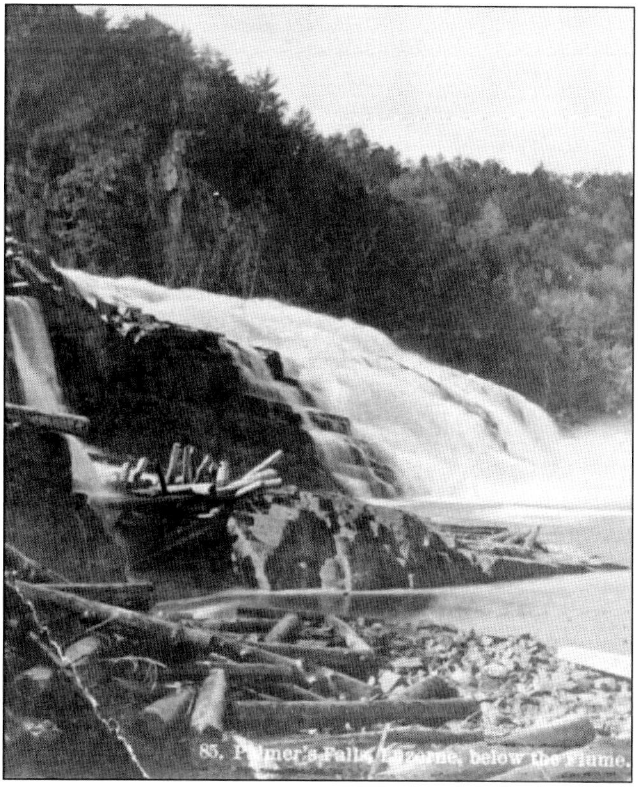

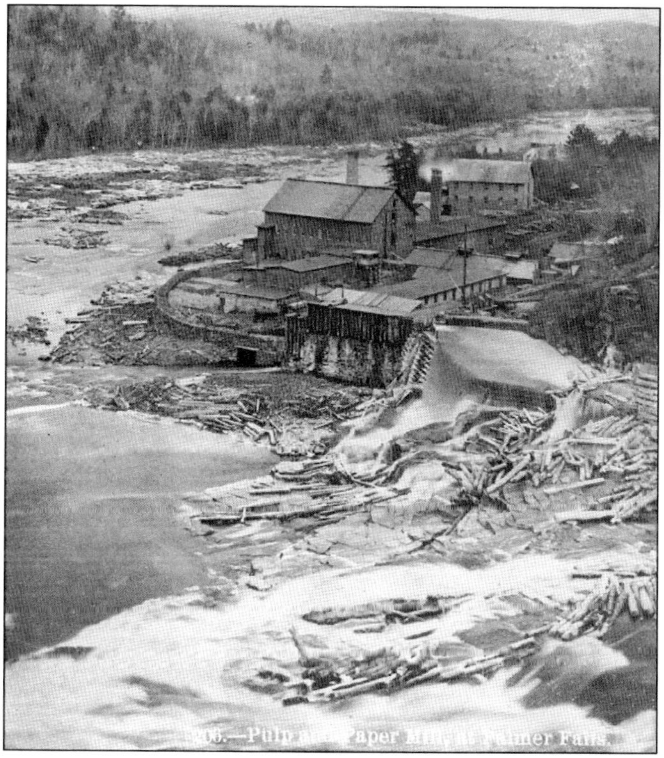

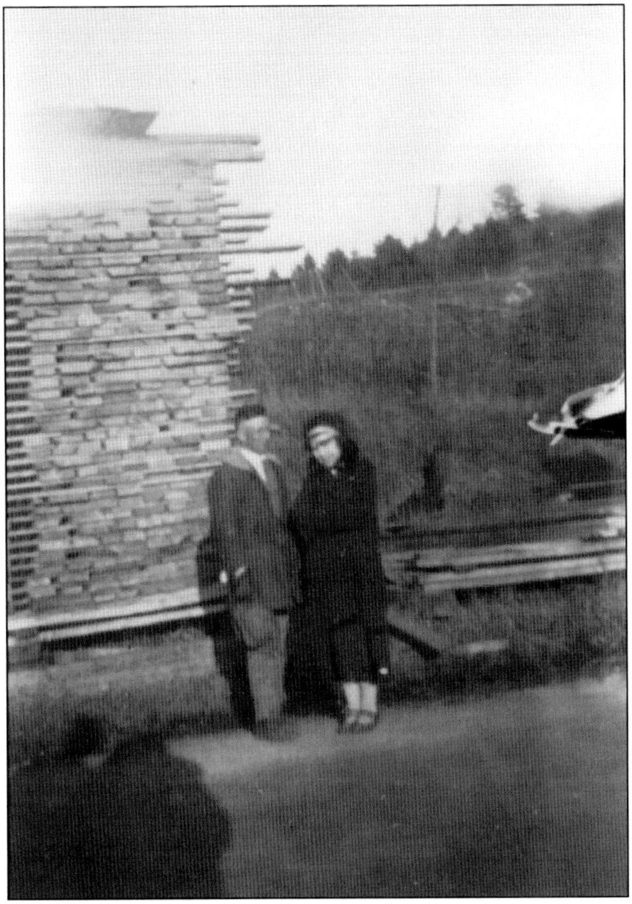

In the first half of the 1900s, it was not uncommon when driving through the Adirondacks to observe logs and lumber piled up at the lumber companies along the way. Great piles of sawdust could also be seen, sometimes smoldering or burning at the mills. The lumber, cut to standard sizes, was piled with air spaces so that it would dry without warping.

Logging companies created miles and miles of their own railroad lines. Around 1890, companies recognized that rail lines could move the huge logs more efficiently and enable them to get logs out of previously uncut, deeper woodlands. Railroads were only in use until the virgin timber was cut, sometimes for only a few years. The rail lines contributed to the deforestation of areas that otherwise would have remained in their primal state.

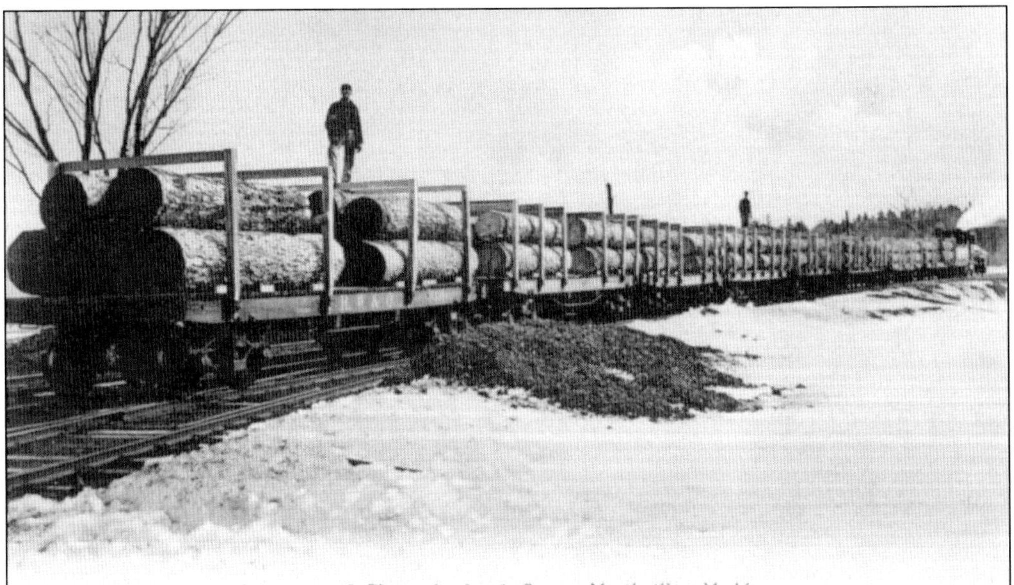

No. 626. A Train load of Logs, Northville, N. Y.

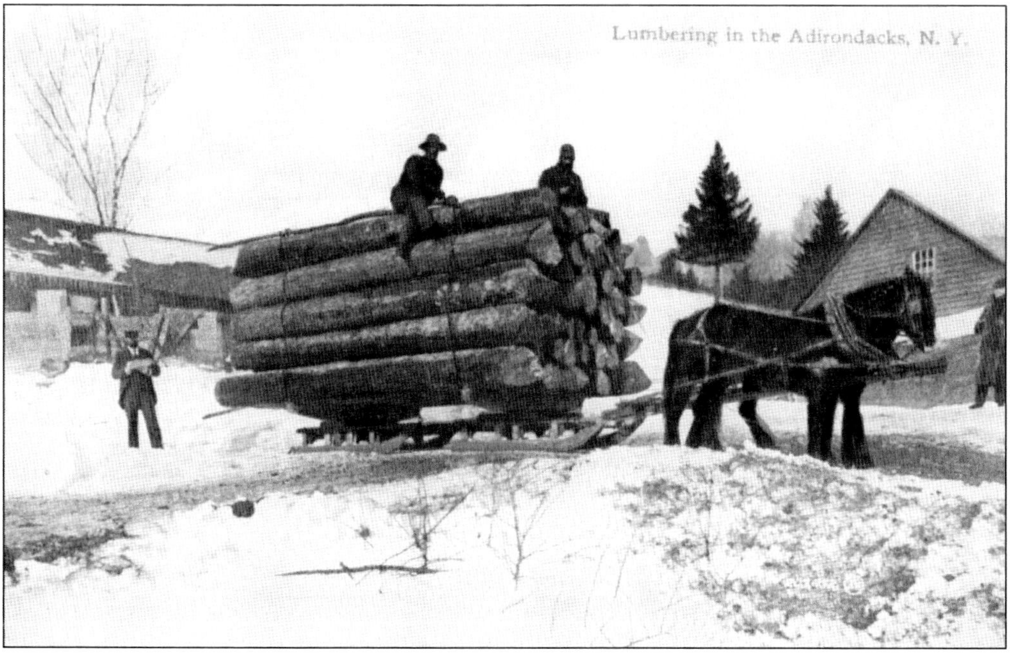

A stiff-kneed two-sled was used at the turn of the 20th century to haul logs from the interior Adirondack woodlands. Two bobsleds were hooked together by a wooden tongue, and the logs were chained together and tightened on the load. They were pulled down two-sled roads by oxen (and later horses), and chains or U-shaped irons were used for brakes. When all else failed, a rope tied around a tree was used to ease the load down a hill. Throwing sand was another option. The stiff-kneed two-sled could be used for carrying loads of cut wood and other goods with the addition of a crib. Hunters found them useful to transport big game.

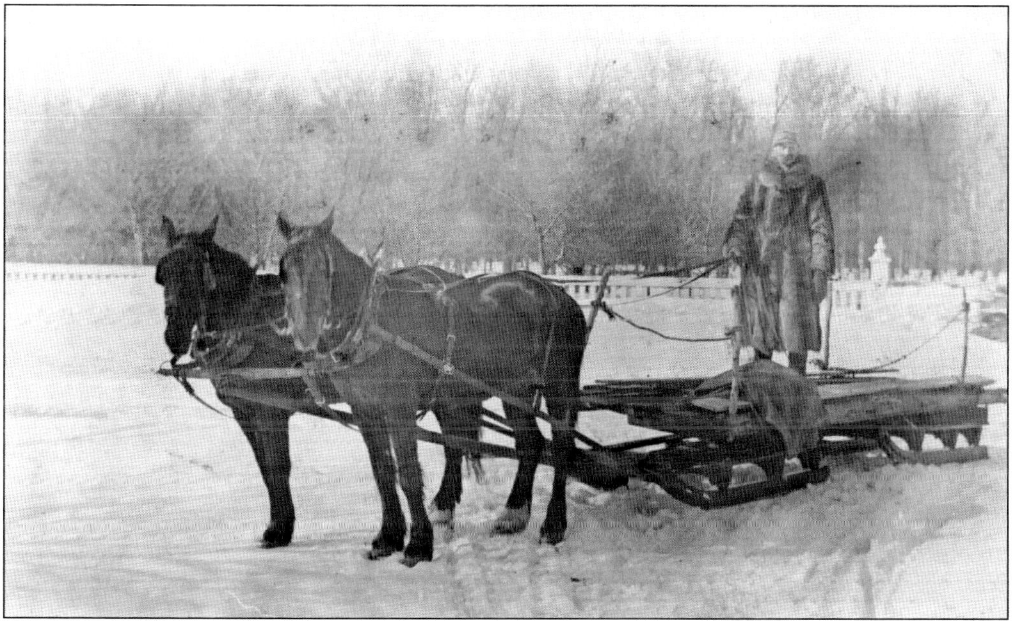

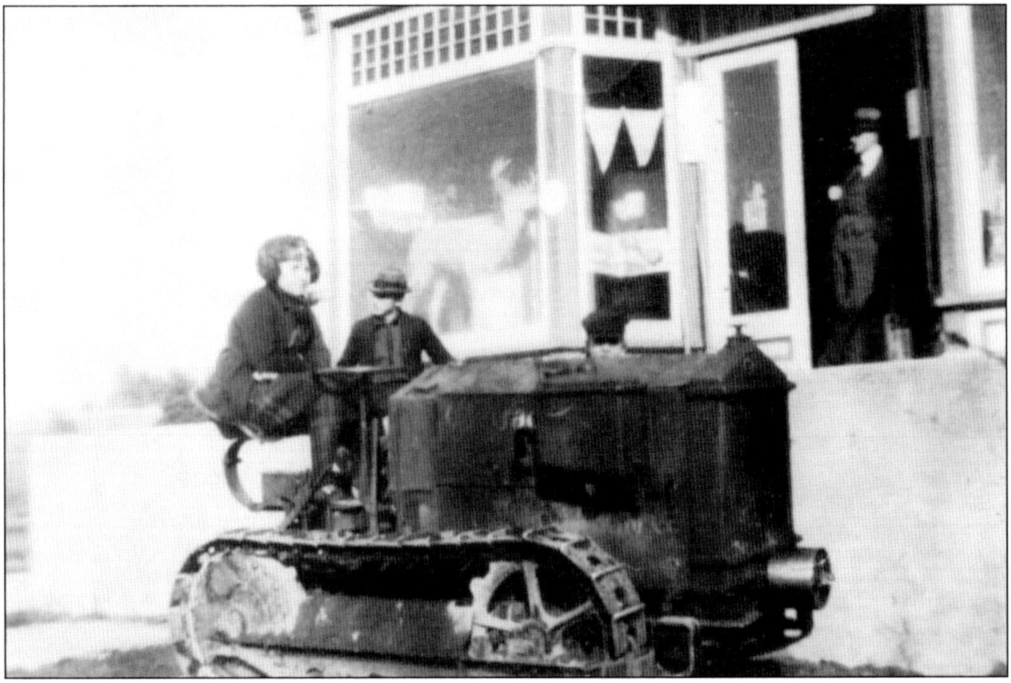

Heavy tractors came into use, replacing horses and oxen, although some still found that the animals did less damage to the environment. A young lady drives a tractor in this photograph.

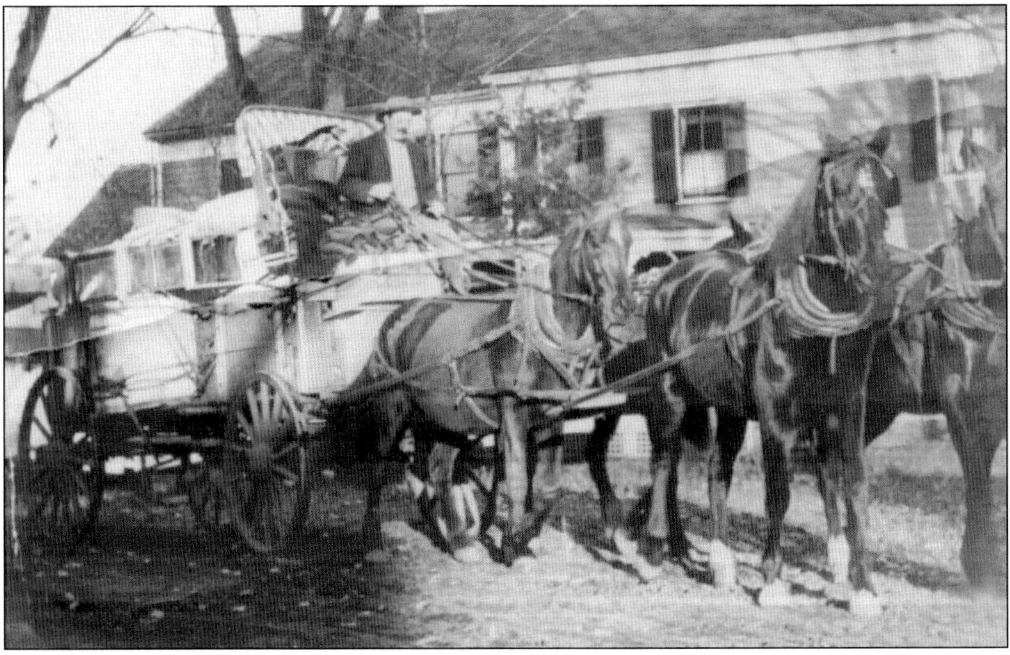

Heavy freight wagons with double teams of horses were called upon to move goods in Adirondack country. Beating a path through the woods to build their log cabins, early settlers arrived by horse and wagon with their worldly goods. Wealthy camp owners had furniture and construction materials hauled to their large lakefront estates. Products of the woodland tanneries had to be drawn by freight wagon to the nearest railhead.

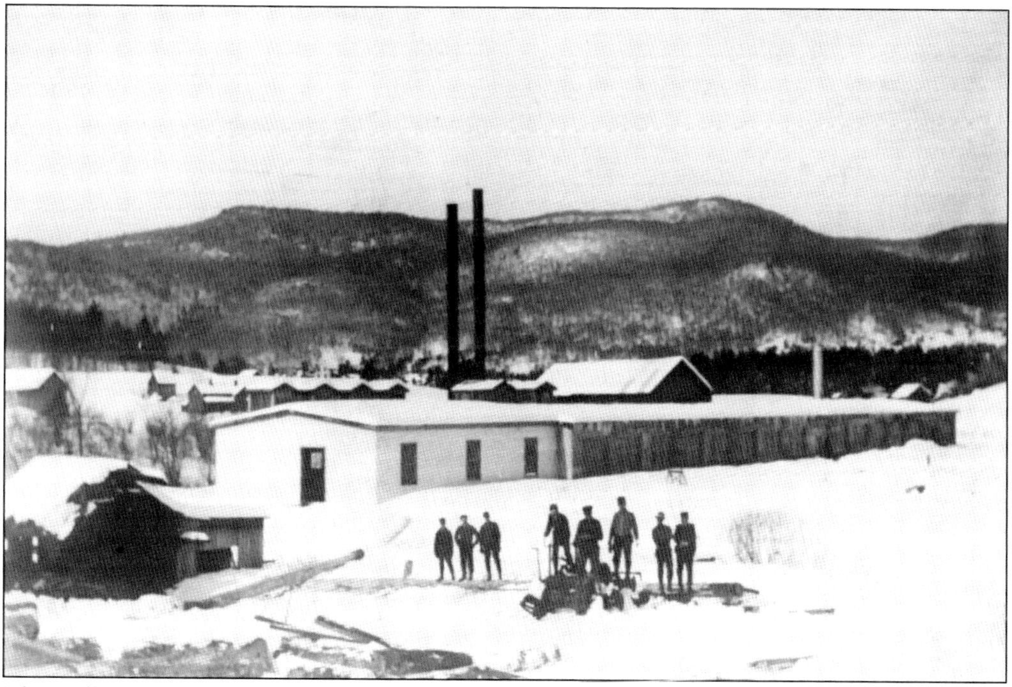

The mill site at Wells on the Sacandaga River evolved over the years, reflecting the natural Adirondack industries and the public needs at different periods of history. In 1821, it became Barnadoes Bratt's sawmill. It was sold to Jacob VanArnam in 1830, and he soon added a gristmill and a pottery. It next became a tannery and furniture factory, with several different owners over the next 36 years. The house, shown below, was known as the "tannery house" and stood adjacent to the mill, where the Catholic church is now located. Pictured above, it was converted to a veneering mill in 1899. In 1915, it became a Woods Product Corporation, adding a four-story bobbin factory. By 1917, it was the Adirondack Lumber Company, which finally closed its doors in 1976.

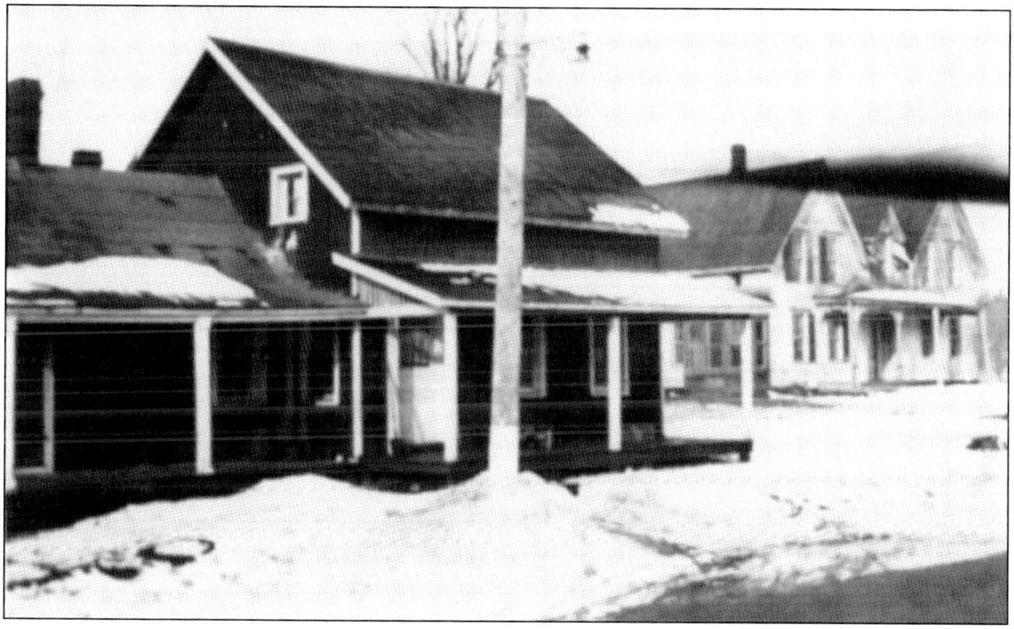

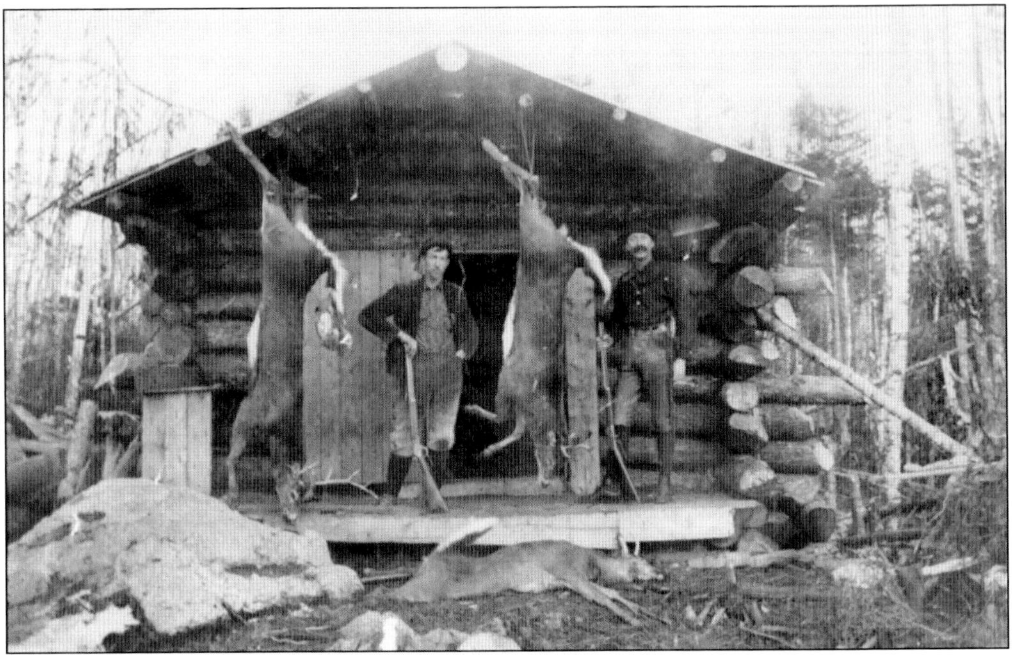

The Adirondack tradition of family hunting camps began in the 1600s with the Native Americans, including the Mohawks and the Algonquins. White trappers and hunters soon joined them, and hunting camps began to invade the wilderness. It was not uncommon to have a large hunting camp with 40 or 50 men on a deer drive. Camping styles ranged from rustic, tar-papered shacks and wall tents to large log cabins. Hunting skills were passed down from one generation to the next, and much of the survival in early settlements depended on a successful hunting season. Some say that there is a hunting story behind every tree in the Adirondacks.

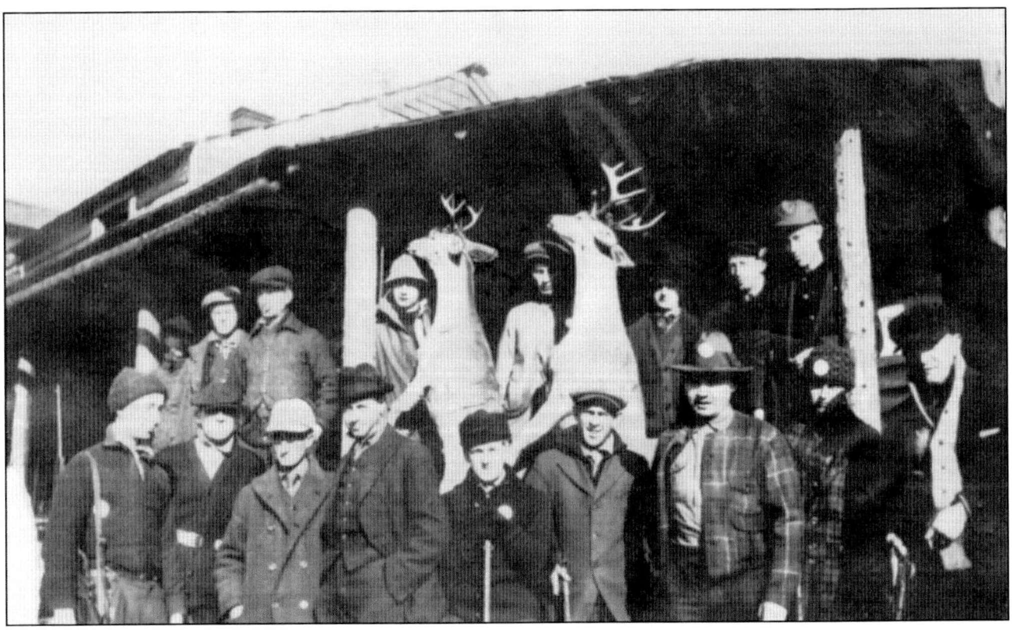

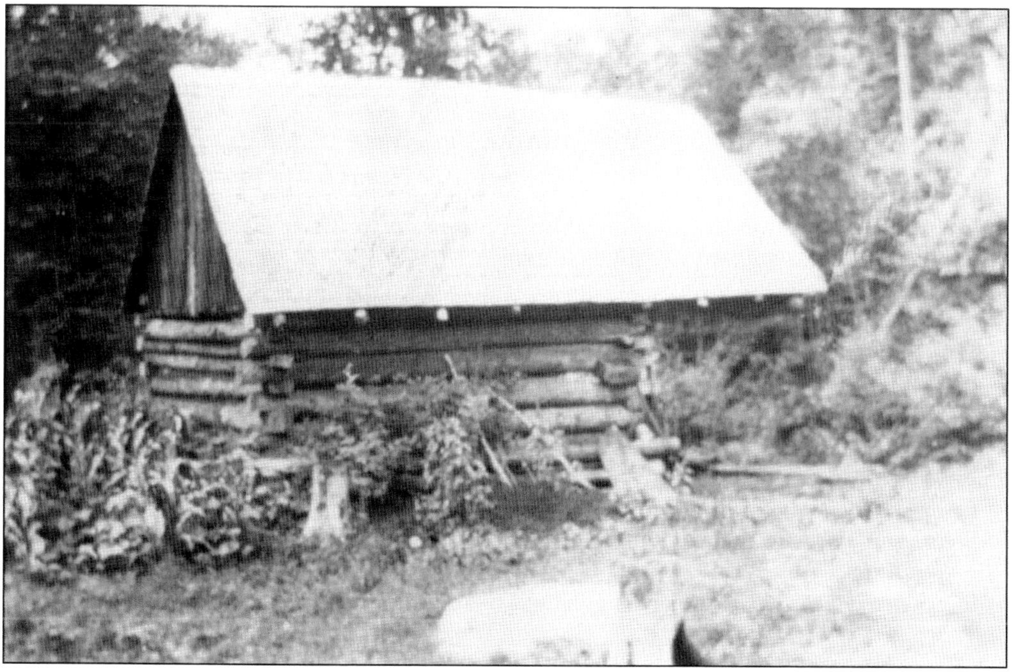

Log cabins—whether for hunting camps, vacation camps, or homes—were natural and efficient in the wilderness. The first settlers found construction of log cabins to be the best way of getting a home in the forested wilds with changing seasons. Sportsman-architect William S. Wicks wrote *Log Cabins: How to Build and Furnish Them*. The majority of his designs were meant for construction within the Adirondacks. Some evidence exists that dates the log cabins back to the 1700s. Long Lake had a cabin settlement in the 1830s, and Griffin had four log cabins in 1835. An 1876 log building can be seen at the Adirondack Museum, and an 1878 log cabin is still used as a home in Wells.

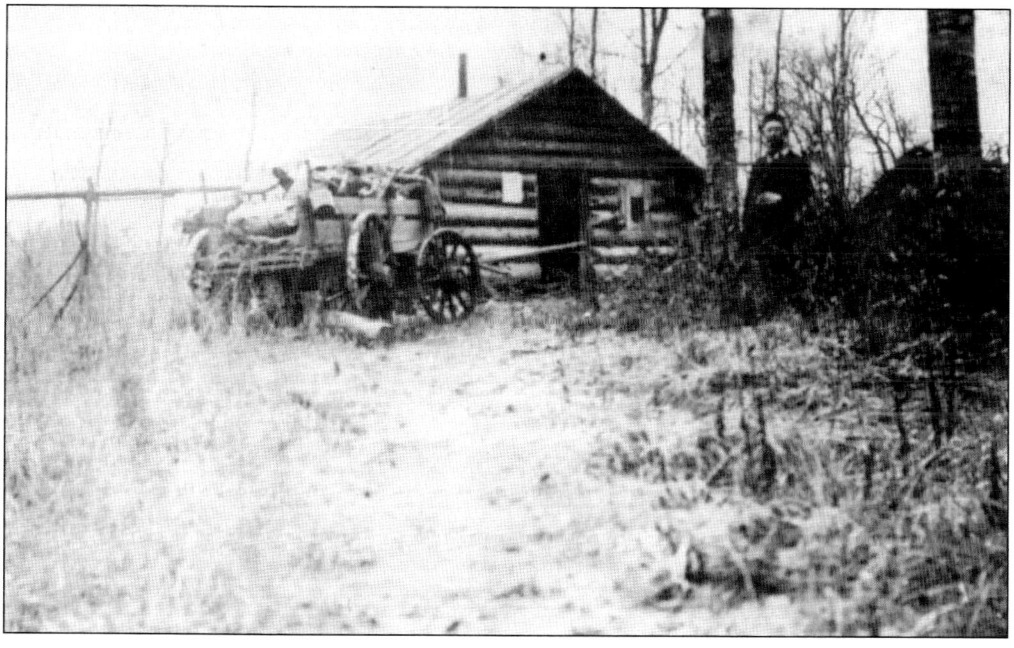

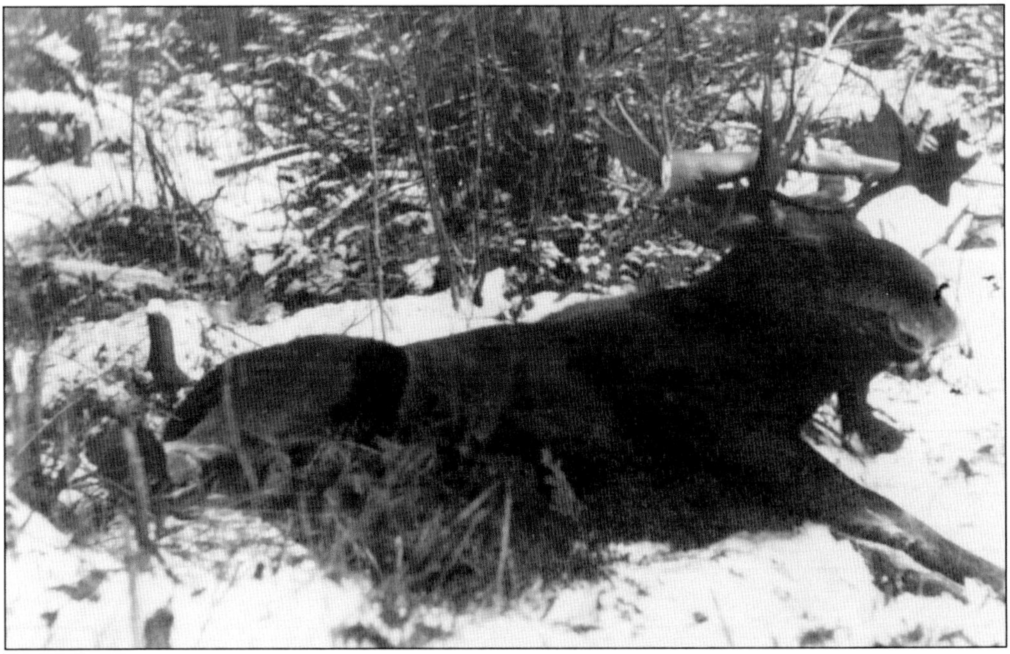

Moose, once abundant in the Adirondacks, were extirpated through hunting and disease by the 1850s. New York governor Horatio Seymour claimed to have taken the last moose in 1859, but an Adirondack guide reportedly took the last moose in 1862 near West Canada Creek. Expensive reintroduction proposals were forthcoming, but the moose made a big comeback during the 1980s on its own. They are now well established in their Adirondack territories, and the day may come when moose hunting season will reopen.

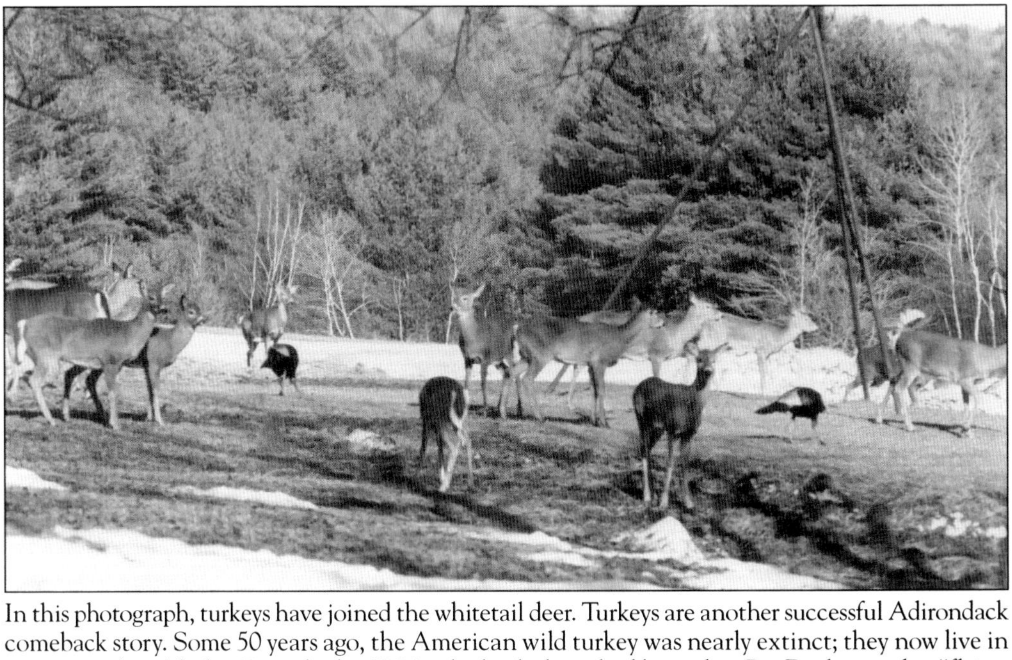

In this photograph, turkeys have joined the whitetail deer. Turkeys are another successful Adirondack comeback story. Some 50 years ago, the American wild turkey was nearly extinct; they now live in every state but Alaska. By early the 2000s, the birds described by author Pat Durkin as the "flying boxcars of the bird world" were forming big flocks in the wilds of New York's mountains.

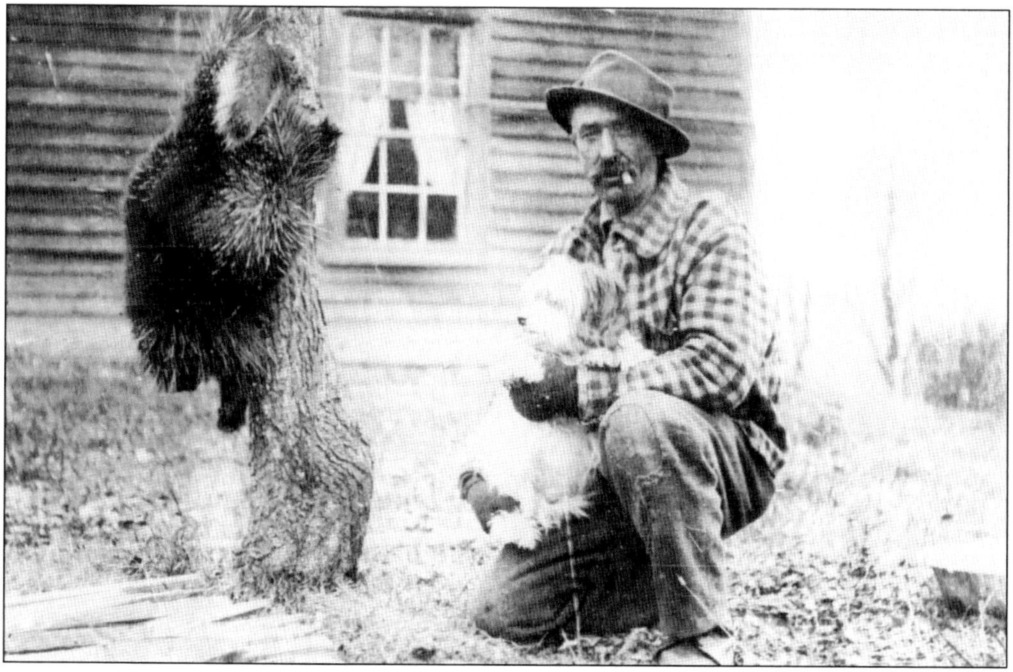

Big game gets most of the attention in the Adirondacks; yet, other wild creatures are part of its hunting history. Slow-moving porcupines wandered through the woodlands and could be easily taken by hungry hunters. One guide was known for his delicious porcupine recipe but, unfortunately, it went to the grave with him. Called "patridge" by Adirondackers, ruffed grouse were the game birds of choice and could be hunted in both summer and winter. Adirondack storyteller Abner Greenfield once claimed to have taken 12 patridge at once by shooting a tree branch, splitting it, and catching the toes of the 12 birds.

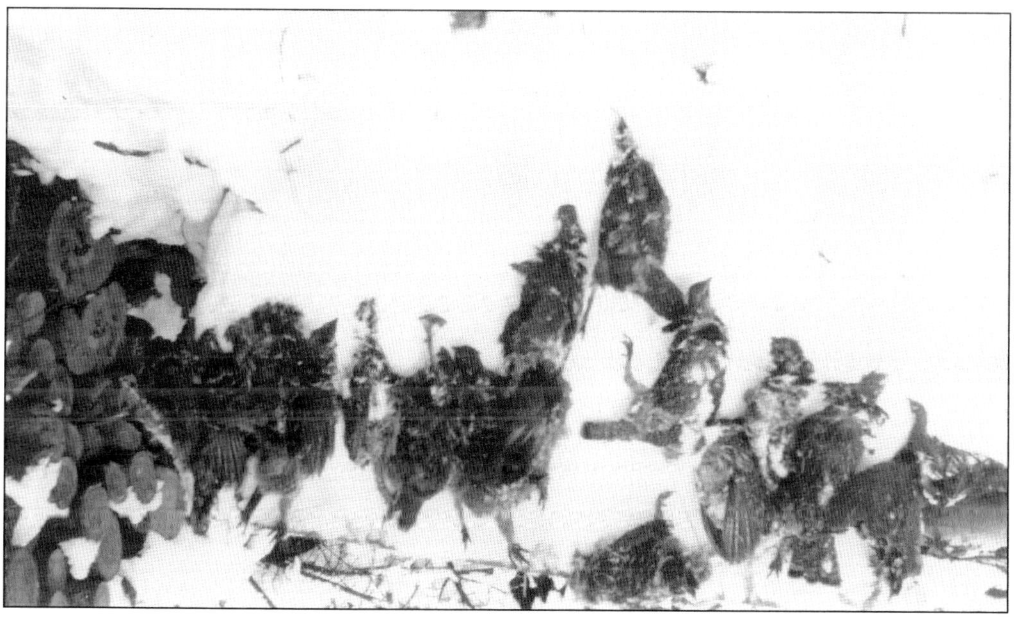

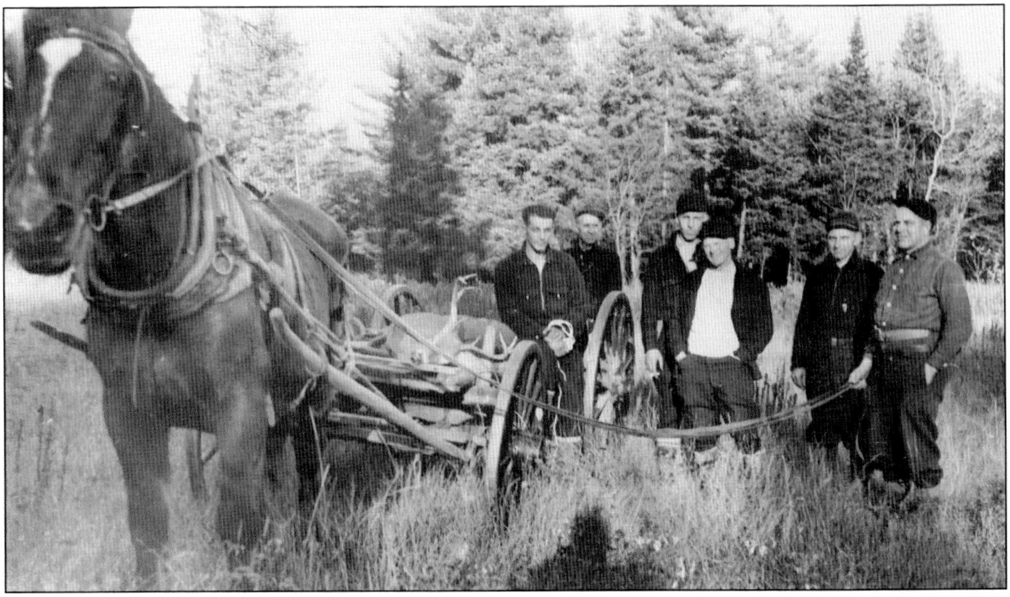

Transporting big game, in some cases, called for the use of sleds, sledges, or wagons. Local farmers provided horses and could add to their annual income by assisting "city hunters" during the hunting season. Farmers also rented cows to the hunting camps for a fresh milk supply while they were hunting. Often, local residents were hired to guide the hunting parties, and many of the young got an early start in Adirondack guiding. Hunters coming from cities took the train as far as the Northville Station of the Fonda, Johnstown & Gloversville (FJ&G) Railroad in the southern Adirondacks and then rode stagecoaches into the hunting country to the north. Deer were taken by stagecoach to Northville and transferred to the train for the ride back to the city. Records kept of the number of deer transported by trains provide a good indication of the success of each deer season.

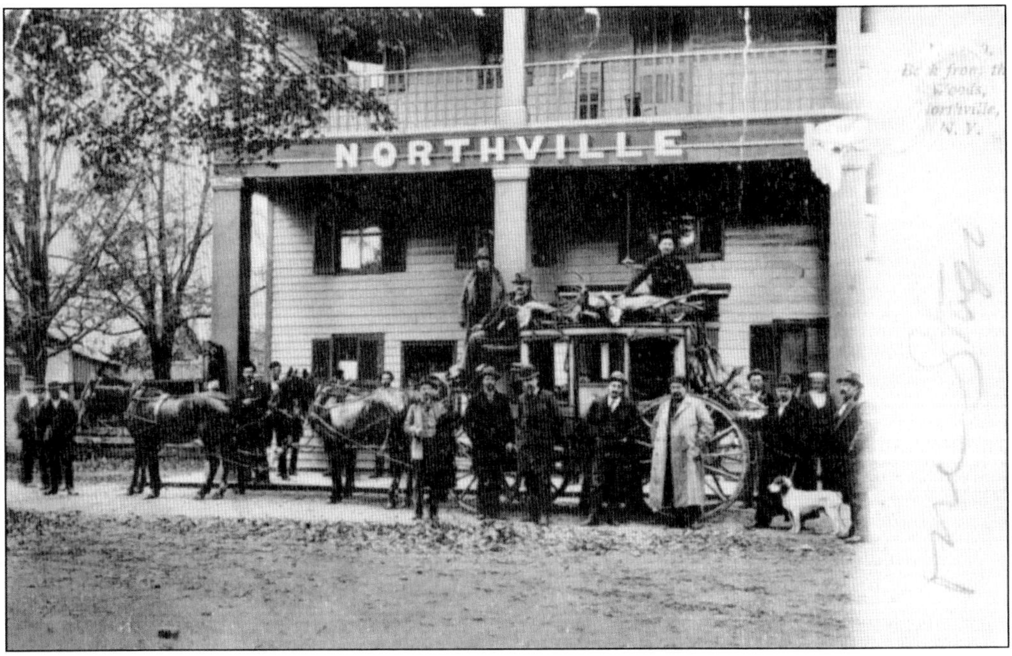

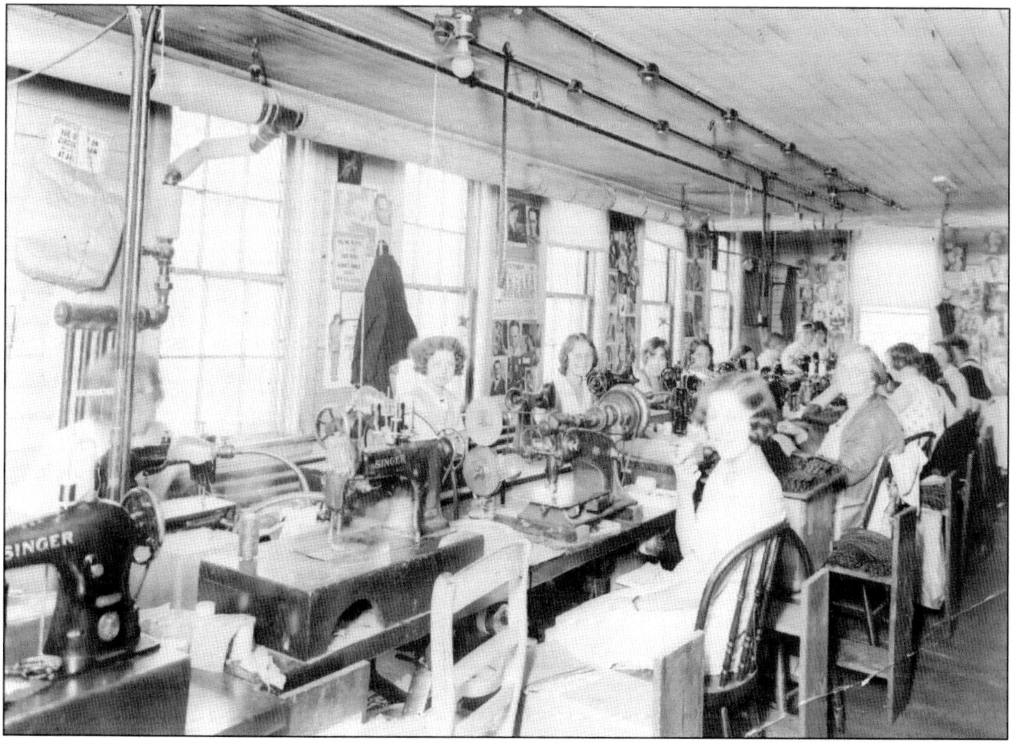

Many of the deer hides from the Adirondacks were tanned in the county and made into gloves and clothes. Tanneries sprang up across the southern Adirondacks but moved to the cities when tanning methods changed. Located near Adirondack hunting grounds, Fulton County was known as "Leatherland, USA." Also known as the "Glove Capital of the World," the county was a major manufacturer of leather products for some 100 years. Originally, gloves were sewn at home, but with increasing demand, factories were built as shown in the photograph. Glove shops employed thousands of women to sew, while men were hired as glove cutters and leatherworkers. Today, only a few tanneries and shops carry on the leather tradition. Below, workers pose in front of the Dixon Glove Shop in Mayfield.

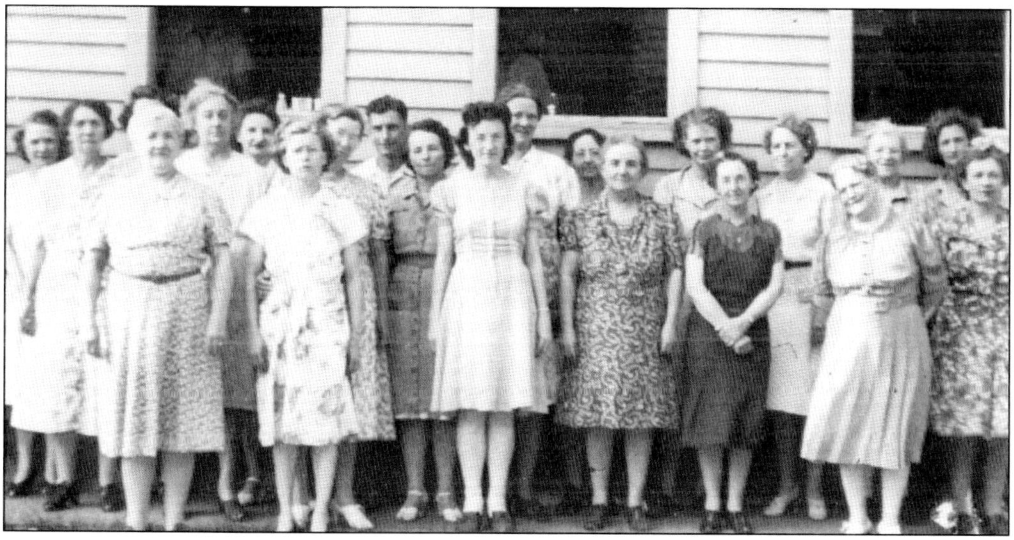

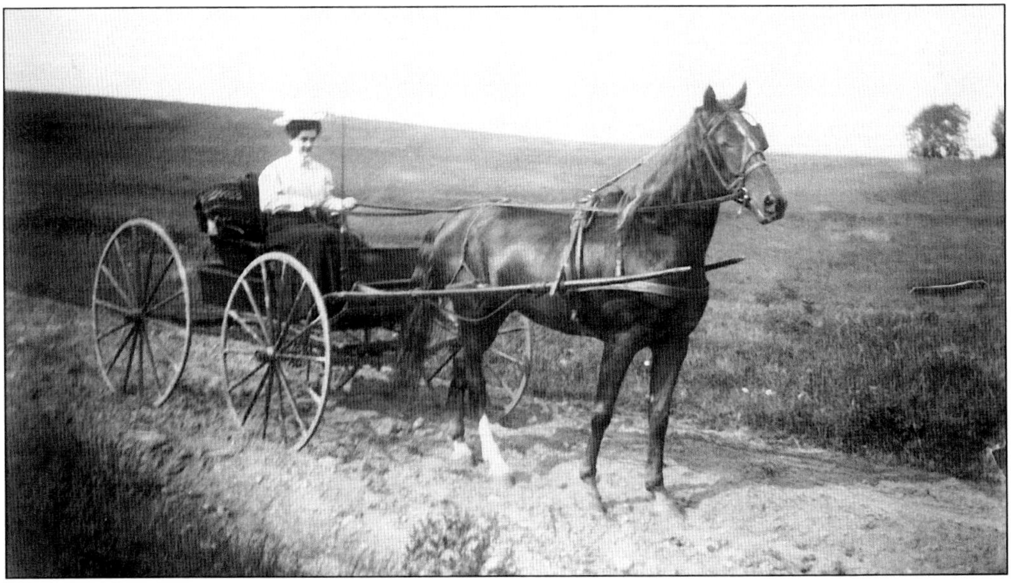

Before the advent of automobiles in the Adirondacks, horsepower was the main method of transportation. Roadways and bridges were constructed to connect Adirondack settlements, and it became everybody's job to keep the roads open for horses and oxen. Settlers were required to keep sections of roads open near their homes. Their responsibilities were based on the number of tillable acres and the size of their homes; an overseer was hired to tax those who did not do their assigned work. In the winter, the roads were rolled and compacted so that the horse and sleighs could get through. Melting snow often made the roadways turn to deep mud in the springtime, limiting their use. Once the newfangled automobile took over, the horse and buggy gave way to waterways and railroads as hamlets grew and businesses prospered.

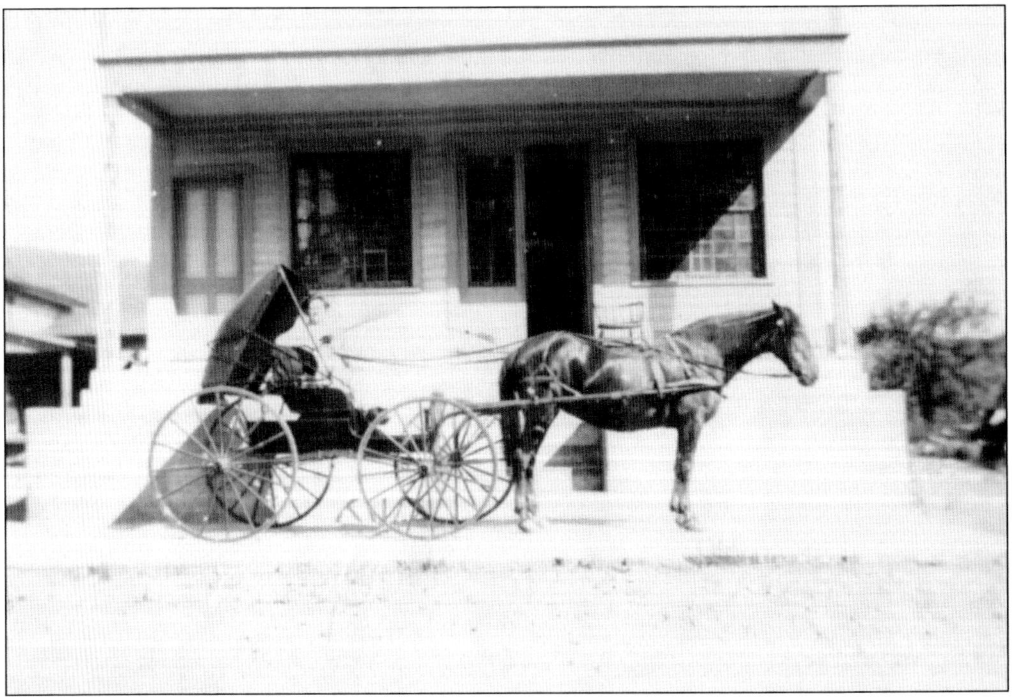

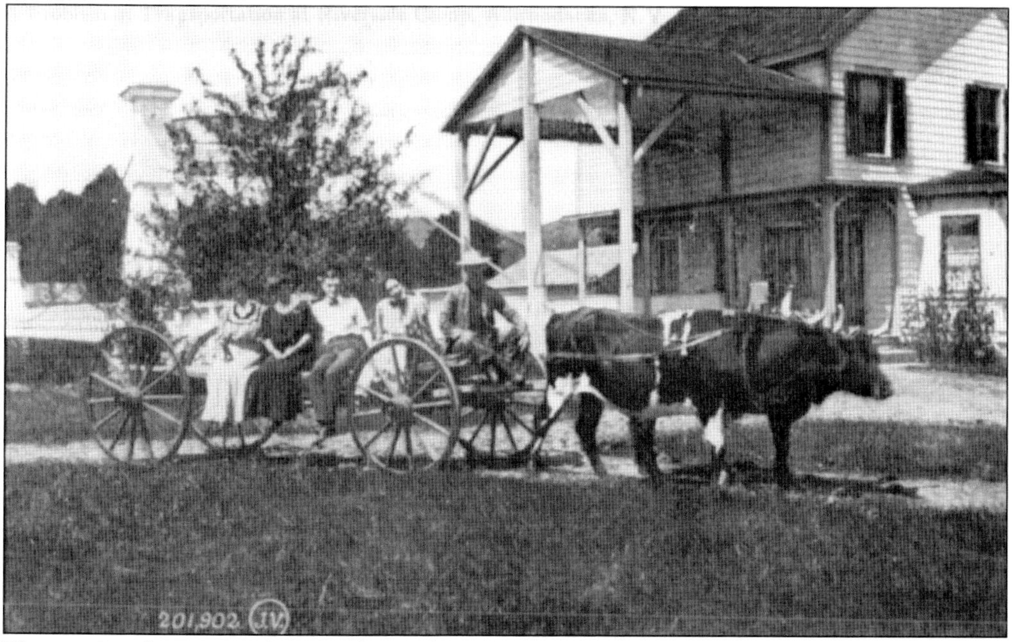

The ox played a major role in civilizing the Adirondack wilds. Oxen pulled wagons, plowed the roads, cleared the stumps, worked in the mines, plowed the gardens, and transported logs. Oxen are easy to train with voice commands, and a simple yoke was used to hitch them to the load.

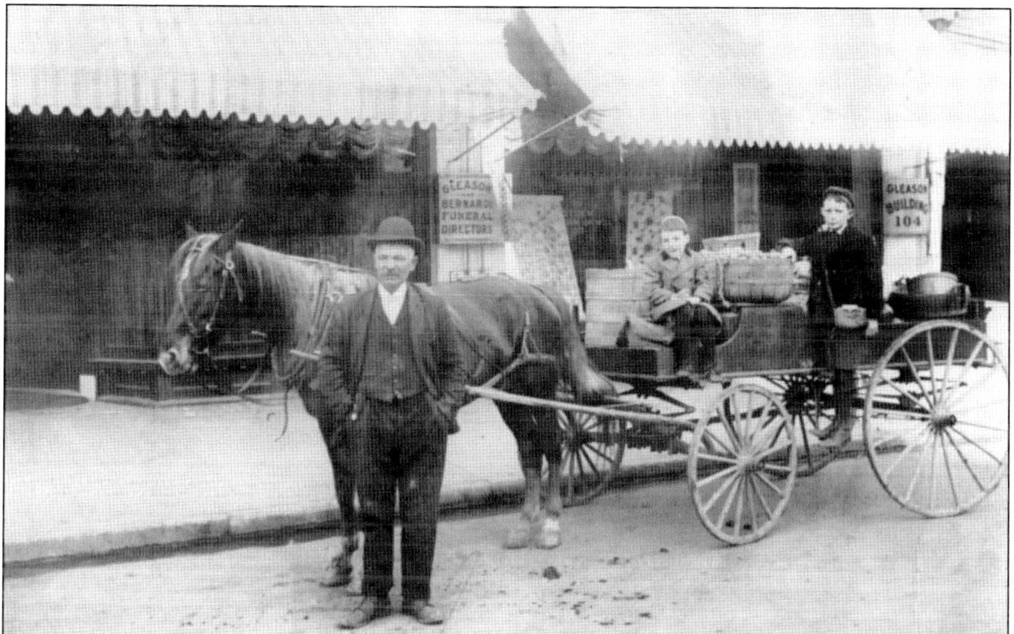

Products of the Adirondacks found their way to city markets, usually transported by horse and wagon or sleigh. Potatoes appear in this photograph; the Adirondacks had a major potato industry. Town weavers took their samples to the surrounding cities to get orders; the author's great-grandmother took her weaving to Utica. Passenger pigeons, venison, and trout from the Adirondacks were in big demand at New York City restaurants.

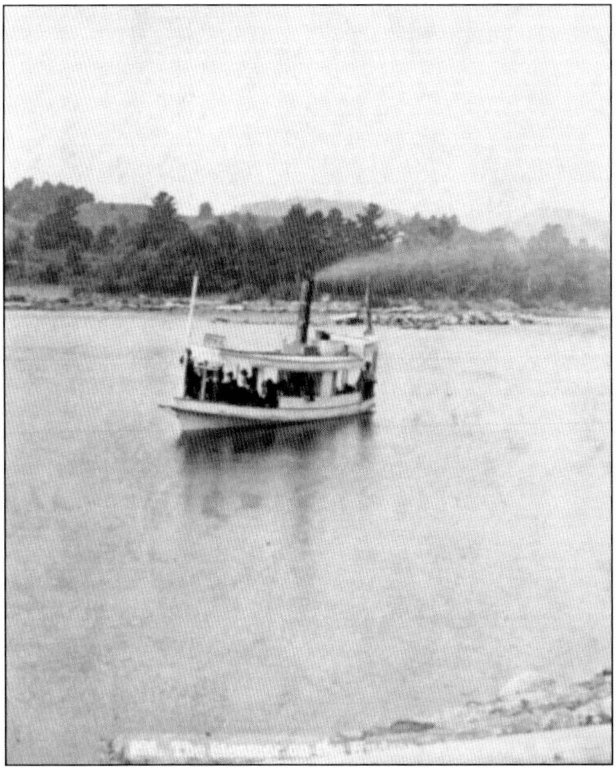

Travel on Adirondack lakes and rivers in the 1800s and 1900s was accomplished by the widespread use of steamers—boats of all sizes propelled by steam power. The steamer in the photograph on the Hudson River at Luzerne reflects the accomplishment of Robert Fulton, who traversed the Hudson River in 1807 to prove the value of steam in water transport. The Fulton Chain of lakes in the central Adirondacks is named in his honor.

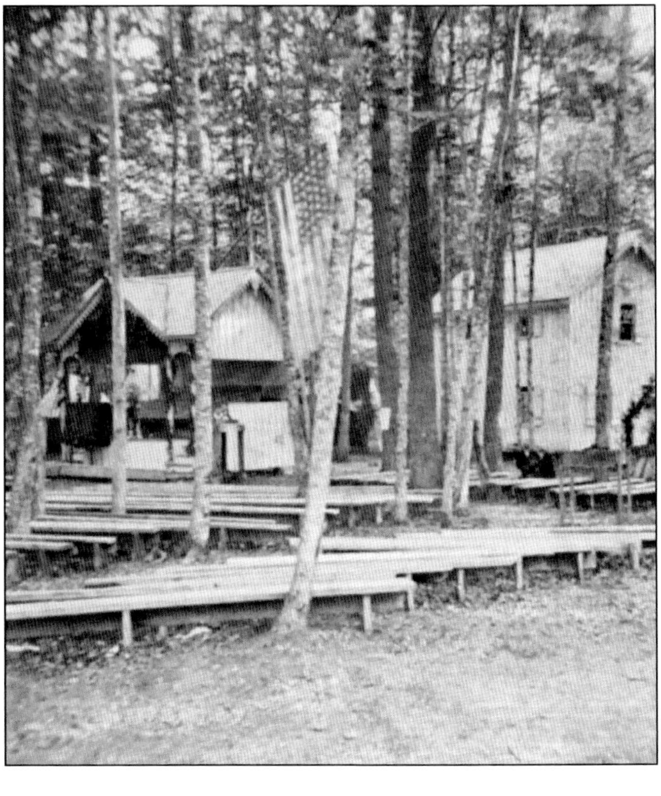

Religious groups found the pine groves of the Adirondacks a perfect location for old-time camp meetings. Gatherings began with tent accommodations on platforms and then evolved into the building of small gingerbread cottages. Shown here in 1884, the Methodist campground at the Sacandaga Park later moved to Round Lake as the park became an amusement center. Rustic benches and fire pits were a part of the outdoor services in the Adirondack woodlands.

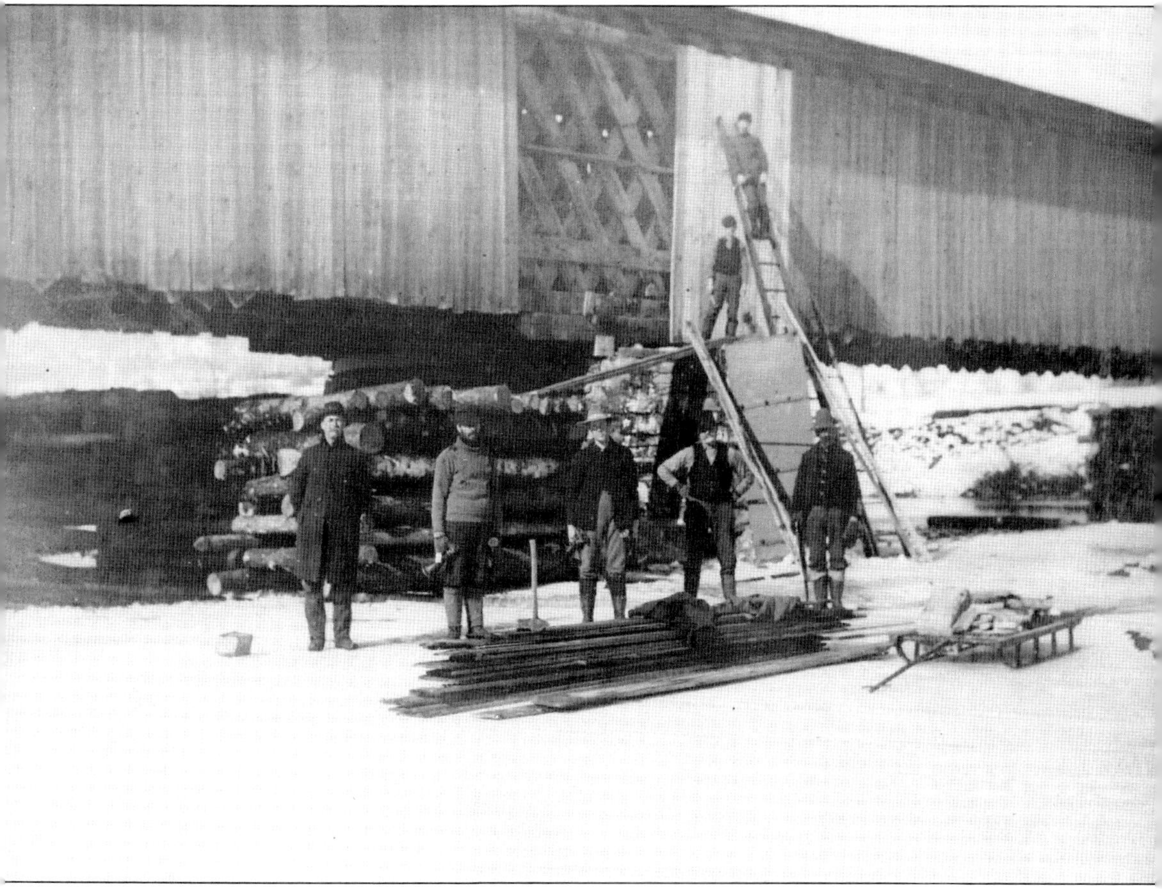

Once land travel overtook the once preferred water travel in the Adirondacks, roadways were constructed between settlements and the "outside world." There were many lakes, rivers, and streams, requiring that bridges be built. Covered bridges were often constructed because they would last longer. The 1866 covered bridge across the Sacandaga River at Wells made the southern Adirondacks accessible. Once the train reached Northville, passengers had to ride a stagecoach to reach Lake Pleasant and other popular spots to the north. After 20 years of service on the Sacandaga, the bridge shown here was raised by two feet, and stone piers replaced the wooden foundations. In 1929, the covered bridge was replaced by a steel bridge that was in use for the next 81 years. A modern flat bridge with decorative stonework was built in 2010. The wooden latticework visible in the photograph was taken to Piseco where it was dismantled in 1929 and used to build trusses in a summer home.

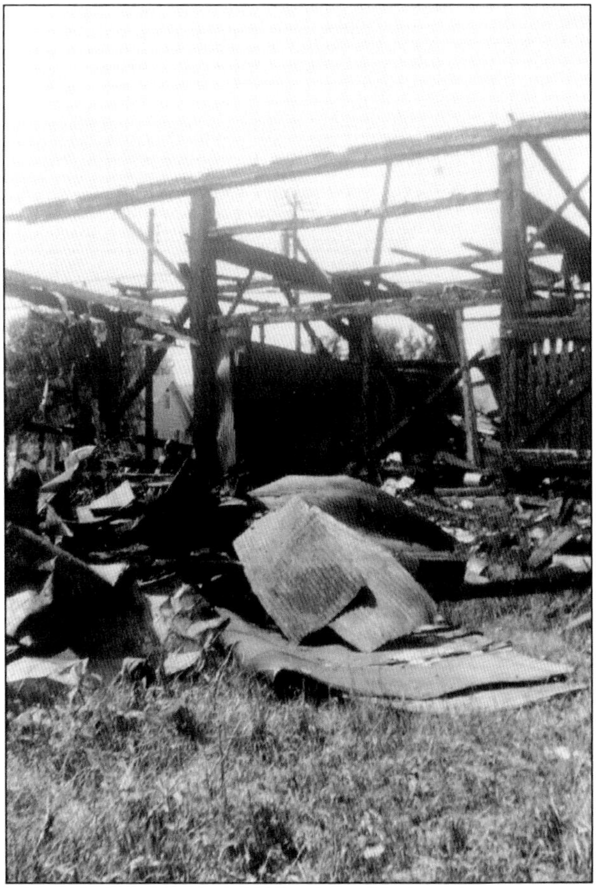

In the days of horses, oxen, and other farm animals, barns were an important part of the landscape. Every settlement had its share of well-built structures, often raised before the house. Caring for animals was vital for survival in remote, mountainous country. Building a good barn took over a year of preparation. Logs had to be cut for beams and joists, and lumber was needed for the floor and sides. Roof shingles had to be split with a froe and mallet. The work was labor-intensive, and neighbors were often called upon for assistance, especially on the day of the barn raising. An experienced "barnmaster" was hired to supervise the construction. Unfortunately, most of those original barns have succumbed to fire or the ravages of time. Old-timers were known to say, "When the roof goes bad, the barn goes." They were right.

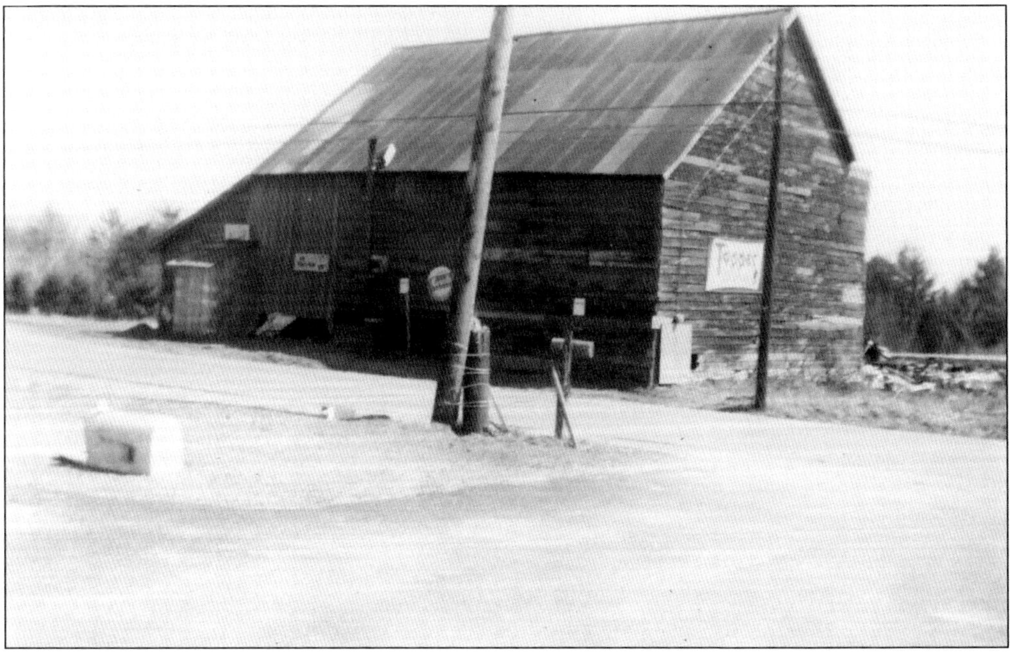

There are 945 dams in the 12 Adirondack counties, and they create ponds and lakes that are larger than their natural size, with around 378 of them of significant size. Lake Pleasant, Pharoah Lake, Lake George, Lake Durant, Lewey Lake, Galway Lake, Harrisburg Lake, and Brant Lake are some of the popular lakes created by dams. After several proposals for dams on the West Branch of the Sacandaga River, including Salmon River, Lake Luzerne, Gooley Mountain, Panther Mountain, and Higley Mountain, a 1969 study recommended that no more reservoirs be constructed in the Adirondacks. Water has become a priority resource in today's world; when it was proposed to sell Indian Lake dam, there was great interest from downstate communities in gaining that water.

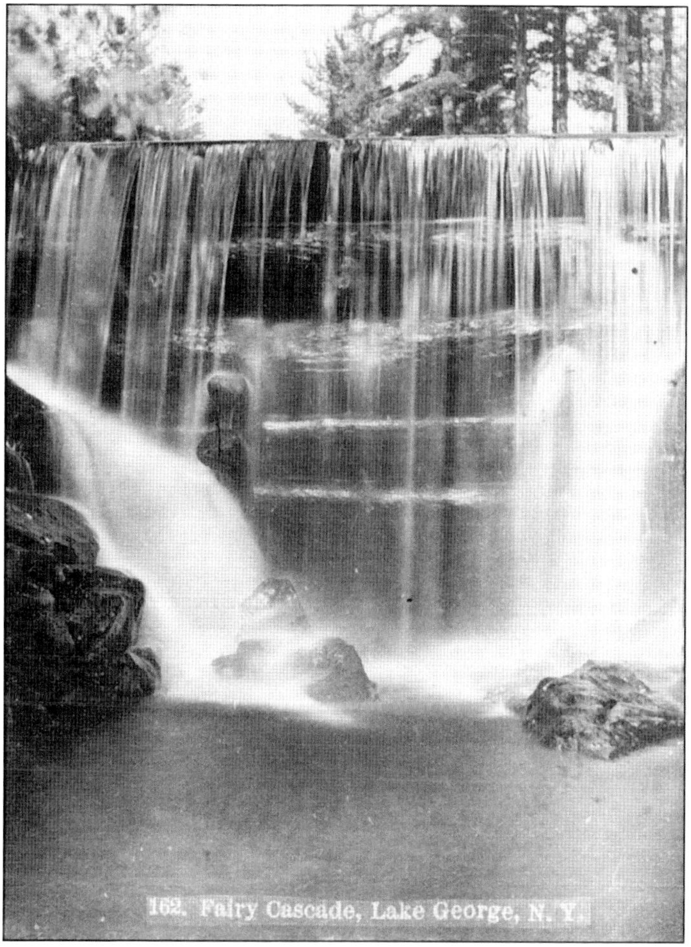

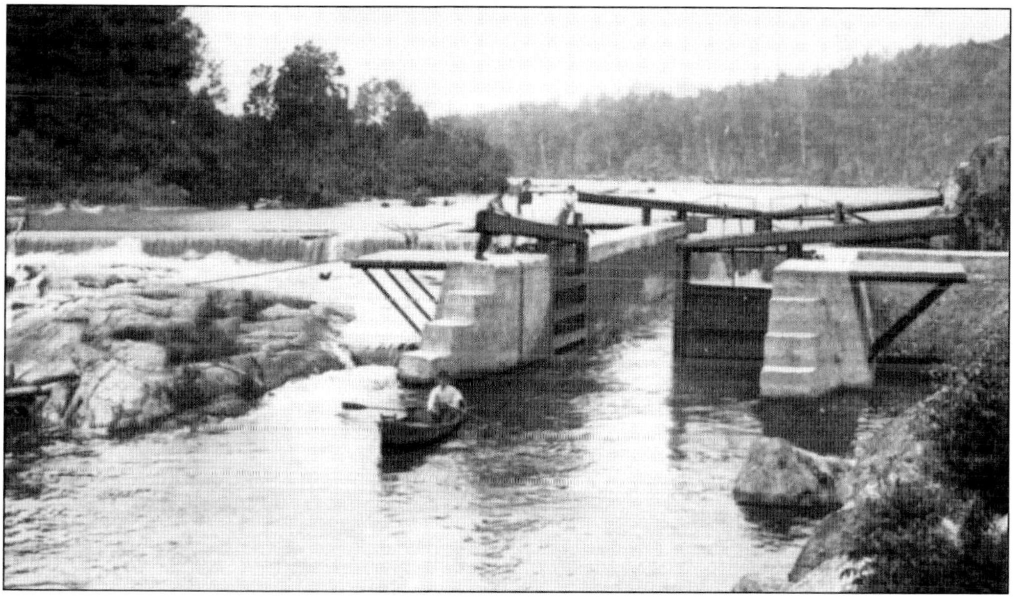

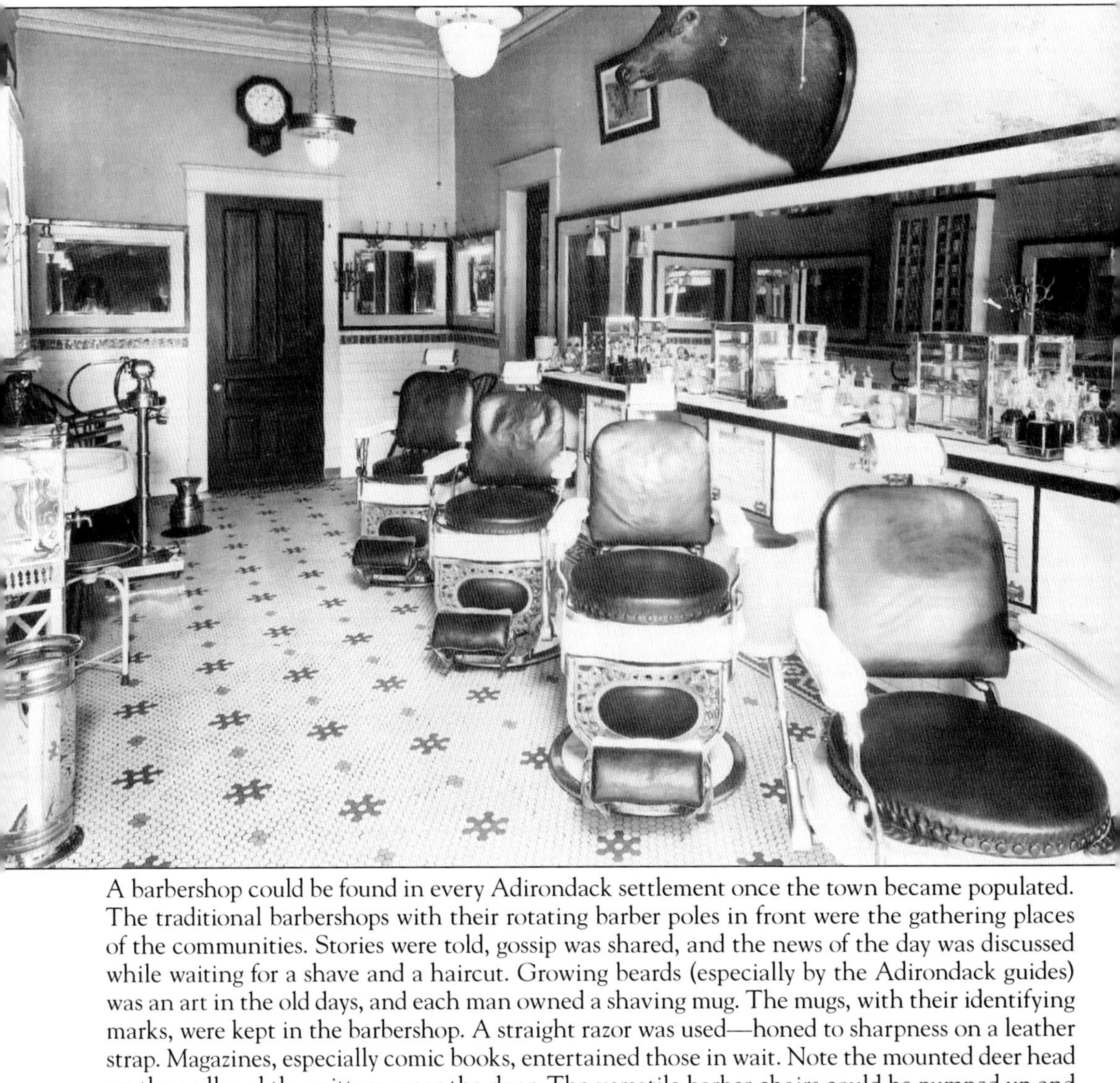

A barbershop could be found in every Adirondack settlement once the town became populated. The traditional barbershops with their rotating barber poles in front were the gathering places of the communities. Stories were told, gossip was shared, and the news of the day was discussed while waiting for a shave and a haircut. Growing beards (especially by the Adirondack guides) was an art in the old days, and each man owned a shaving mug. The mugs, with their identifying marks, were kept in the barbershop. A straight razor was used—honed to sharpness on a leather strap. Magazines, especially comic books, entertained those in wait. Note the mounted deer head on the wall and the spittoon near the door. The versatile barber chairs could be pumped up and down and swung around while the barber plied his trade. Today, such barber chairs have become highly collectable. Much of the Adirondack past was shared in barbershops.

Two

The People

The cast of characters in Adirondack country runs the gamut. Throughout the years of development, rich and poor, young and old, natives and outsiders, residents and visitors, and governmental workers and businessmen all found their niches in the fabric of Adirondack life.

A Broadway show of the Adirondacks might include such players as the wealthy camp owner, the Adirondack guide, the summer tourist, the winter sportsman, the hunter, the angler, the trapper, the hermit, the invalid, the resort worker, the ranger, the game protector, the logger, the tanner, the road worker, the caretaker, the miner, the artist, the writer, the boater, the hiker, the camper, and the preacher, among others—including the retirees and the children.

The Adirondacks had their share of those who made their marks on history. The other Adirondack books in the Images of America series by the author include stories of Boston clergyman/author Rev. William Henry Harrison "Adirondack" Murray; the true Adirondack hermit Noah John Rondeau; Adirondack guides Nick Stoner and Oliver Whitman; the first female guide, Julie Preston; the backwoodsman French Louie; the storyteller Mart Moody; Adirondack furniture maker Lee Fountain; the world-famous skater Sonja Henie; and circus dwarf/actress Cynthia Nickloy, among others.

Many of the nation's parks are mired in traffic and congestion. This is not so in the Adirondacks. The six million acres are crisscrossed with good highways that rarely become burdened with heavy traffic. People move freely throughout the mountains on the highways and waterways and hike, snowmobile, ski, and bike trails. The Adirondack Park has been called "the people's park." Its public and private land belongs to the people, and state-owned lands are open to all.

Cultural attractions, events, good schools, health-care facilities, community organizations, and churches are all found in Adirondack country. And modern technology is now connecting the remote, forested land to the outside world.

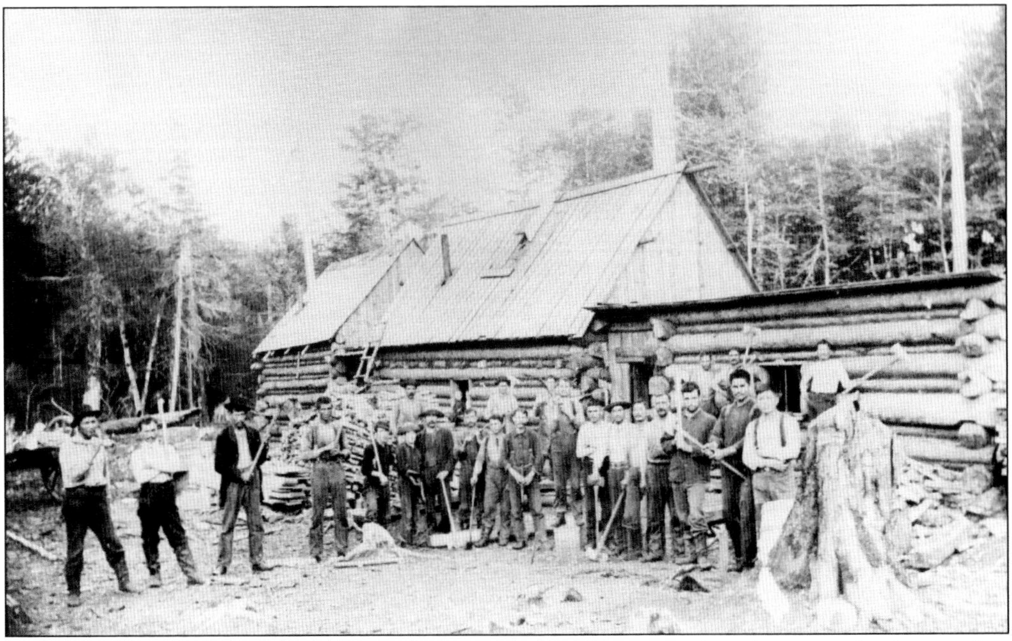

In the 19th century, the proliferation of tanneries played a major role in bringing the first settlers to the mountains. Tanning villages came with the tanneries. Tannic acid, used to tan animal hides, was made from the bark of hemlock trees. Axemen were called "fixers," while "spudders" scored the bark with the axes and ripped off the four-foot sheets with spuds.

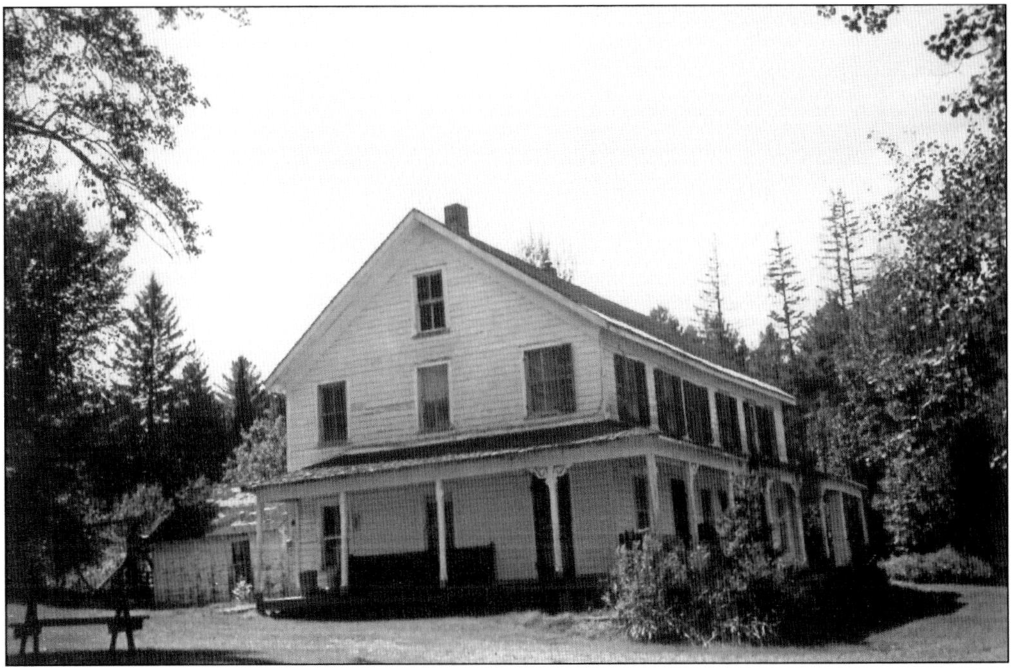

The tanning village of Griffin had a once thriving population of 600— more on Saturday nights, when the lumberjacks came to town. When the tannery went out of business and lumbering slowed down, the village was abandoned. Some of the homes were sold and moved to the nearby village of Wells. The few buildings that remain are in use as summer camps.

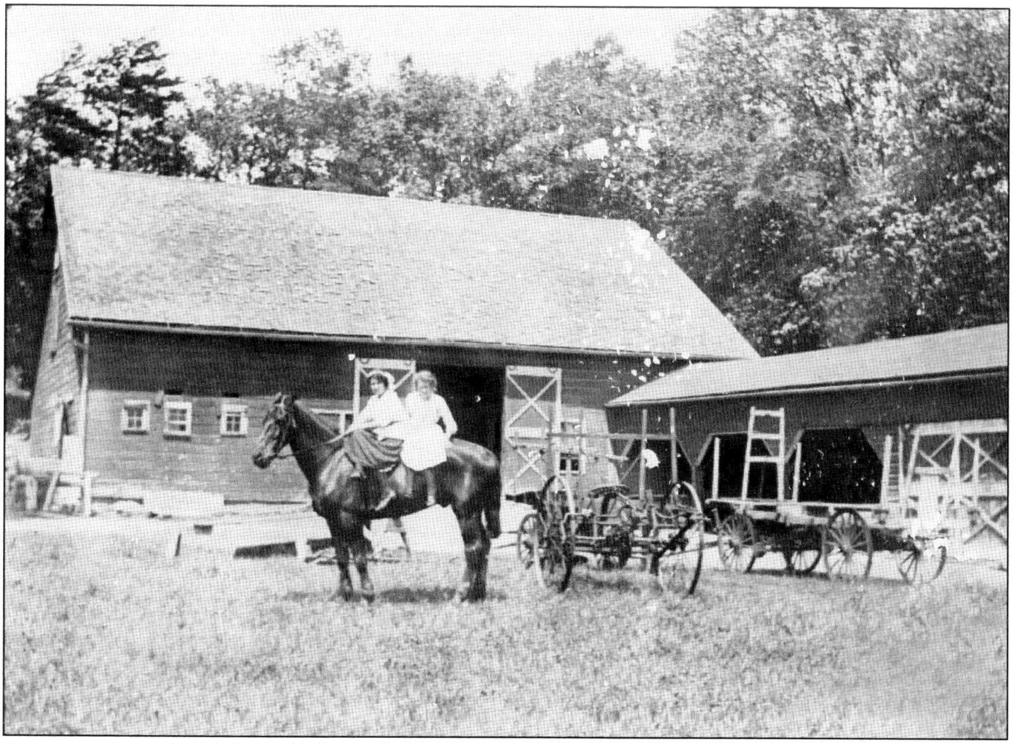

Some came to the Adirondacks to farm; it was believed that once the land was cleared of the trees, the rich soil would grow big crops. Settlers found that farming was highly labor intensive. The rocks kept "growing" each year, while the growing season brought Jack Frost too early in the fall. Horses were kept for use in the woods and for transportation. Several types of vehicles were also used.

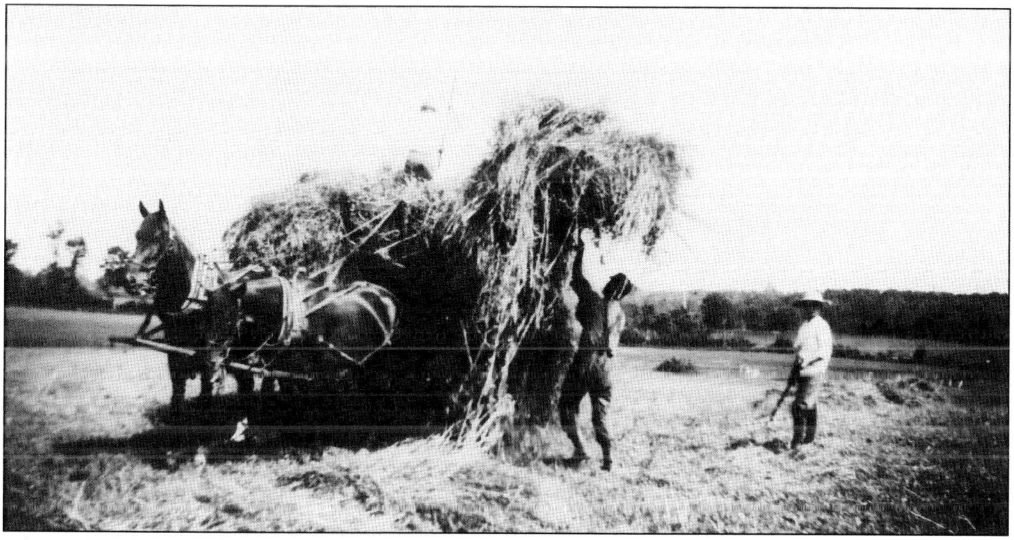

The Adirondackers pulled out stumps and planted hayfields and gardens. Farmers often got together to harvest crops. They borrowed equipment from each other and bartered one crop for another. Wells was once known as "Pickleville" because of the large number of cucumbers grown on the Sacandaga River flats and sold out of pickle barrels in general stores.

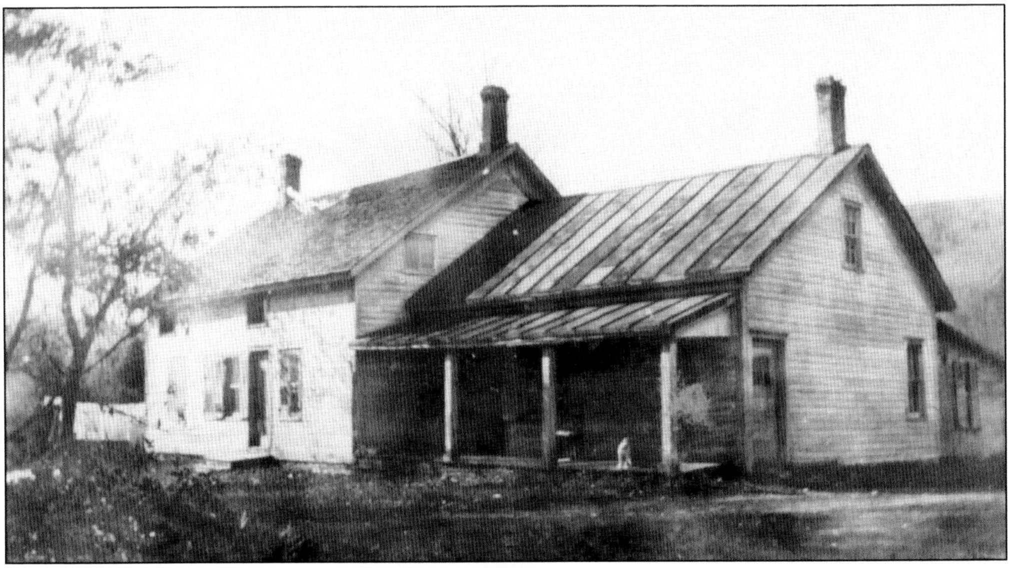

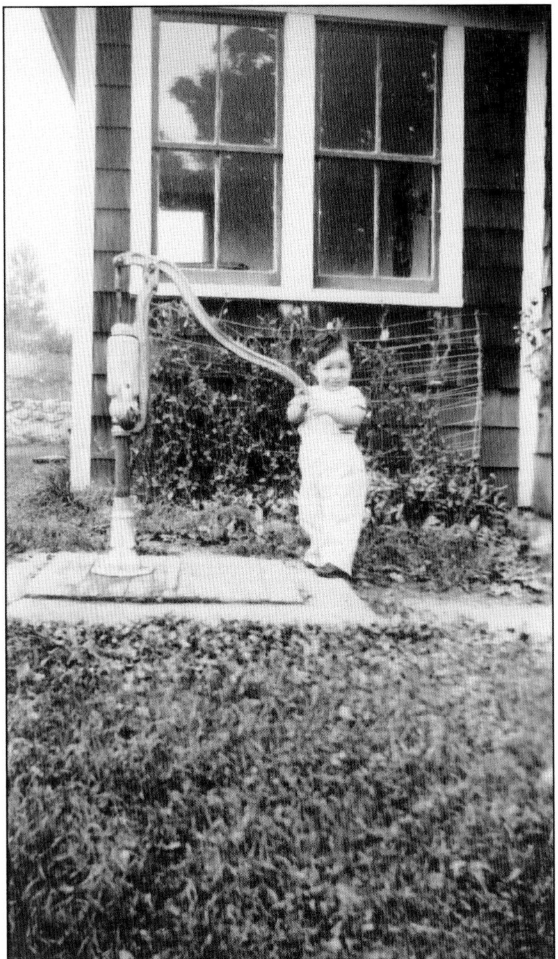

John Hosley grew up on a farm located on the west side of the Sacandaga River at Wells. His parents, James S. Hosley and Lina Burton Hosley, farmed the rugged Adirondacks in the late 1800s and early 1900s. They found farming in the mountains a challenge, with the rocky soil and short growing season. On their farm, they had a sugar bush for maple syrup and limekilns for potash.

Municipal water supplies were unavailable in the Adirondack settlements; it was necessary to find water using an apple twig for dowsing and digging the well by hand. An inverted cone-shape hole was dug until water was reached, and then a round stone wall was laid up. Dirt was filled in around the stone, and a water pump or a crank was installed on the top with a bucket on a rope.

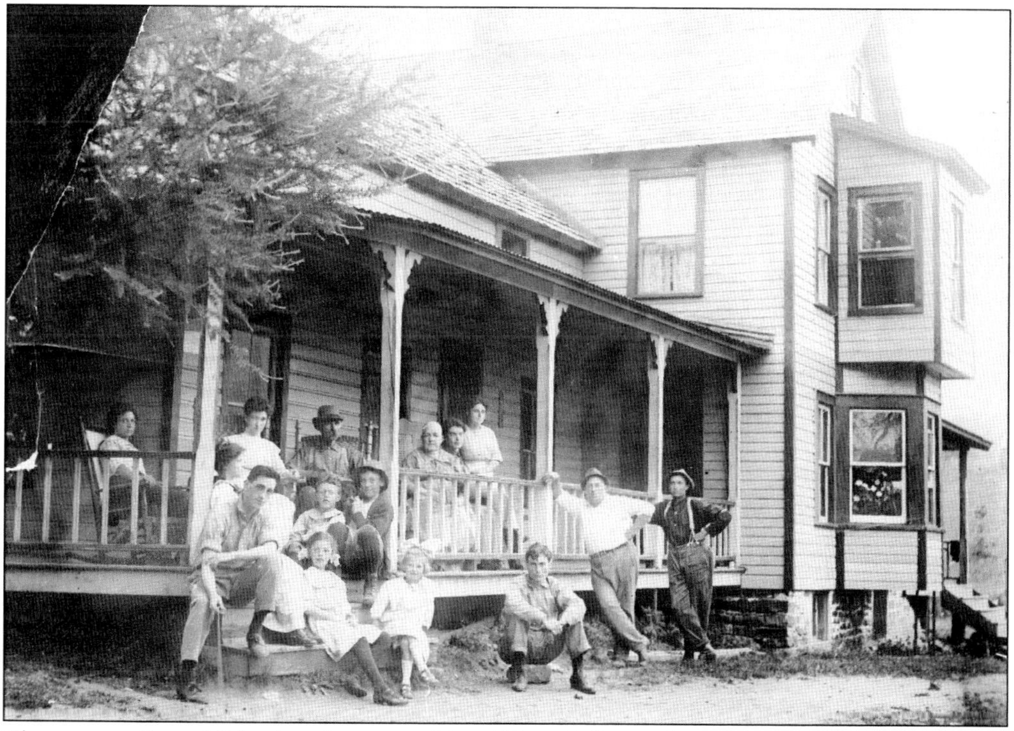

The once well-established settlement at Hope/Hope Falls on the Adirondack Trail (Route 30) was the site of large tanneries and seven sawmills. As early as 1845, more than 600 people resided in the town. Stately homes, two stores, a school, hotels, and a church made up the settlement. This large family homestead once stood across the roadway from the schoolhouse, which still stands today.

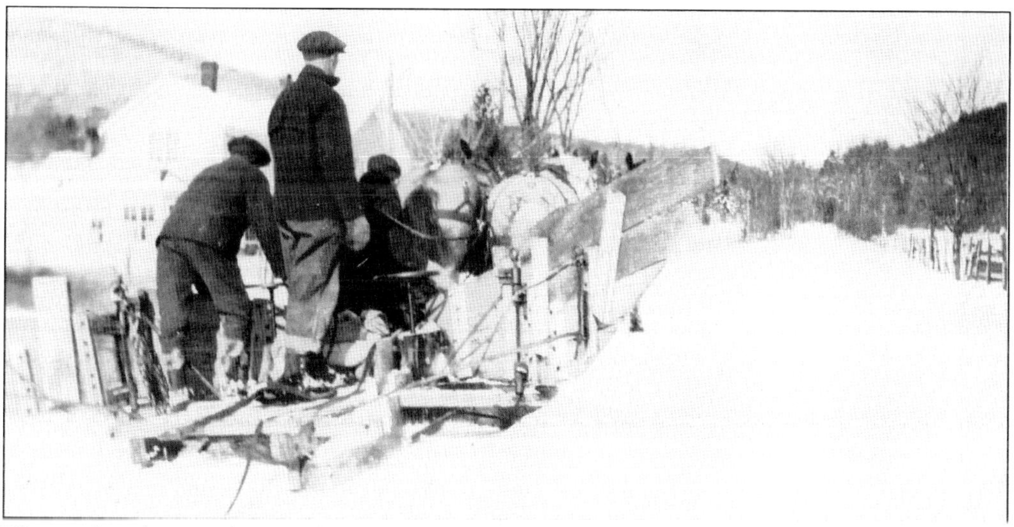

Those who chose to live in the rural Adirondack region faced the task of keeping the snow-covered winter roads open. Horses and oxen were used to pull large wooden plows or snow-rollers to prepare a frozen roadbed. When the snowdrifts reached great heights, they were shoveled by hand. There were times when the horses were down in the snow, and tangled harnesses had to be removed to get the horses up again.

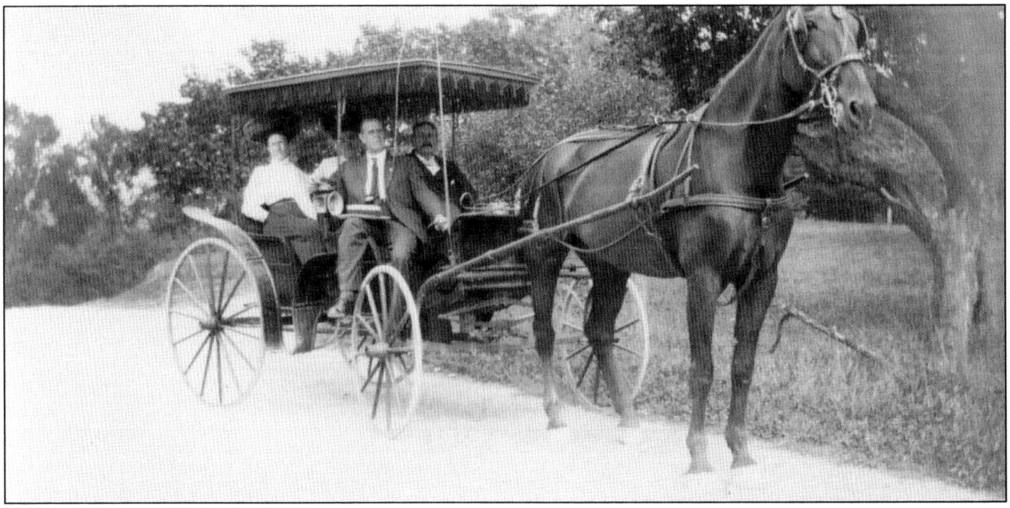

Many people know the song "The Surrey with the Fringe on Top," from the 1943 musical *Oklahoma!* Hitching up the horse to a light carriage with four wheels, two seats, and roof for a Sunday afternoon drive brought Adirondack families together. Surreys were used to go to church on Sunday and to prayer services. Box socials at the schoolhouse also brought out surreys.

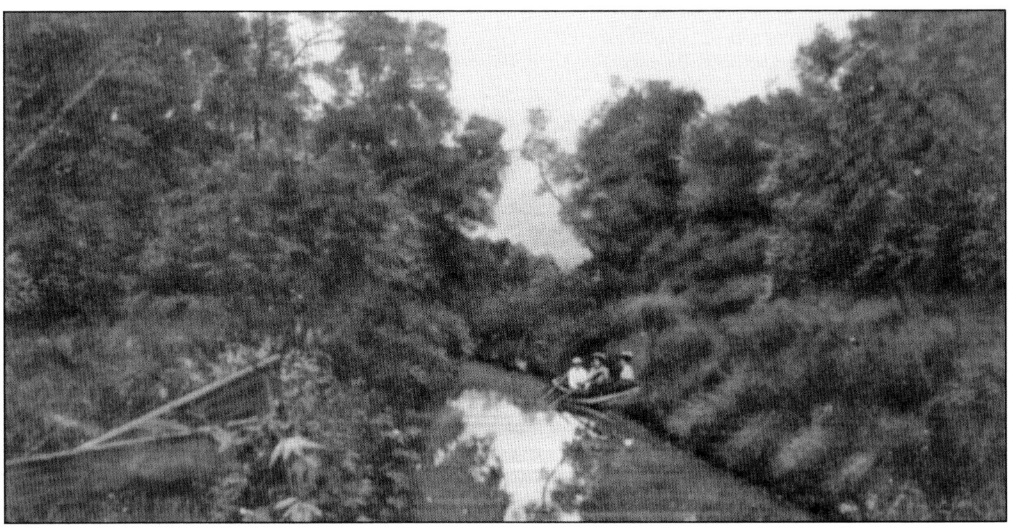

After an early surge of "men only" enjoying the Adirondacks, women of all walks of life found the forested mountains and lakes to their liking. Wealthy city matrons, college girls, settlers' wives, and women who simply loved the out-of-doors came to the Adirondacks for everything from vacationing at comfortable camps to roughing it on wilderness trails. The ladies in this photograph are enjoying a guide-boat trip up the Kunjamuck Stream.

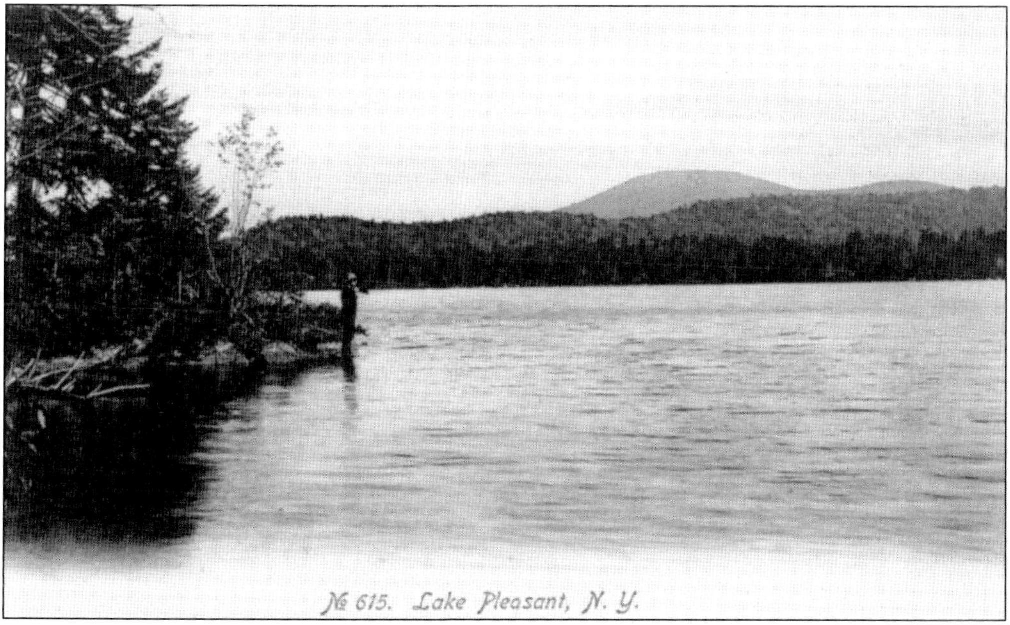

A lone fisherman stands on the shores of Lake Pleasant representing the thousands who have found good fishing in the Adirondacks since the days of the 1840s Lake Piseco Trout Club. The Reverend George W. Bethune was an avid fisherman and a member of the club. He became the American editor of Izaak Walton's *The Compleat Angler* and included a report on the club in the 1880 edition.

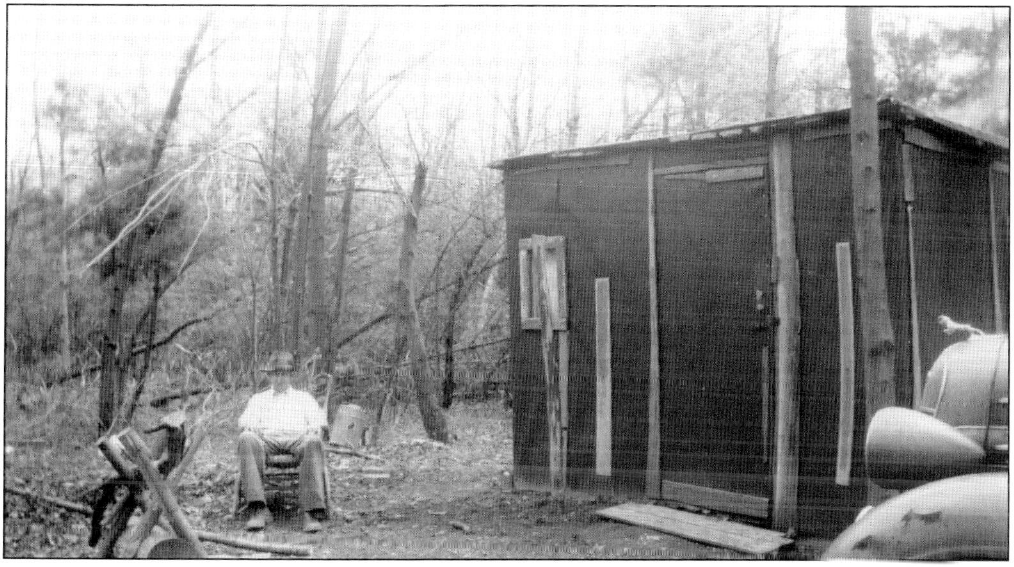

Adirondackers enjoyed their backwoods camps that could range from the elegant "great camps" on Adirondack lakes to tar-papered shacks back in the woods. The camps were well used during the hunting season and enjoyed by many during the summer season. Water was found in a nearby mountain spring and a privy (outhouse) was hidden in the nearby woods. Kerosene lamps and lanterns provided light, and cookstoves burned the plentiful wood.

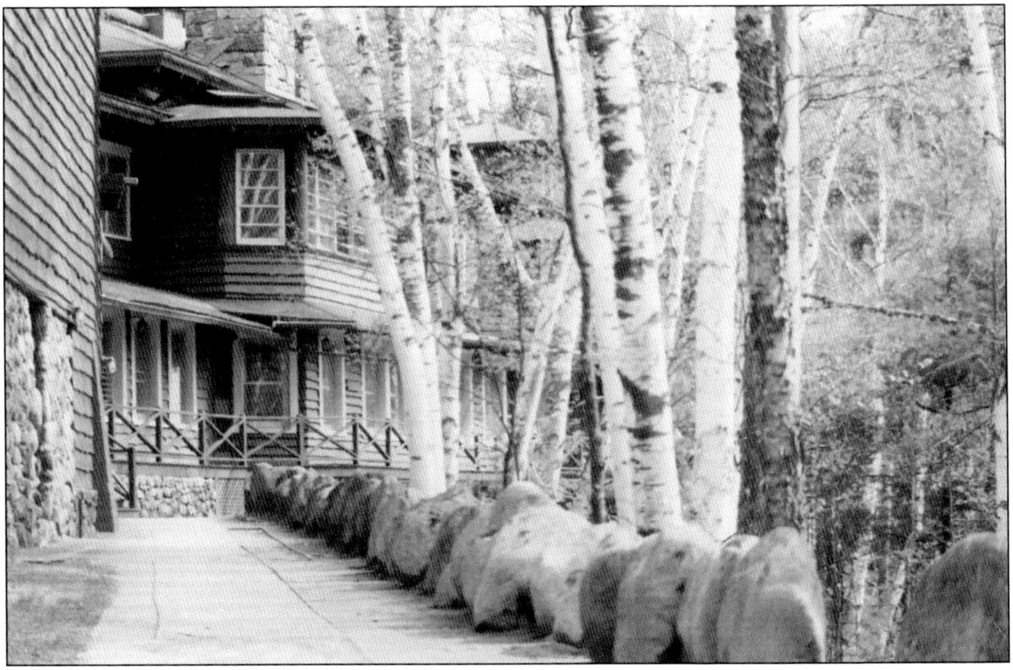

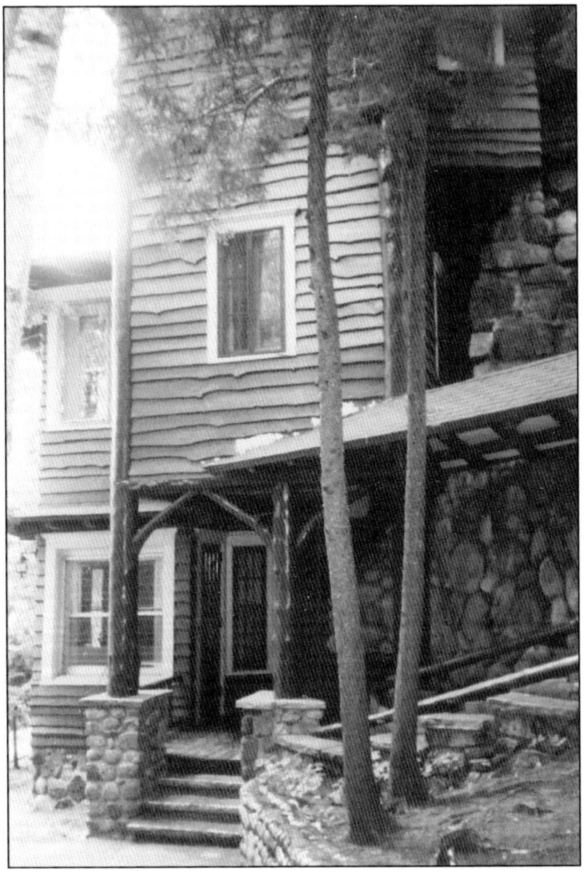

The Durants, Vanderbilts, Rockefellers, Huntingtons, Posts, Whitneys, Webbs, Pruyns, and Litchfields, among several others, built wilderness estates on the Adirondack lakeshores. Construction and maintenance of the giant rustic buildings in these "great camps" provided employment for many people. Usually, over two dozen buildings were on the estate, each fulfilling a specific purpose. By separating the uses of the buildings, such as a kitchen building from a sleeping building, the whole camp was not lost when a fire occurred. The Post estate shown here was once owned by the people of New York State but is now in private hands. Majorie Merriweather Post originally developed it as a summer home on Upper St. Regis Lake. Located on a rise between two lakes, it was named Topridge.

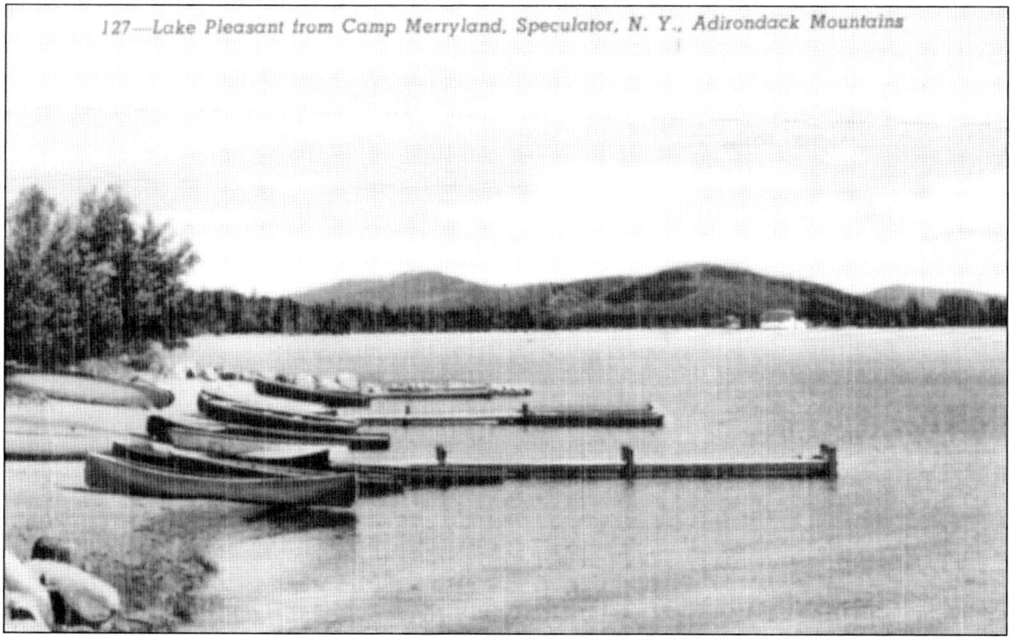

Charlie Brown was somewhat a legend in his own time; he had amazing knowledge of the Adirondack woodlands and Adirondack birds. His storytelling endeared him to folks of all ages. He was the owner of Camp Merryland, an Adirondack resort on Lake Pleasant, where he rented out cottages. He prided himself on being able to name all of the birds that landed there, and his garden of flowers was a showplace.

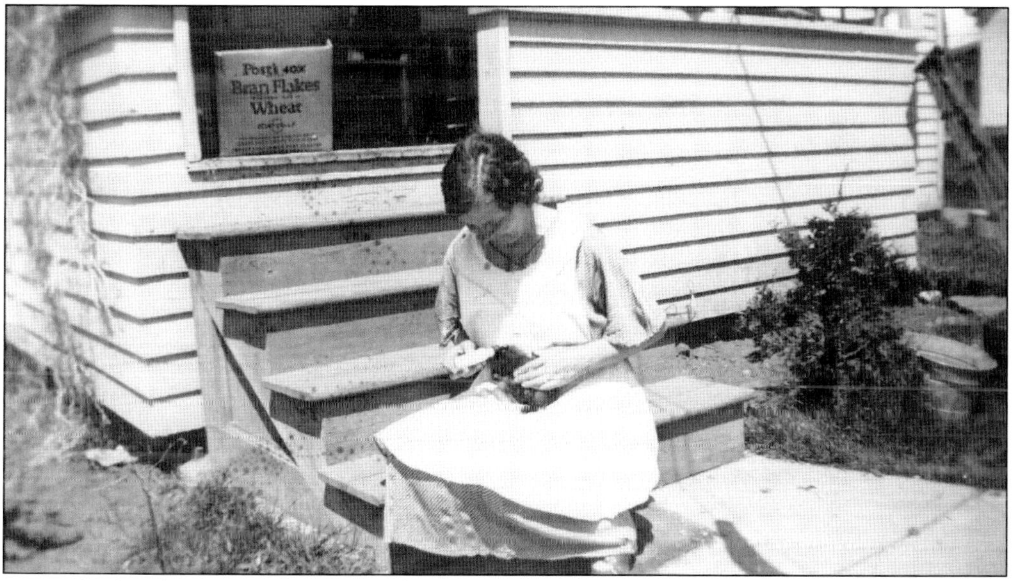

Animals played an important part in the lives of the rural Adirondack people. Settlers depended upon them for food and money. Horses, cows, pigs, and dogs were kept for domestic uses and to create income. The housewife shown here is feeding a baby silver fox from a bottle. Silver foxes were raised both domestically and commercially for their valuable furs.

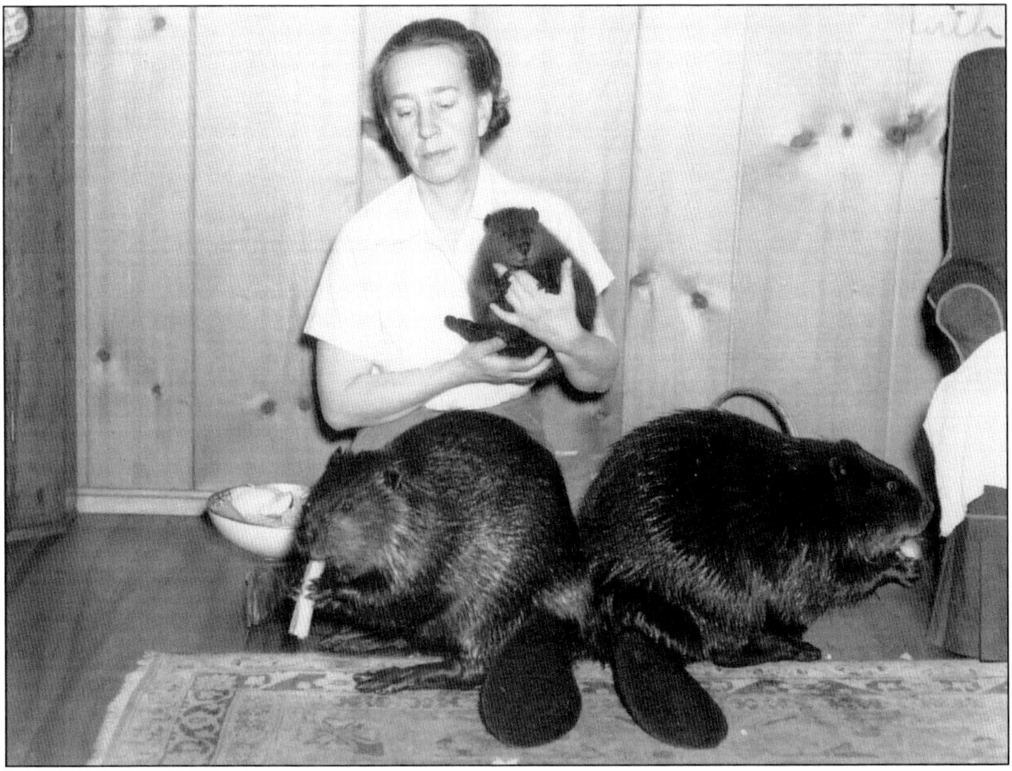

For many years, "Beaver Lady" Dorothy Richards opened her home Beaversprite, near Dolgeville, to the Adirondack beaver. A waterway was constructed from a beaver pond to her kitchen so that beavers could swim in and join her for dinner or to welcome visitors. She created a sanctuary for the beavers and wrote the quintessential book on life with beavers. She found them to be highly intelligent and neat in their own way. When water got tracked onto her floor, the beaver would go to the closet and get a mop cloth to wipe it up. Schoolchildren got to meet the beavers up close, and if they were good, Dorothy approved their presence. The beavers were given names such as Hank, Chuck, and Eager. The natural history center on the property still offers summer lectures today.

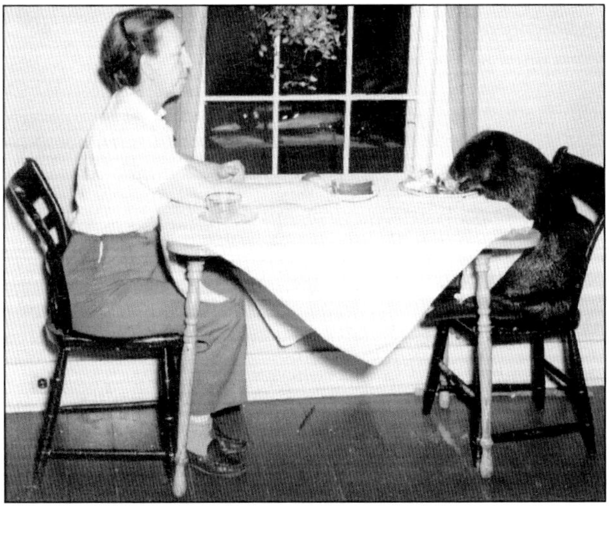

Beatrice Whitman Fremont was born at Wells in the Adirondacks in 1899. Like many of the Adirondackers, she was in the fifth generation and lived there all her life. Her father, village blacksmith Charles Whitman, was born there in 1853 and lived to be 93. The Whitman family migrated to the Adirondacks in 1792 to "get rich" in the tannery business.

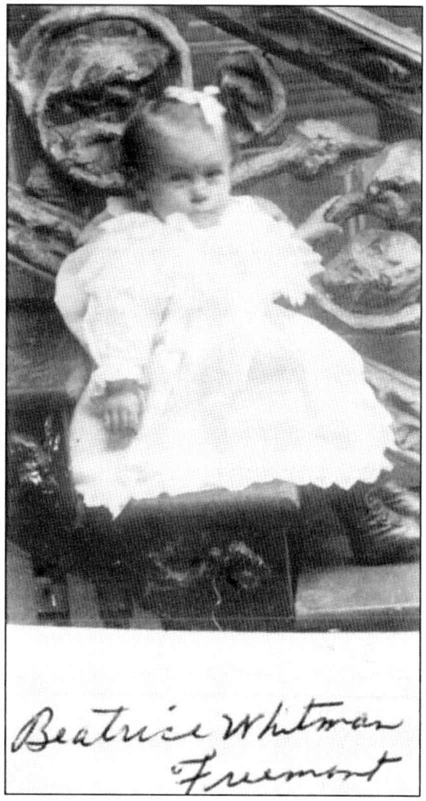

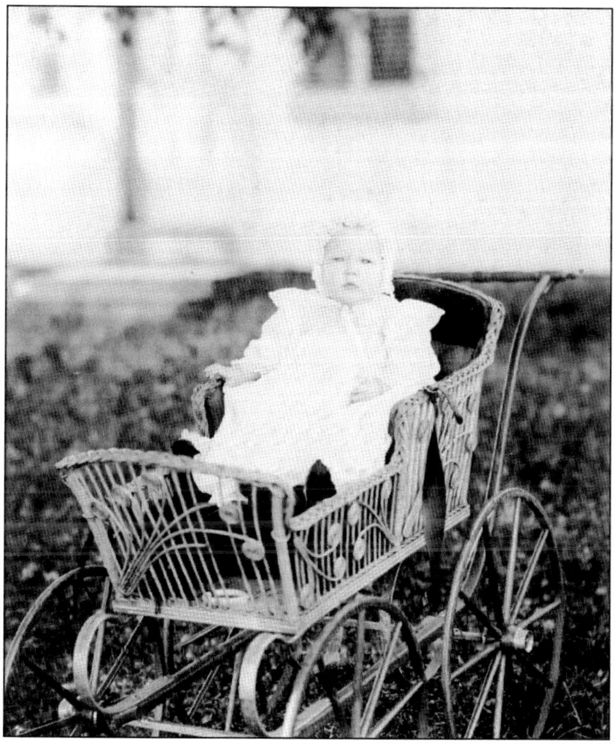

Bessie Hosley Brown descended from another longtime Adirondack family; she was a fourth-generation Hosley. Benjamin Hosley had moved to Wells from Edinburgh, New York, in 1841 to build a hotel. Sampson Hosley's hotel was a great stopping off place for the southern Adirondack stage line. The 1898 Hosley House still stands in Wells. The Hosley family became known for their fine hotels.

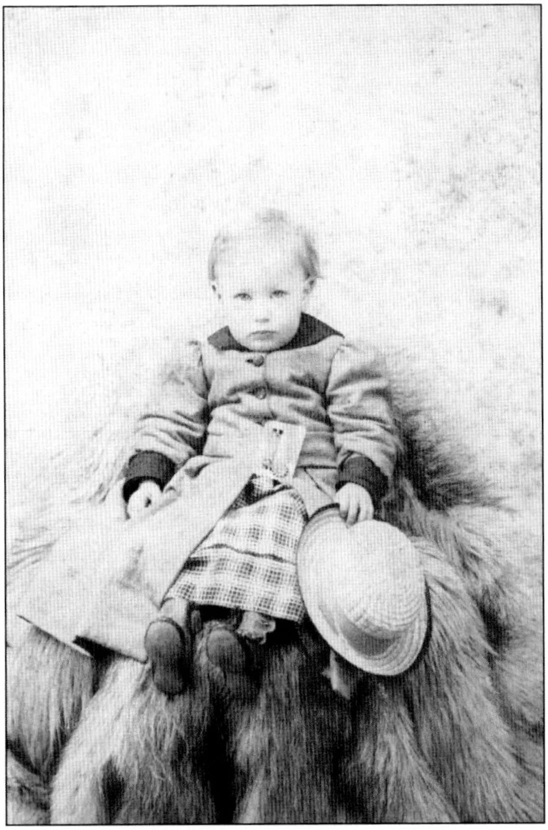

Little boys of the late 1800s were often photographed in dresses; the clothing catalogs of that day did not offer pants until the age of three, and long pants were not allowed until boys were nine years old. In this 1880 photograph, fifth-generation Adirondacker John Hosley models the fashion of the day; it is a far cry from what one might expect on a backwoods Adirondack boy.

Three Adirondack girls pose in their finery in front of Bill Greenslet's barbershop in Wells in 1910. The skirts may have been homemade; most girls of that day were taught to sew at a young age. There were seasons of the year that called for the heavy sweaters, and, with homes heated with a woodstove in the kitchen and a parlor stove in the living room, warm clothing was necessary.

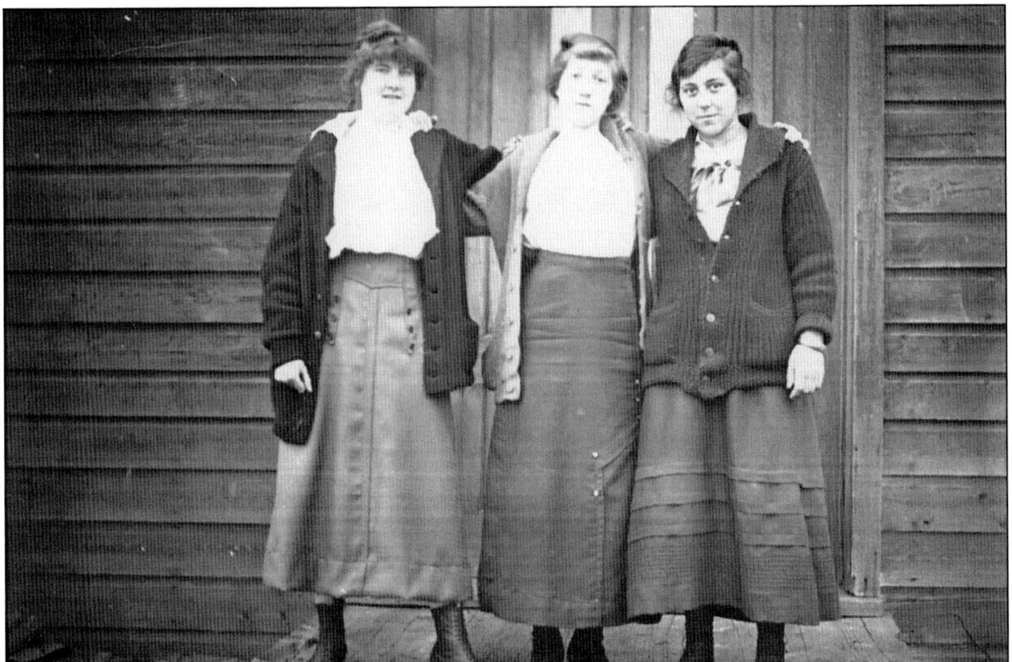

In the sitting rooms and parlors of the turn of the 20th century, various pieces of furniture were in widespread use, including lounges, couches, and bed lounges. Regular lounges had a padded back and slightly angled resting arm on one end. Bed lounges are similar, with the addition of comfortable springs instead of the usual horsehair or straw filling. The couch shown here has a rug-like covering.

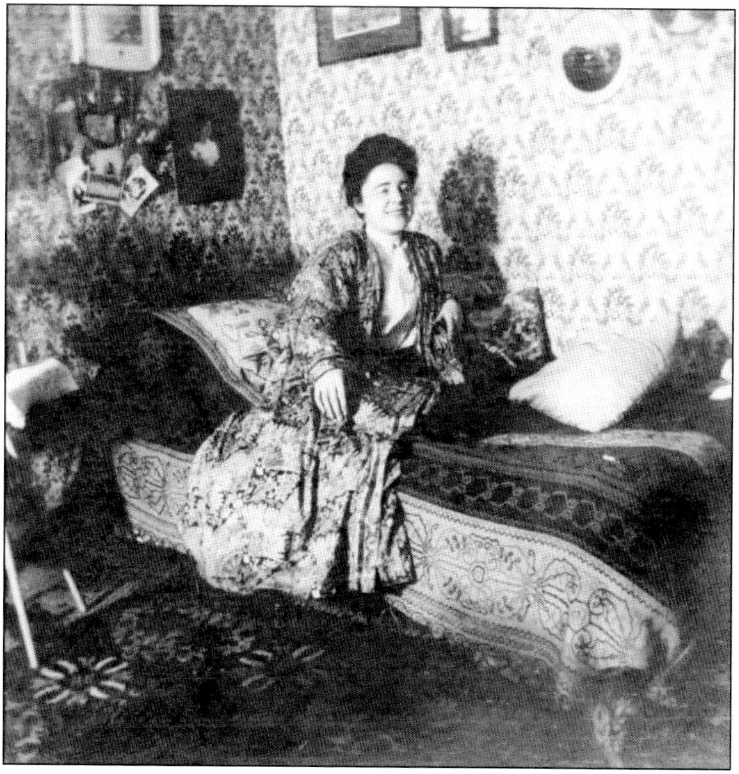

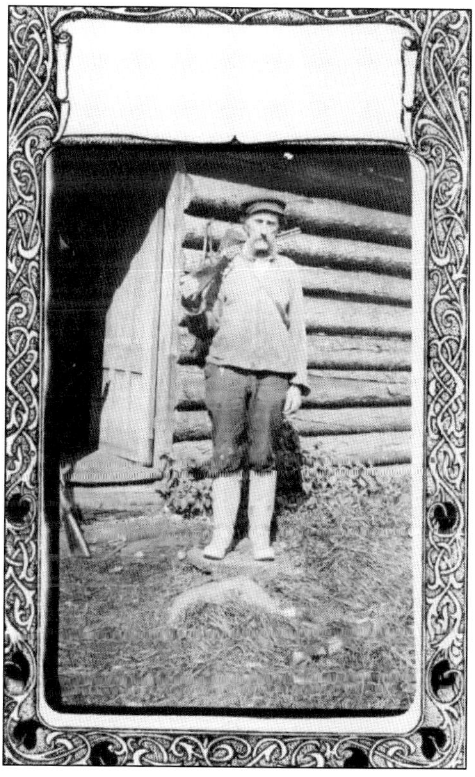

Hamlet Whitman, another member of the longtime Adirondack clan, has dressed up in his hunting outfit. Ham settled his family in the wilds at the end of a dirt road in 1850, without obtaining a clear deed. When he passed away, his land reverted back to the forest preserve. It is a story that was often repeated in a day when squatters could settle on Adirondack lands.

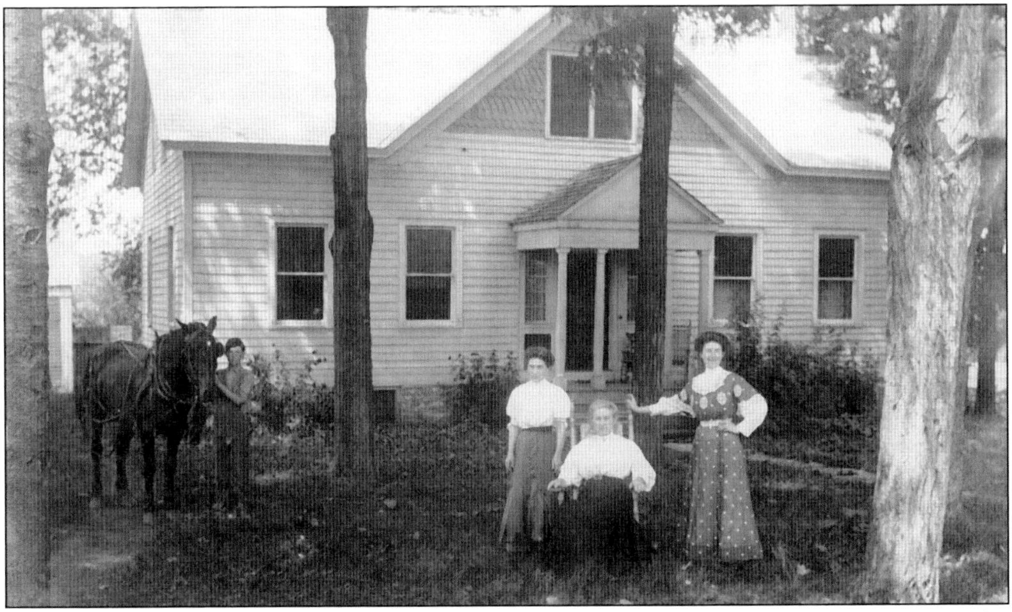

These well-dressed ladies pose in their finest in front of this Adirondack homestead. Not to be outdone, the family horse was brought out of the barn in her finest harnesses. Horses were an important part of the Adirondack family life, serving as their main source of transportation, working in the gardens, and harvesting the great Adirondack logs. Adirondackers took good care of their horses.

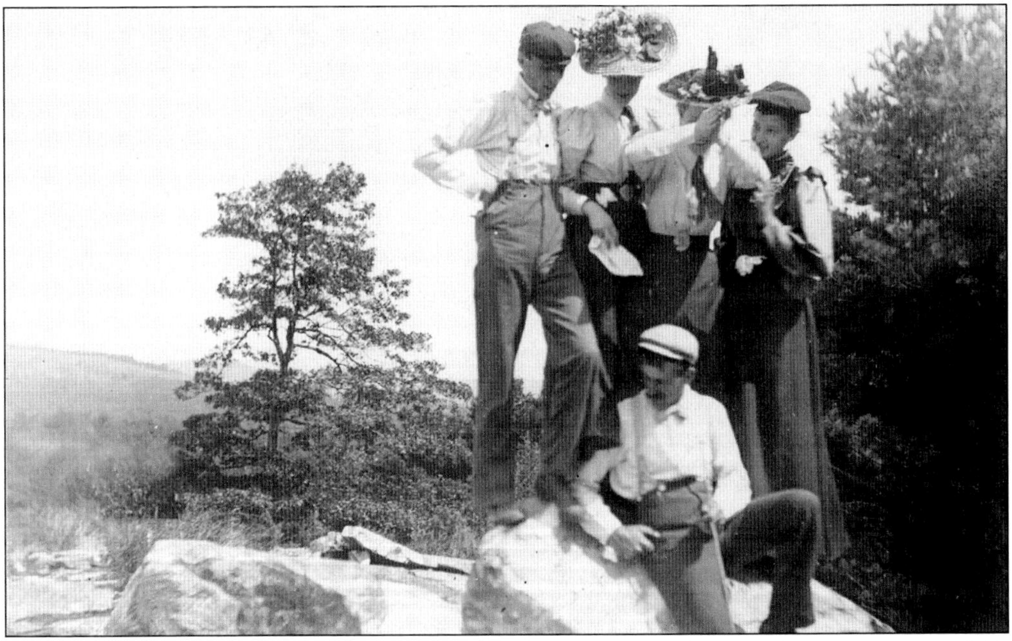

Another well-dressed Adirondack group is enjoying the out-of-doors in the Adirondacks. Life was a little slower in those days, and leisurely excursions could be made out of the urban areas to the country. A Sunday afternoon excursion to the mountains was often made while still dressed in "Sunday best." Hats were in style for both ladies and gentlemen. High fashion was often the norm at the Adirondack resorts.

Family continues to be important in the Adirondack communities. Many of the Adirondack families go back several generations. Extended families, including grandparents, parents, children, and grandchildren, often lived under the same roof. This family photograph was taken at Tupper Lake in 1903. Family names, including Hosley and Brown (among many others), were scattered in Adirondack country and are still found there today.

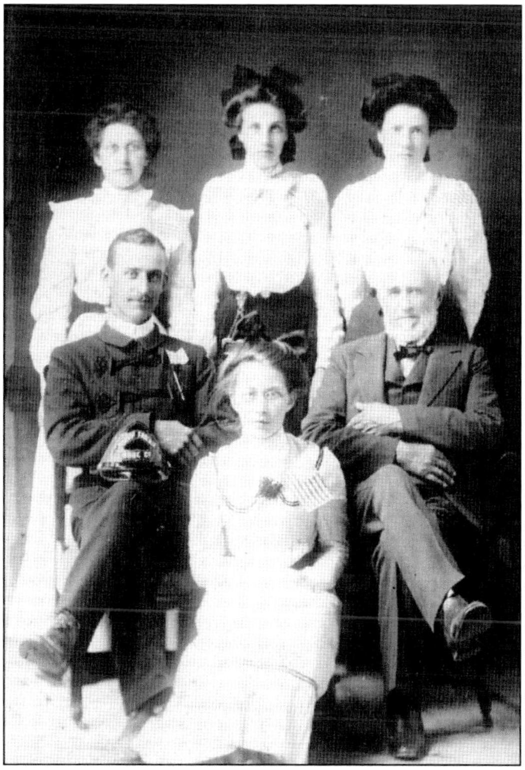

Another city group has decided to cool off in an Adirondack lake. They have shed their hats to avoid losing them in the water. Other beachgoers can be seen off in the background, also still dressed in their Sunday clothes. Skimpy bathing suits and sunbathing were not a part of the Adirondack scene in those early days. Wading in the cool water was enjoyed instead of swimming.

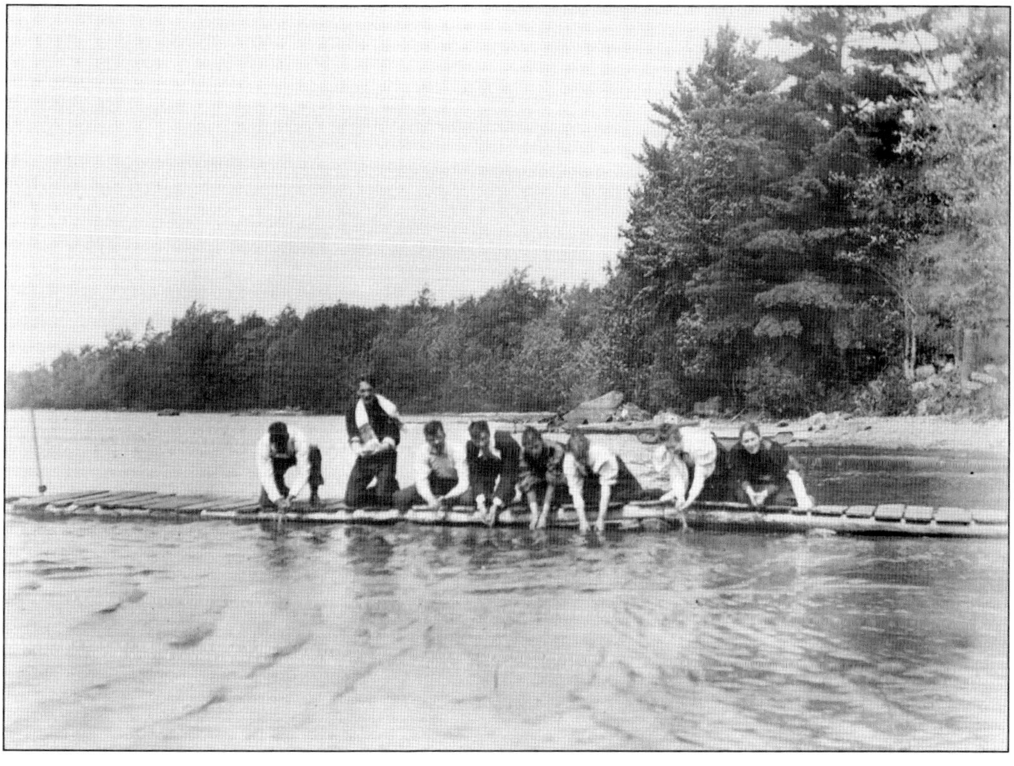

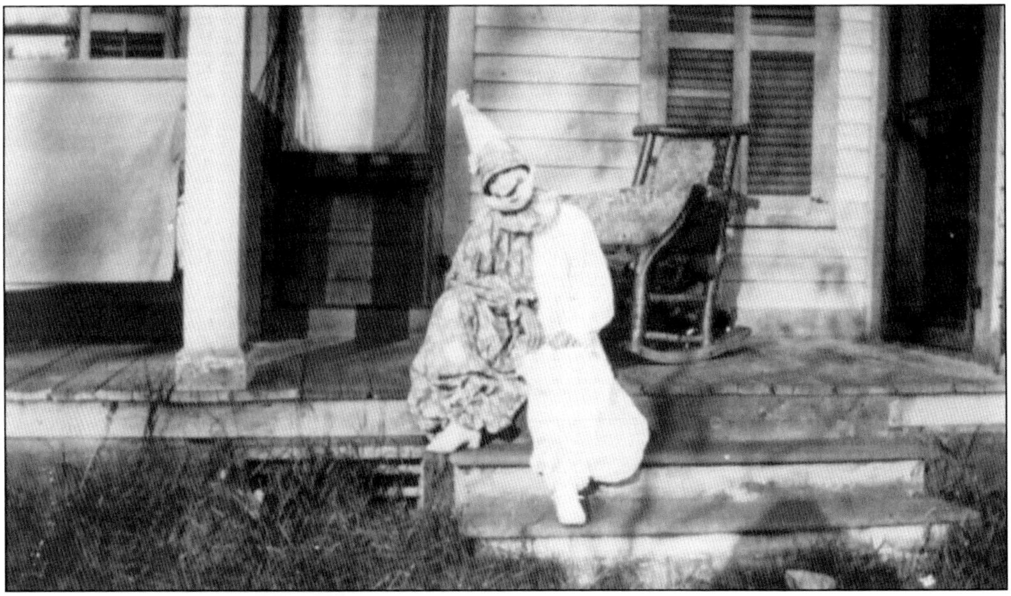

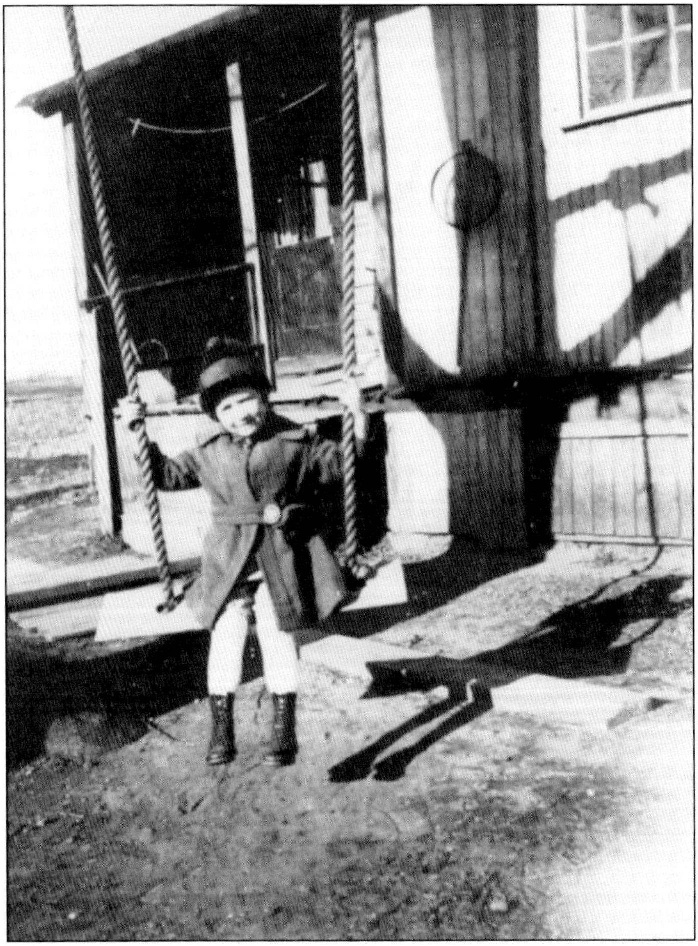

This clown is a mystery. The porch may be a sleeping porch for a TB patient, and the clown may be there to entertain. TB patients came to the Adirondacks in the latter part of the 1800s for the curative powers of the fresh, pure air. The rustic birch rocker, similar to those made by Lee Fountain, identifies this scene as Adirondack.

Rope swings were popular in the Adirondacks. They were created by tying a large rope to one of the level, lower branches of a tree and adding a board seat. Whenever there were children in the home, there was a rope swing. Some had broad seats wide enough to hold two people at once and were big and strong enough for adult use. Swinging was especially fun when a sibling gave the swing a push.

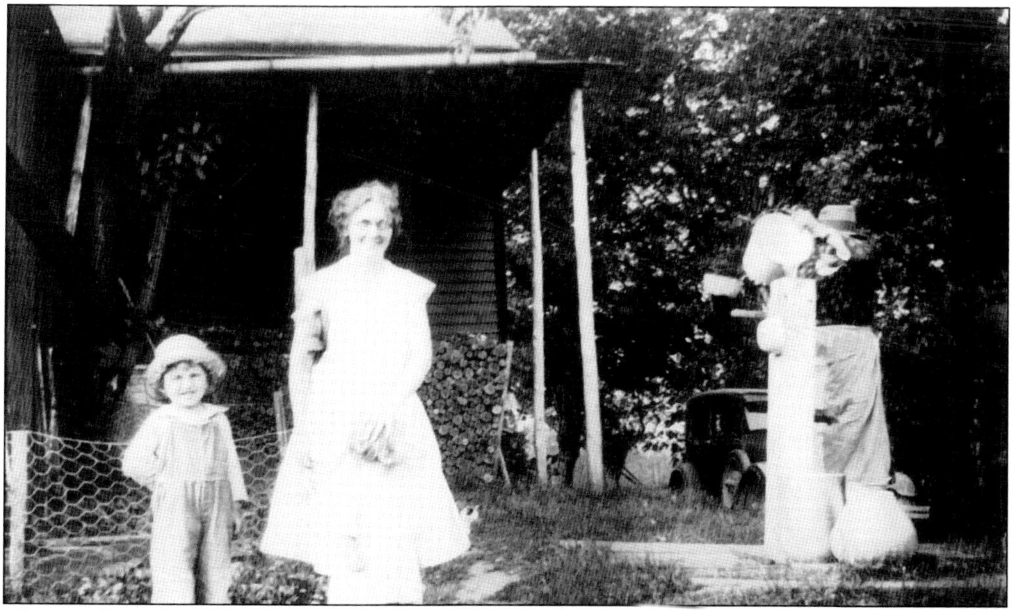

This small chicken-wire fence encloses the area where chickens were kept for their meat and eggs. A pile of wood for the kitchen is stacked on the porch. The person at the well appears to be priming the pump—pouring water in the top to get the water flowing. A gutter along the edge of the roof leads to a rain barrel for extra water for the animals.

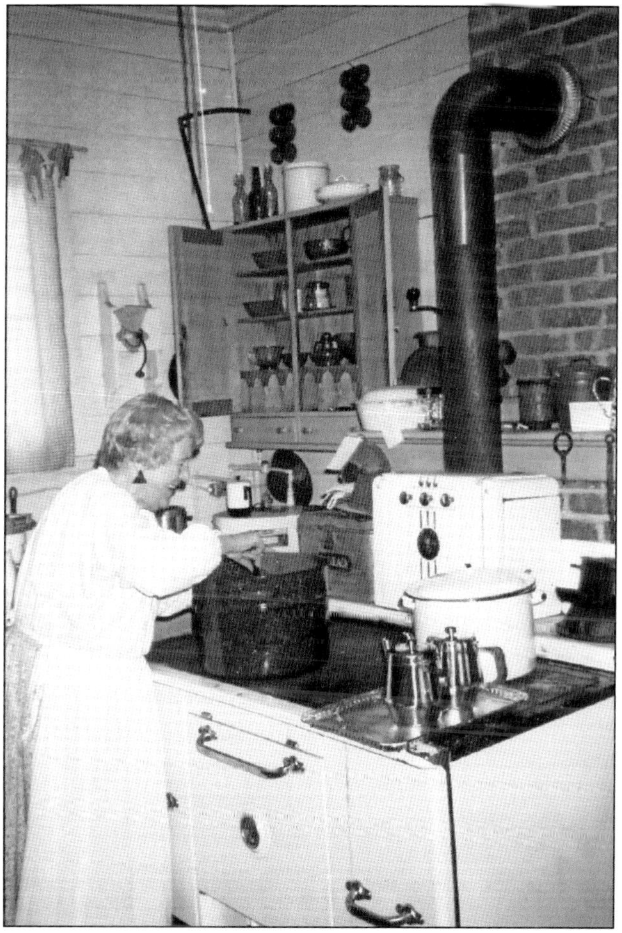

The cookstove was the center of the household before electricity came to the rural mountain lakes of New York State. The lady of the house was able to bake bread and cook meals on the fire for relatives, travelers, hired help, and others. The stove shown here is still in use at the Rice Homestead Museum at Mayfield.

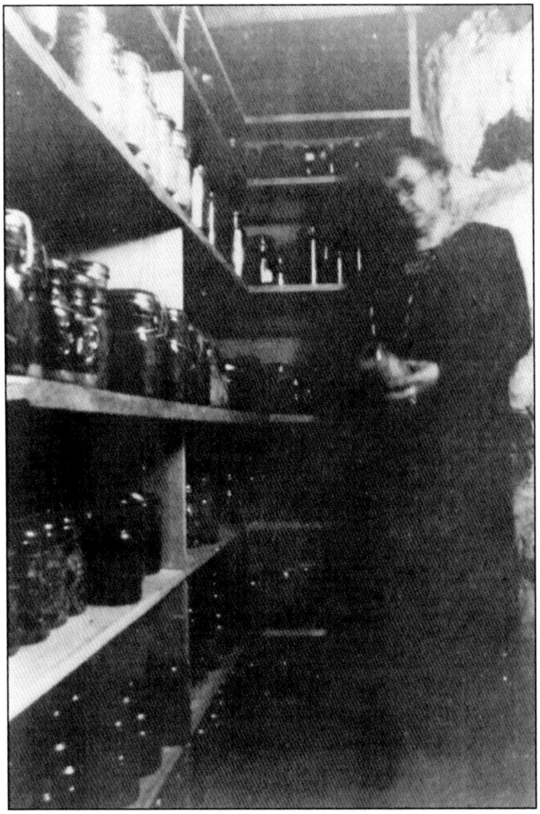

Canned goods lined the Adirondack cellar shelves in a day when preserving food was a way of life. Fruits and vegetables were processed on the cookstove to get the family through the winter. Housewives learned to make jam, jellies, mincemeat, sauerkraut, pickles, and grape juice. They also learned how to can chicken, eggs, sausage, and pig hocks. Some made headcheese and cottage cheese.

In the days before the centralization of New York's schools, each settlement had a village school and surrounding district schools. The children walked to the nearest school when the roads were not too muddy or snowy and when they were not needed at home. School buildings were among the first built in a settlement, and they were used for community events and for church services.

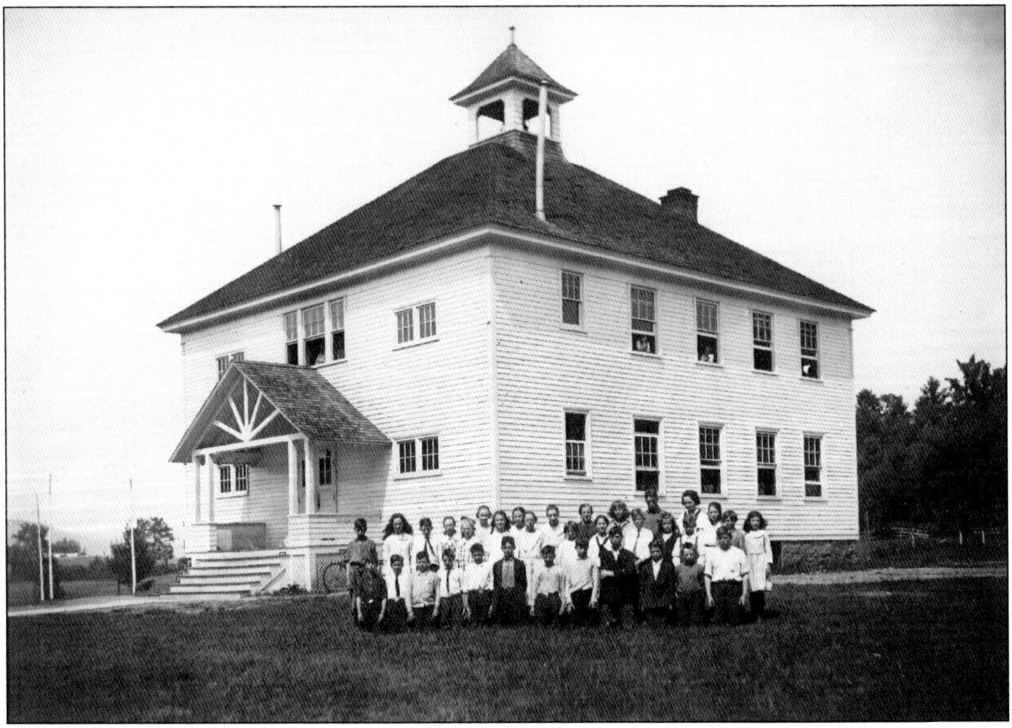

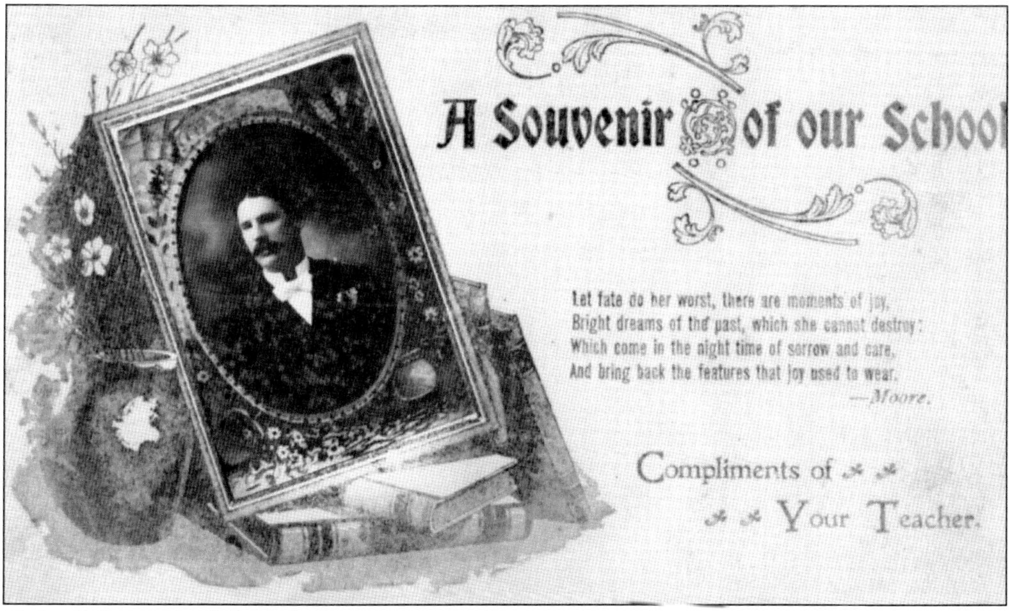

"School days, school days, dear old Golden Rule days" are not the same as they were in the day of the one-room schoolhouse. Most of the community schools ended at the eighth grade. In the summer term of 1898, teacher Thomas H. Cassidy gave a souvenir card to each student listing all of the school's pupils.

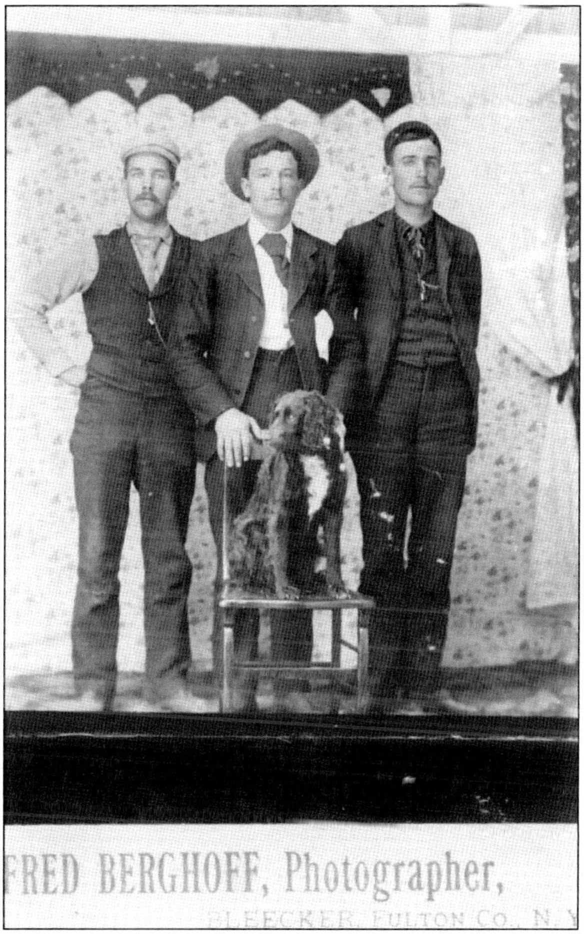

At that time, traveling shows provided entertainment in Adirondack communities. The shows moved from one settlement to another, singing, acting, and otherwise entertaining those who lived in remote areas. Magic shows, singers, dancers, and animal shows including dancing bears were a welcome break from daily tasks. Here, young men perform with their dog in Bleecker in the southern Adirondacks.

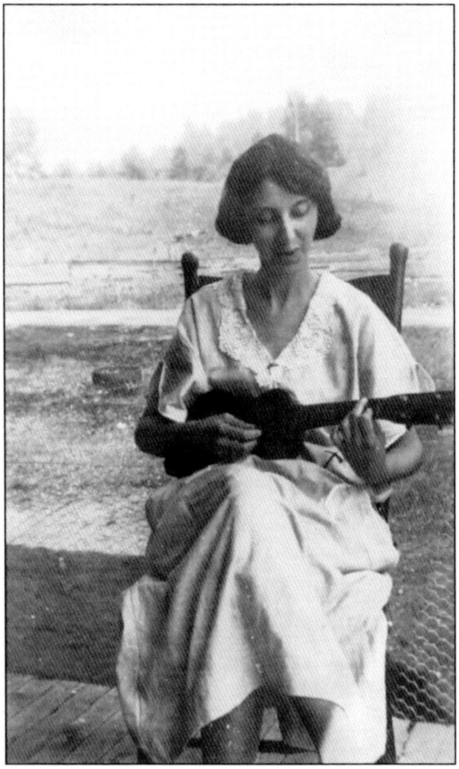

Music was a part of life in Adirondack homes. Extended families often had a band with fiddles, guitars, banjos, mandolins, mouth organs, accordions, and pianos. It was common to jam on the stoop or in the kitchen on a Saturday night. Round and square dancing were sometimes a part of these musical gatherings.

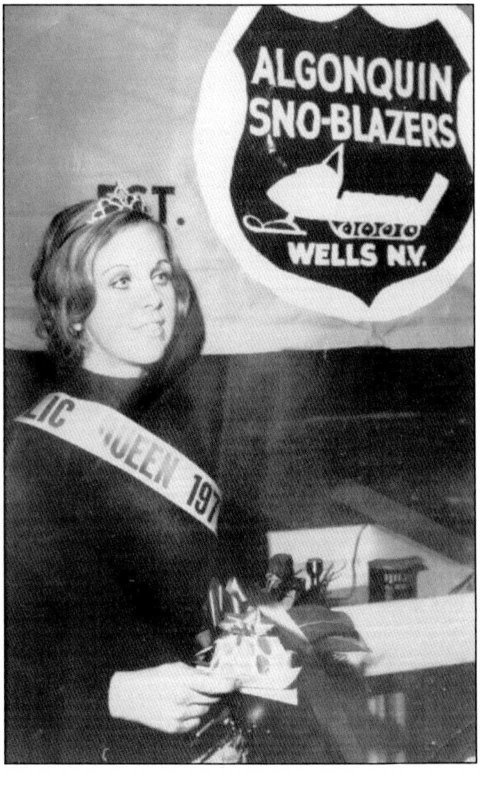

Once the snowmobiles invaded the wintertime Adirondacks, trails and clubs soon followed. The Algonquin Sno-Blazers Club at Wells sponsored its fourth annual Snowmobile Frolic in 1974 and selected Cheryl Scott of Amsterdam as frolic queen. Previously, she had been Miss Plattsburgh and had competed in the Miss USA World Beauty Pageant. Today, the Adirondack boasts miles of well-groomed trails and several active clubs throughout the mountain region. Snowmobiling provides a big boost to the winter economy.

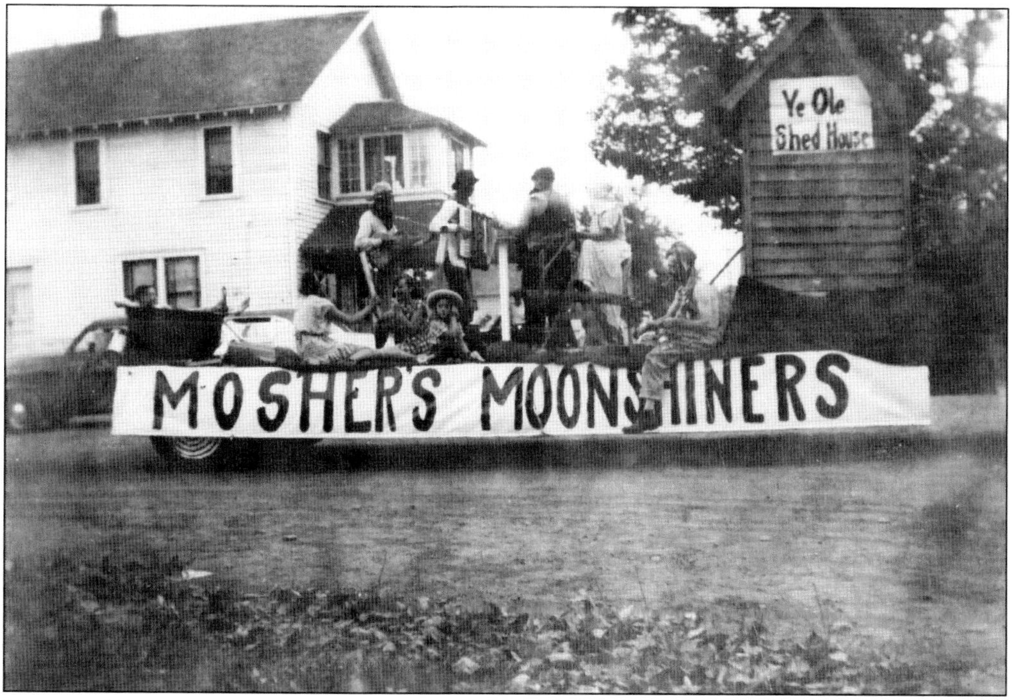

Music and floats played an important role in holiday parades and Old Home Day celebrations. The parades were not complete without the school bands, community bands, and special bands hired from the outside world, along with the creative floats designed by families and community groups. Here, a "moonshiner" float features Moshers Moonshiners, along with a three-piece band. The sponsor of the float was Moshers General Store. Another big attraction at the celebrations was the parades of babies. Carriages were decorated, the babies were dressed in their finery, and proud mothers paraded them through town. The celebrations, attended by residents, former residents, and visitors, also featured games, food, competitions, and displays. Some Adirondack communities carry on the tradition to this day.

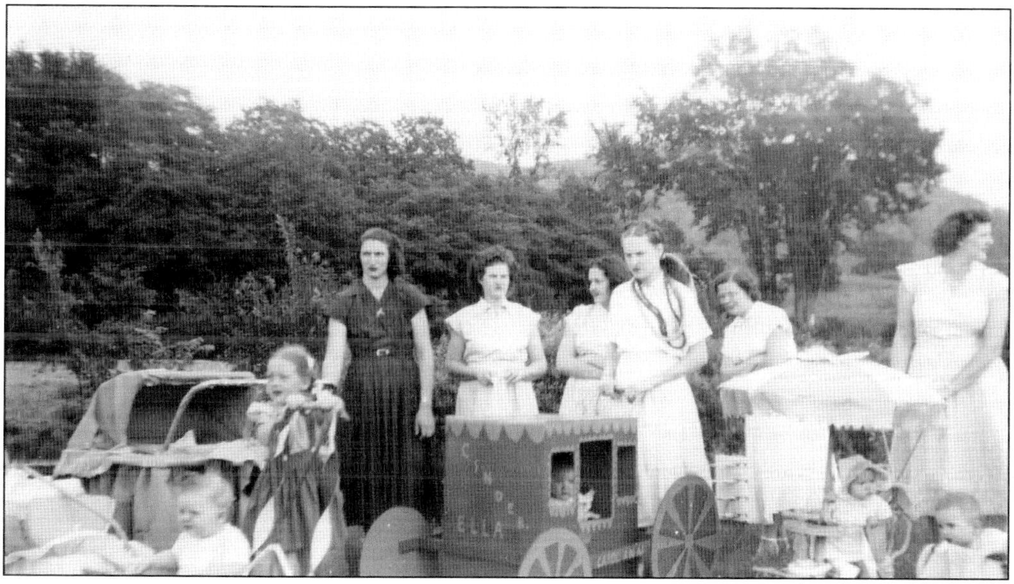

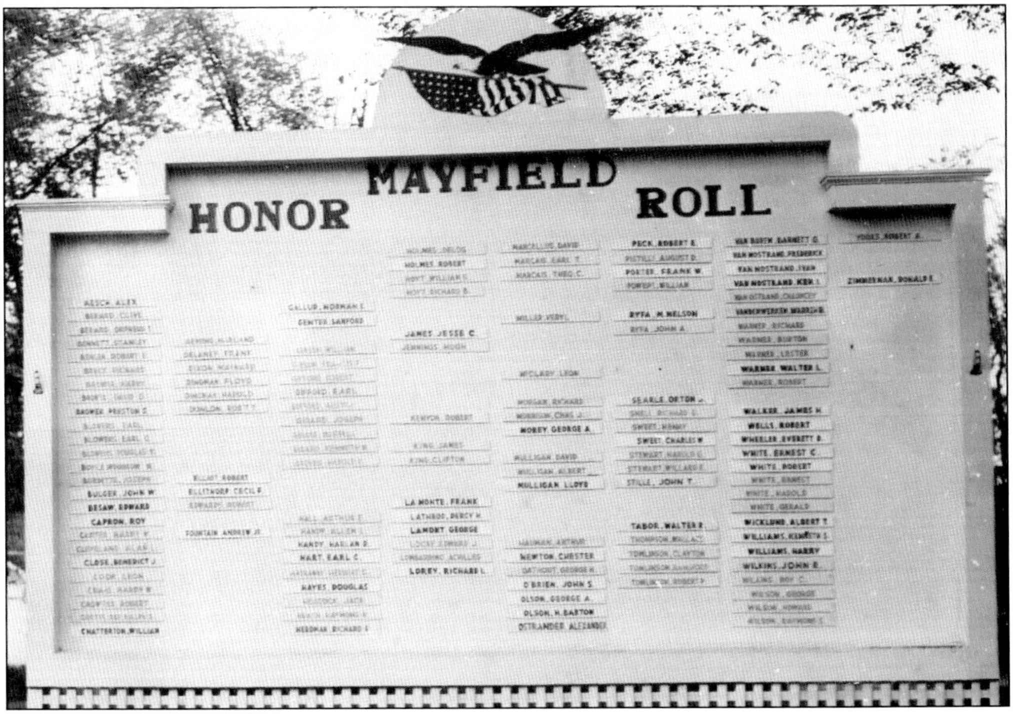

When the Adirondack Guides Association was formed in 1891, honorary president Verplanck Colvin called the guides the best body of riflemen in America. He noted that they were "a safeguard to the state should war arise." He also offered to take a battalion of guides to Cuba to fight in the Spanish-American War. Adirondackers went off to war during the Revolution, the War of 1812, and World War I. Young people continued to serve their country in World War II. Honor rolls were erected in the town squares to recognize those who served.

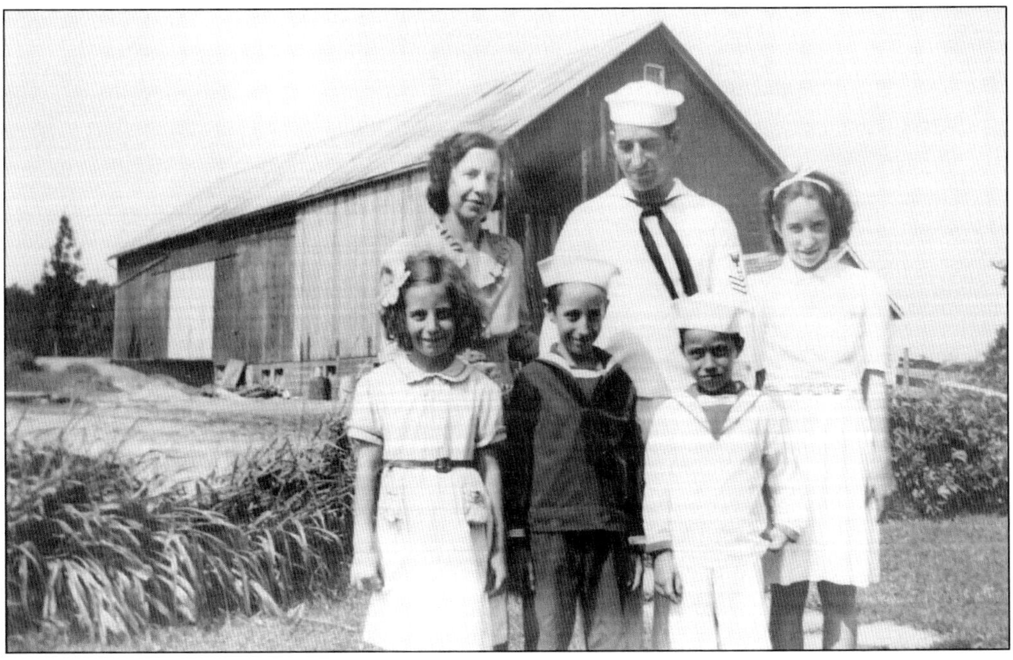

Three

The Places

For some 200 years, the Adirondacks have been a popular destination. Once the world learned about that "Great Wilderness" from the Native Americans, hunters, trappers, and soldiers who penetrated its depths, the influx began.

The Adirondacks evolved from a place of woodland grottoes to world-class golf courses; from hidden trails and high peaks to graveled roadways and groomed byways; from cabins to great camps; and from lean-tos to luxurious hotels. It was a place of rivulets and raging rivers, clear lakes and quiet ponds, and rolling hills and steep mountains, which then became home to lumber camps, mining towns, hamlets, museums, amusement parks, ski centers, parks, monuments, and public beaches. Sanitariums found their place in the health-giving Adirondacks.

Animal lands and amusement parks became tourist destinations. Each summer, from 1900 to 1930, thousands took the train ride to the Sacandaga Amusement Park. Other amusement parks attracted visitors and residents to the mountains. Animal lands ranged from small cages of bears beside a garage to giant 1,000-animal attractions. The beaches attracted the sun lovers and swimmers, and the ski centers brought in winter sportspeople.

In 1957, the Adirondack Museum, one of the finest regional museums in the country, was built at Blue Mountain Lake. In recent years, the Wild Center at Tupper Lake has become a popular natural history destination.

Most who love the forested mountain and lake region have found their own special places within the six-million-acre park—a favorite beach, a challenging waterway, a woodland glade, a view from a mountaintop, a tiny waterfall on a mountain stream.

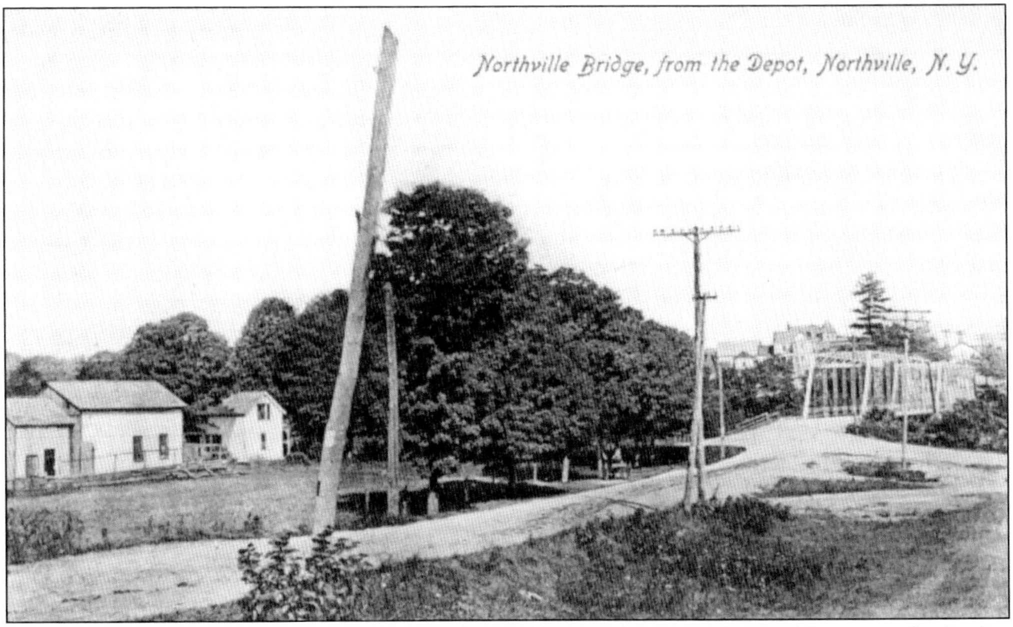

The village of Northville on the Adirondack Trail Byway (Route 30) is visible across the bridge in these photographs. For isolated Adirondack settlements, bridges were (and are) lifelines to the outside world. Northville depends on the bridge across the Sacandaga. Settled in the 1790s, Northville was accessed by an 1860 wooden bridge that was lost in the flood of 1882. The two-span steel bridge shown here replaced the covered bridge and served for 49 years. In 1930, the construction of the Sacandaga Reservoir or "Great Sacandaga Lake" called for a newer, bigger bridge. The second, three-span, steel bridge was called the "blue bridge" after it was painted blue. In 1990, the blue bridge was replaced by a more modern flat bridges, known as an open-deck bridge. The blue bridge and the open-deck bridge are under construction in these photographs.

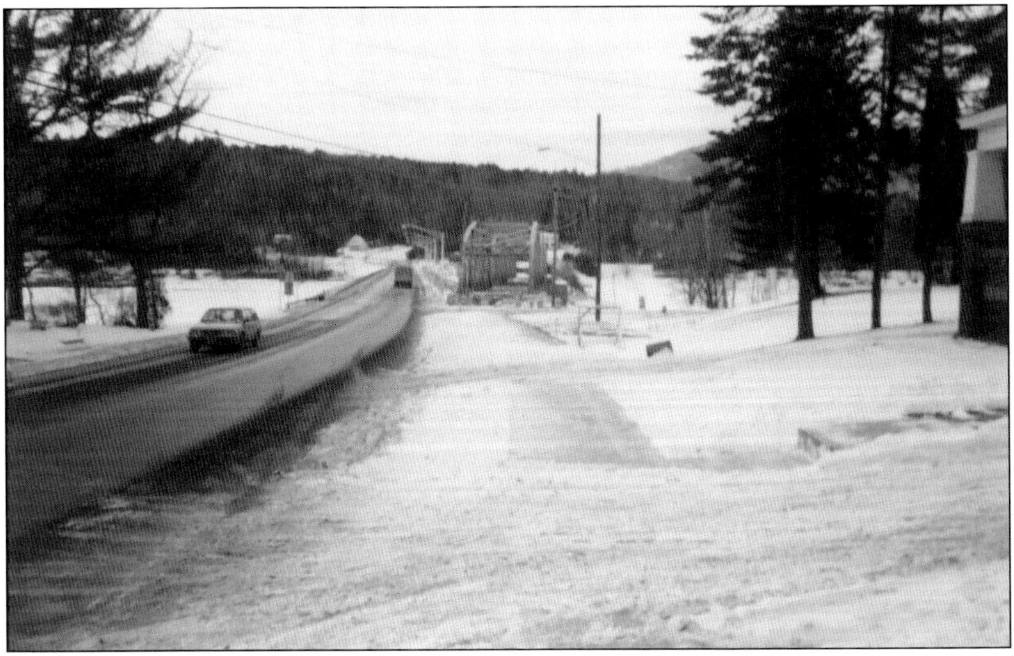

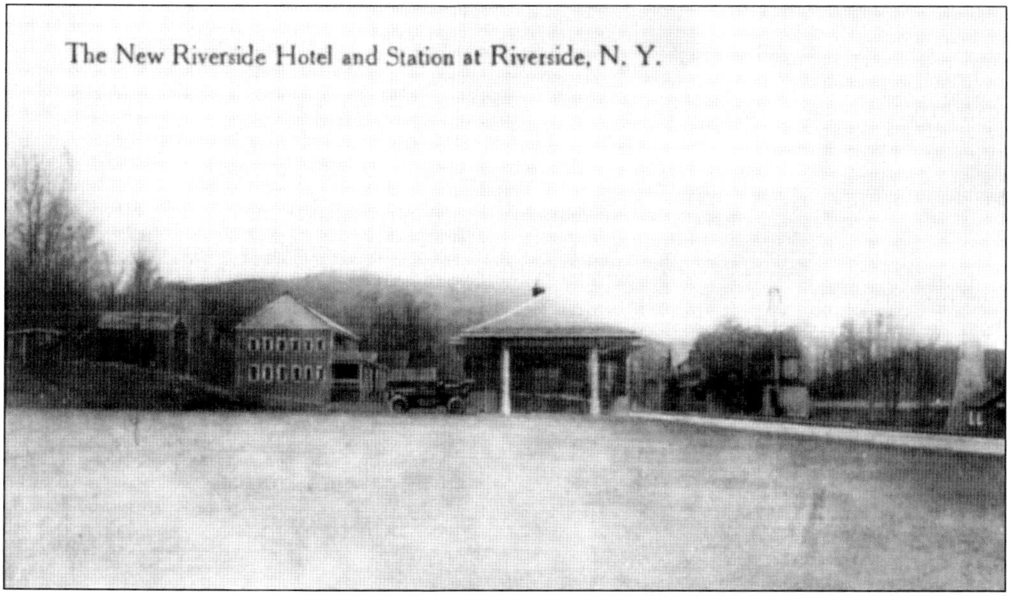

The railroad opened up the Adirondacks to thousands of travelers. The Riverside Station at Riparius on the upper Hudson River was once the busiest station on the Adirondack Railroad. The train reached Riverside in 1870, and the station was added in 1914. Stagecoaches transported passengers from Riverside to accommodations at Schroon Lake resorts seven miles away. Lodgings such as the New Riverside Hotel (shown here) offered fine food and accommodations. Loon Lake benefited from the railroad line and the major highway between New York and Montreal. Those who stopped off for an extended stay enjoyed accommodations like the Loon Lake Colony, which boasted a seven-piece college orchestra, fresh milk and vegetables from its farm, tennis courts, bowling alleys, horses, and water sports.

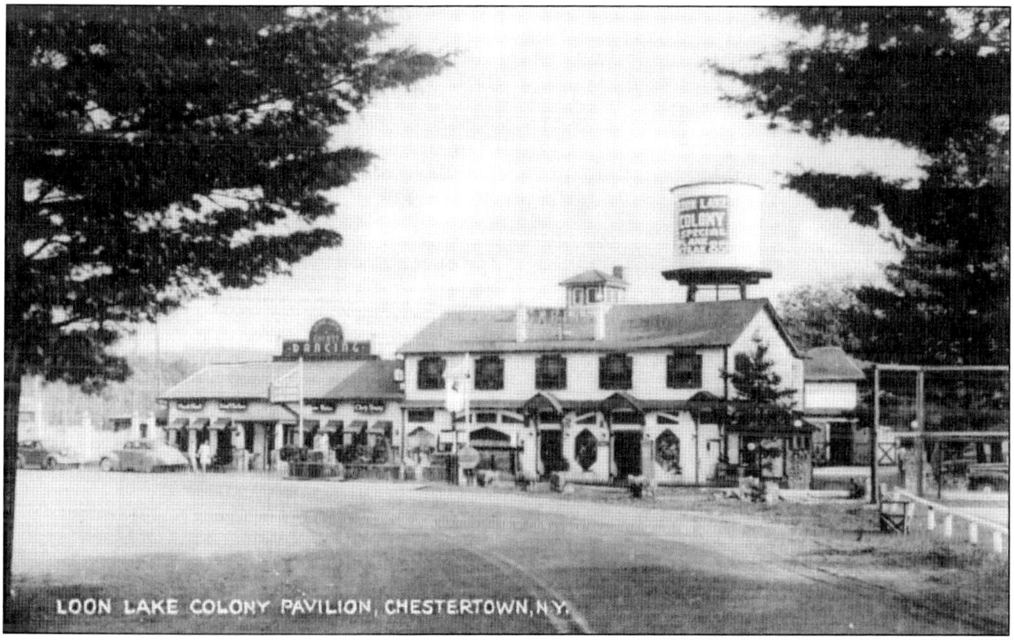

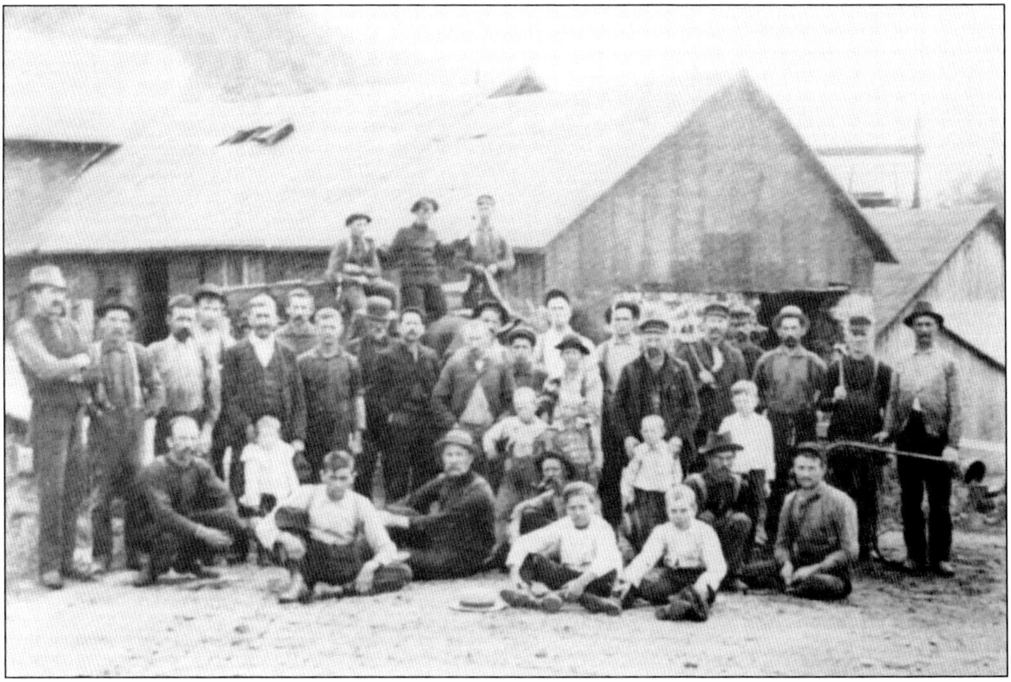

Tanneries brought large numbers of workers Adirondacks. It took many hands to gather hemlock bark and to process hides. Tannery workers received $1 a day to process animal hides. In the 19th century, there were 40 large tanneries in Hamilton County alone.

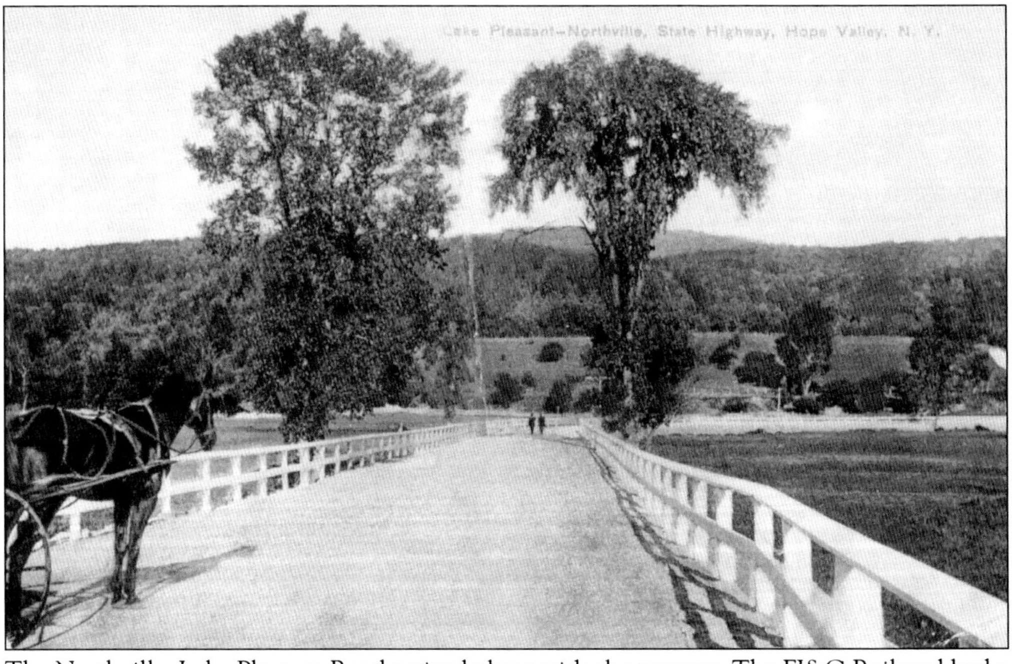

The Northville–Lake Pleasant Road arrived along with the tanners. The FJ&G Railroad had a terminus at Northville where passengers disembarked to take stagecoaches. Wooden fences along the highway kept horses on the roadway, and both wild and farm animals out of the road. Lumber for the miles of fencing was cut at Adirondack sawmills.

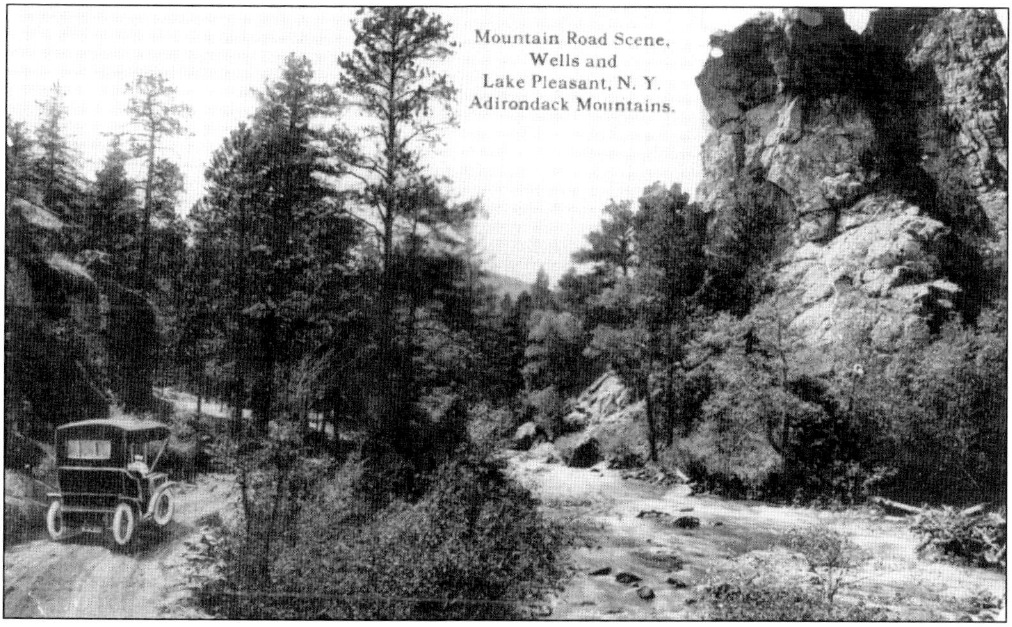

Beginning in 1902, the automobile was met by rough roadways in the Adirondacks. Spare tires had to be carried along to take care of recurrent flats. This mountain road ran along the Sacandaga River between Wells and Lake Pleasant. Today, it is a major section of Route 30, known as the Adirondack Trail.

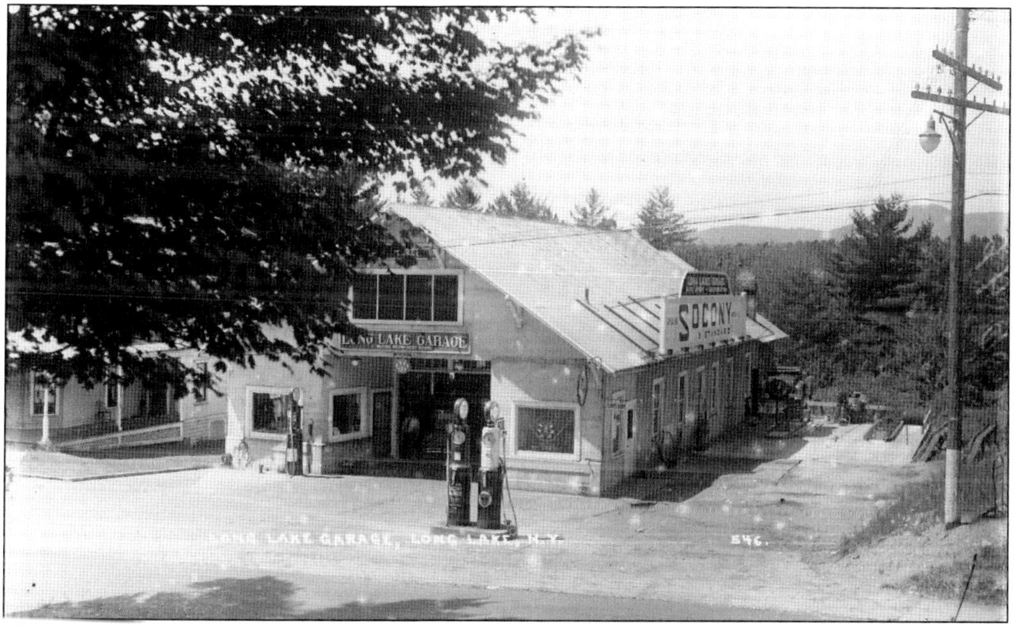

The first automobile entered the Adirondacks in 1902, and it was not long before service stations were needed for the newfangled means of transportation. Sensing the inevitable demand for gasoline and kerosene products, the Standard Oil Company of New York (Socony) constructed a distribution center along the railroad tracks at Northville. Plumley's Long Lake Socony station offered fireproof storage, an auto livery, wrecking car, tires, tubes, and accessories, as well as a ladies restroom.

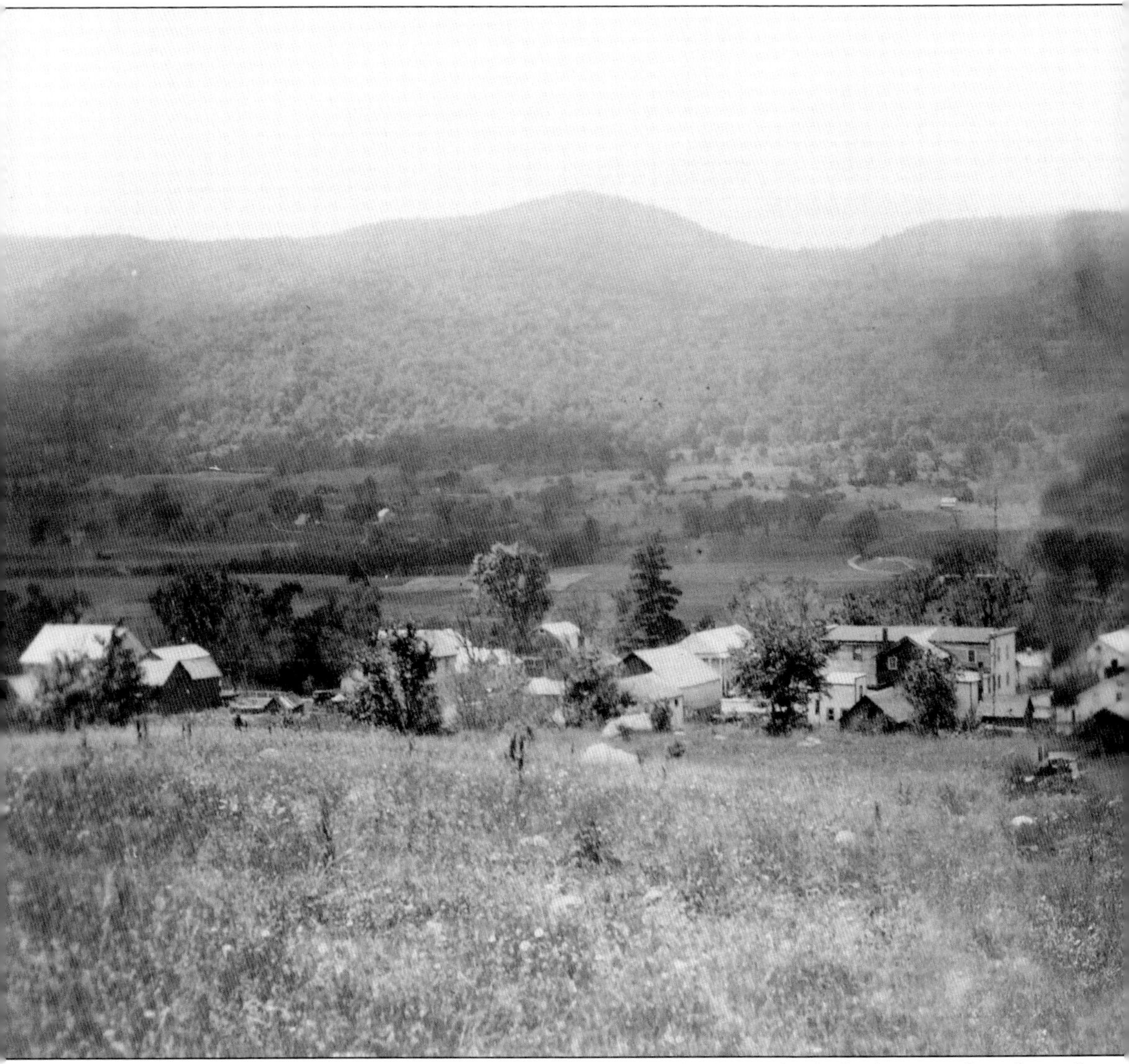

An early, unknown photographer took two photographs from the hillside east of Wells and fastened them together to show a panoramic view the Sacandaga River valley. On the extreme right is the former Hosley House. In the middle of the photograph is the former Baptist church, now owned by the Hamilton County Historical Society. The large building nearby is the Hotel Cochrane, which was razed in 1929 to build a bank. The house south of the bank is the Buyce

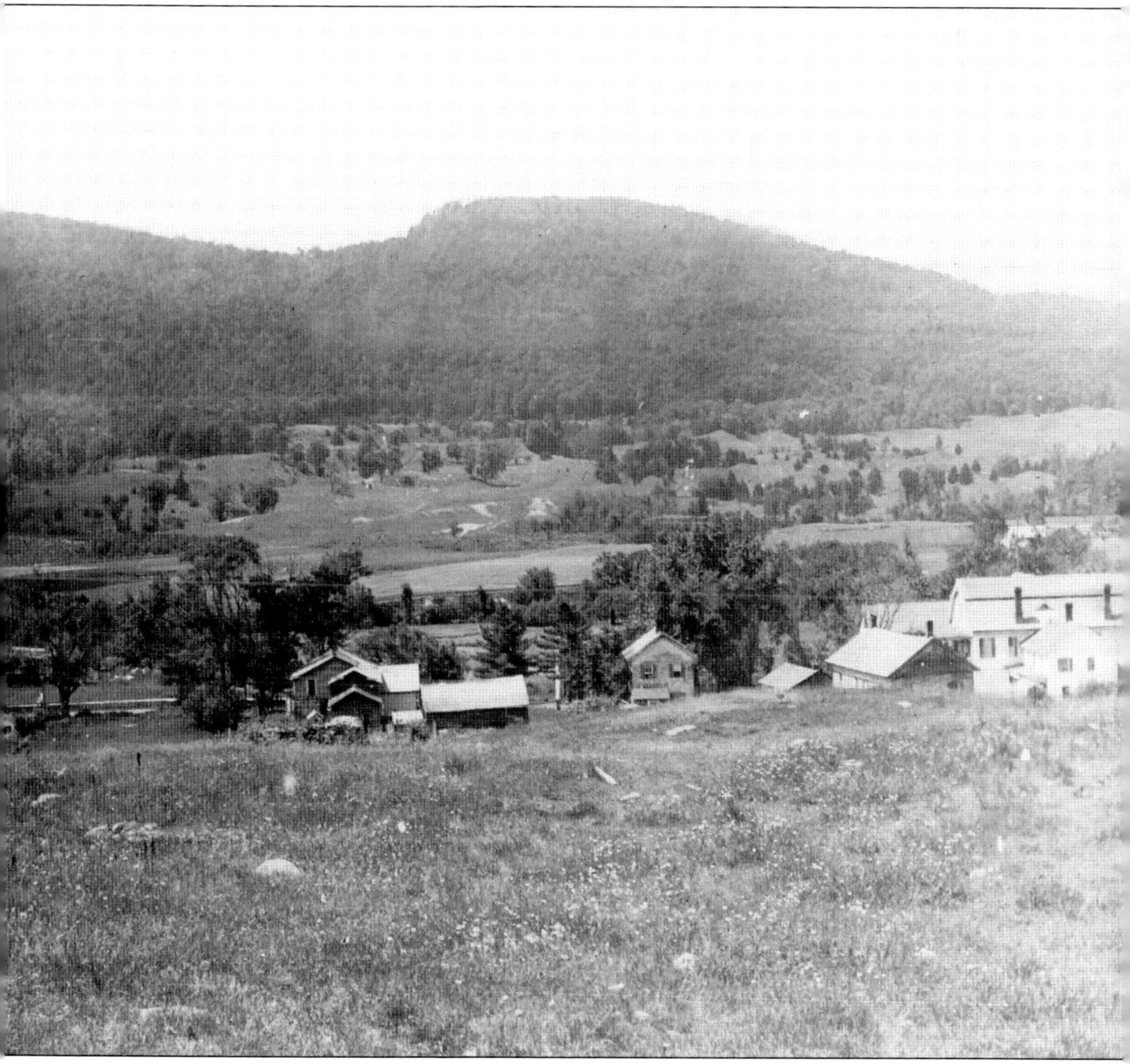

homestead, now the Wells Museum. All the land west of the village is now flooded by Lake Algonquin. Leonard Wells Volk, one of America's greatest sculptors, got his start in Wells, where his father was a stonecutter. He was born in 1828 on the site of the later John Hosley farm. He went off to study in St. Louis at the age of 20 and was Pres. Abraham Lincoln's sculptor. Today, internationally known sculptor John VanAlstine maintains a studio and gallery at Wells.

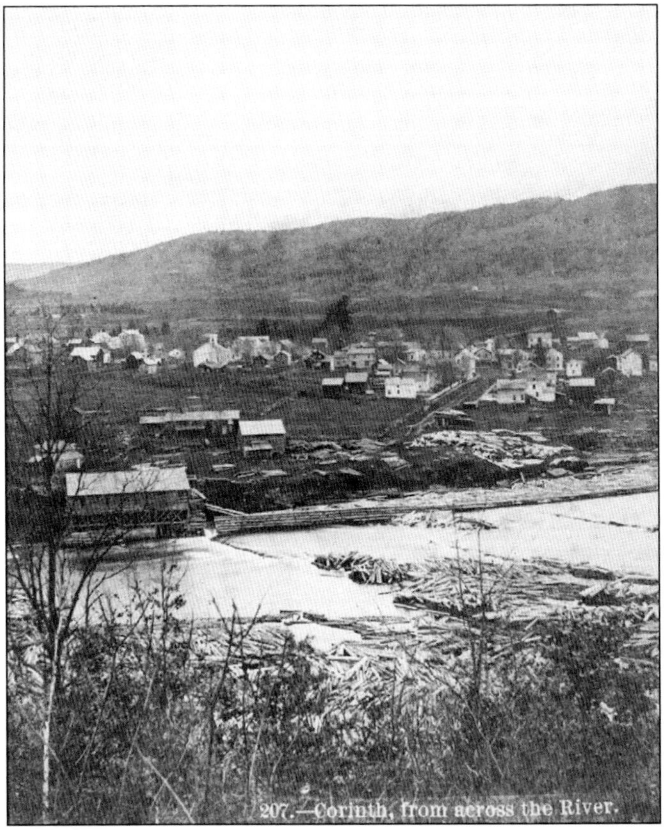

On the Hudson River, Corinth became a logging settlement early in the 1770s. Permanent settlers began arriving in 1775, and it became an official town in 1818. At the second town meeting, citizens put a $10 bounty on wolves. The town became known as the "Snowshoe Capital of America" in 1970. The US Snowshoe Association, organized in 1977, sponsored national championship races at Corinth. Its goal was to make snowshoeing an Olympic event, developing four categories. The association also published a newsletter.

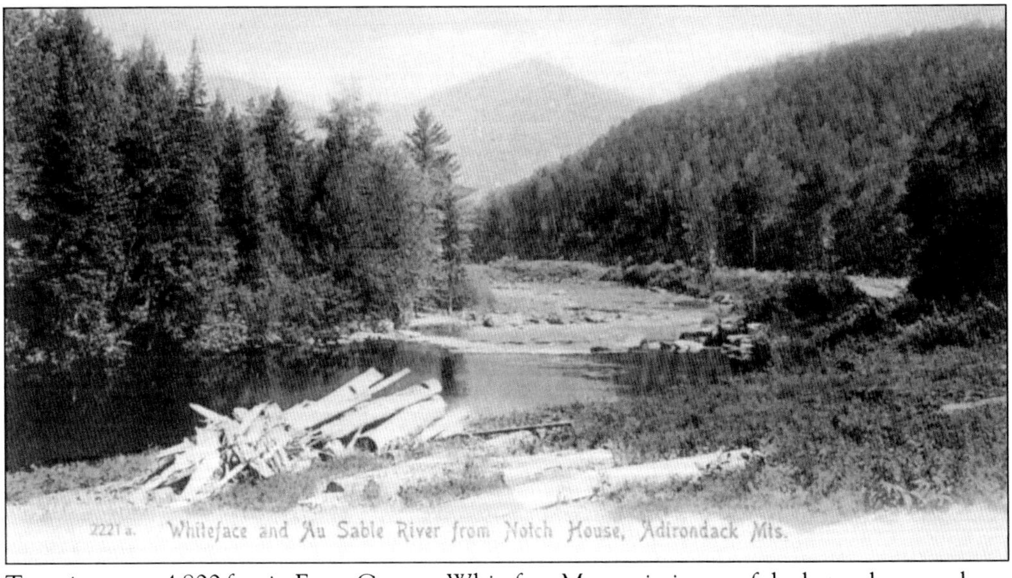

Towering some 4,800 feet in Essex County, Whiteface Mountain is one of the better-known places in the Adirondacks. Besides having an eight-mile paved highway weaving to its summit, it has a 276-foot elevator that ascends through sheer rock to the summit. A 424-foot tunnel provides access to the elevator. In 1814, surveyor John Richards was the first to record a climb of Whiteface. New York State established the road in the 1930s.

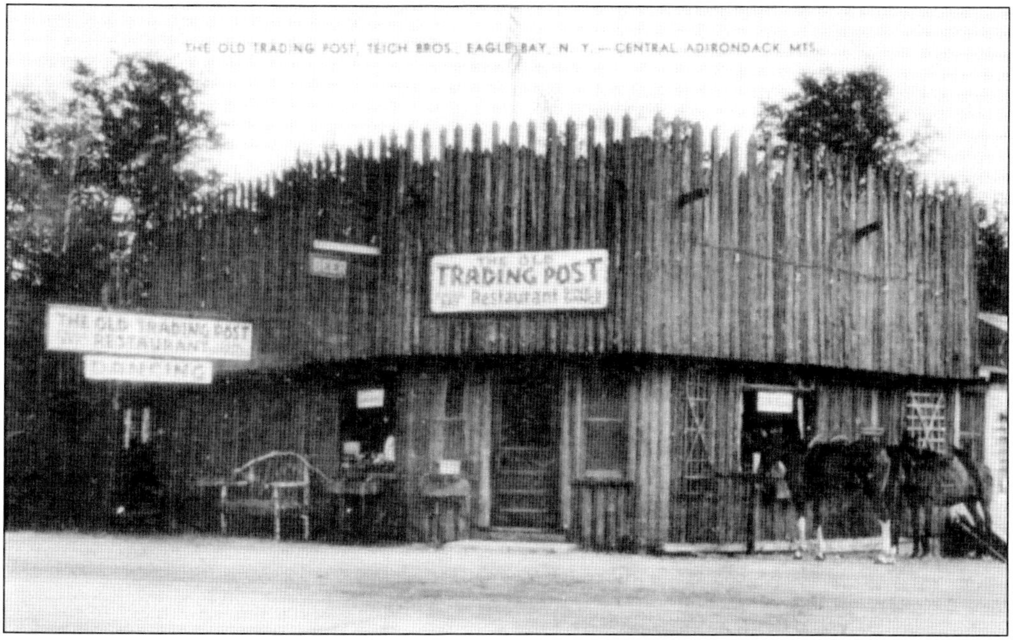

An assortment of tourist stopovers sprang up in the Adirondacks along the roadside. The Old Trading Post on the Central Adirondack Byway (Route 28) was a replica of a log fort. Operated by the Teich Brothers of Eagle Bay, it offered good food, legal beverages, and dancing. Domestic and wild animals were also a big attraction. Horses were tethered on the front rail.

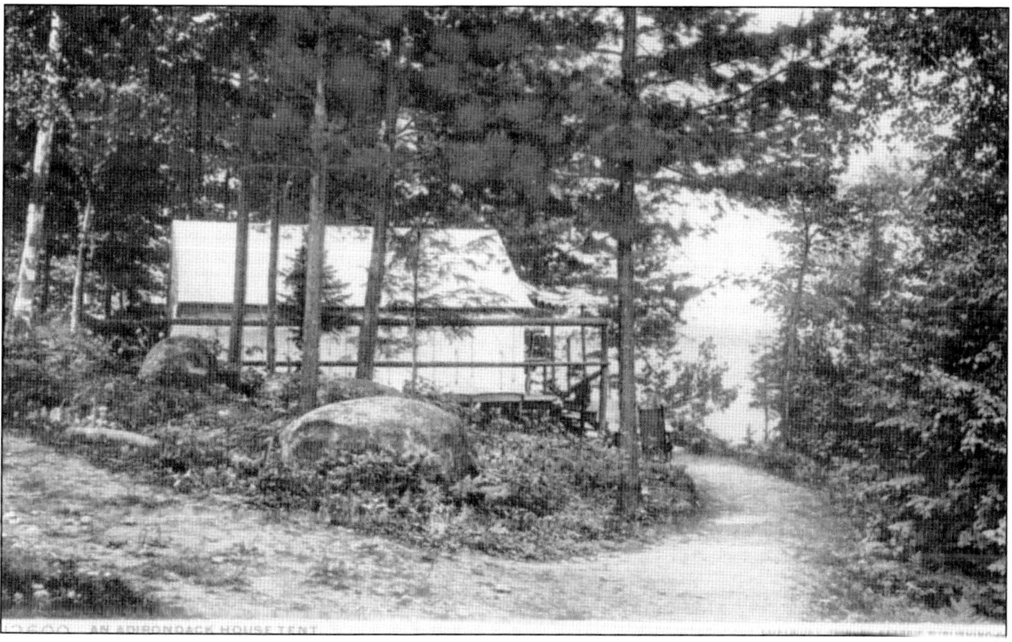

Established 112 years ago on Indian Lake, Timberlock was originally an adult tent camp and still, as a family camp, uses house tents along with regular cabins. The longtime Adirondack venture has had only three owners. Much like other Adirondack family-owned resorts, Timberlock offers swimming, boating, hiking, tennis, horseshoes, riding, and fishing, along with three good meals a day.

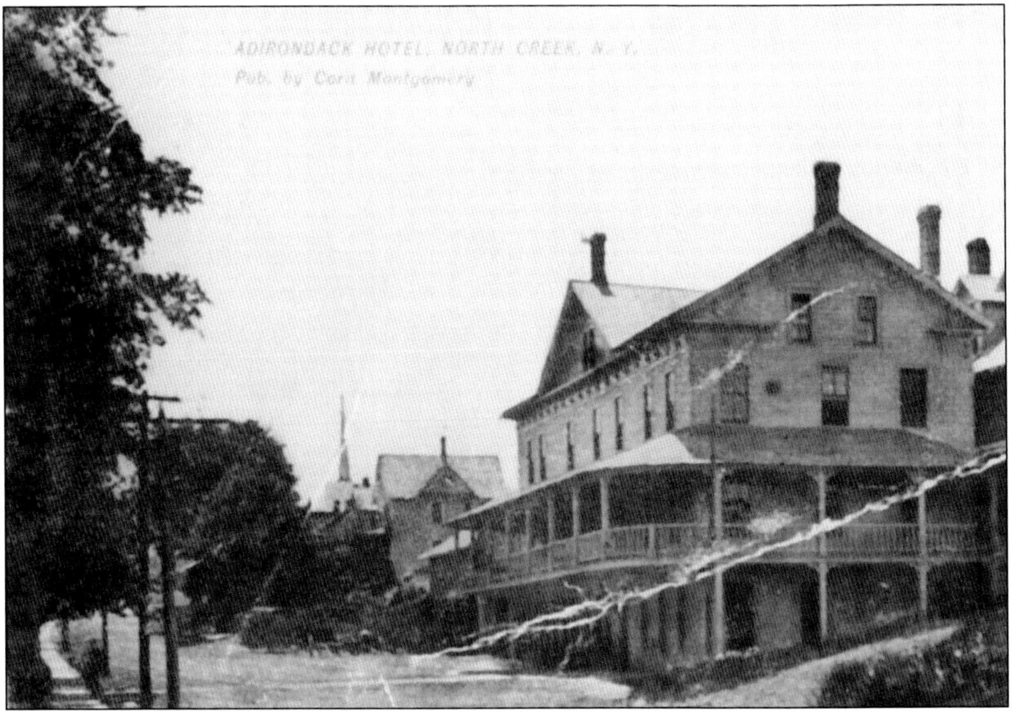

From 1850 to 1950, hotels sprang up throughout the Adirondacks to meet the needs of tourists. In the 1890s, S.R. Stoddard stated in his Adirondack guidebooks, "The American, a short distance from the depot, is the best hotel at North Creek, and provides good substantial fare at the very reasonable rate of $6 to $10 per week; transient guests, $2 per day." The American also provided horses and carriages to reach other Adirondack destinations.

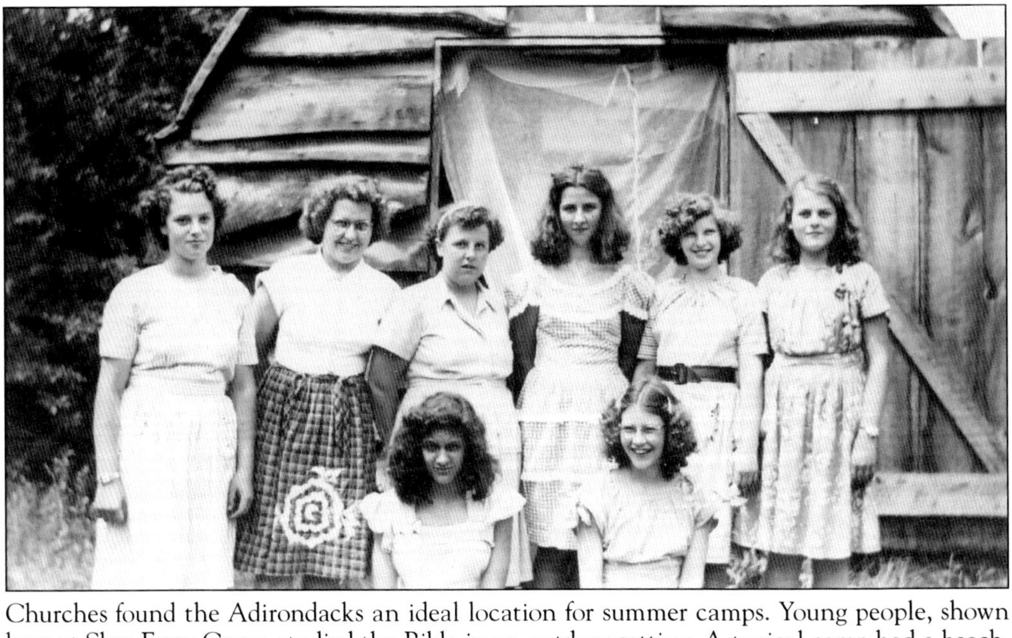

Churches found the Adirondacks an ideal location for summer camps. Young people, shown here at Skye Farm Camp, studied the Bible in an outdoor setting. A typical camp had a beach, mountain trails, and clean air and water, far from hot, urban settings.

The Fort William Henry Hotel stood on the site of Fort William Henry at Lake George. Owned by the Delaware and Hudson Railroad, the six-story hotel had a 25-foot-wide plaza surrounded by 16 Corinthian columns at 30 feet tall. The plaza provided a pleasant location to sit, socialize, and enjoy the view. Note the well-dressed patrons of that day. Built prior to the Civil War, the hotel appears in an 1872 wood engraving of Lake George. It also appears in a well-illustrated descriptive booklet published in 1891. The original hotel burned down in 1909 and was replaced by another hotel in 1911. The 1911 hotel was razed in 1969, whereupon a third hotel was built, which remains on the site today.

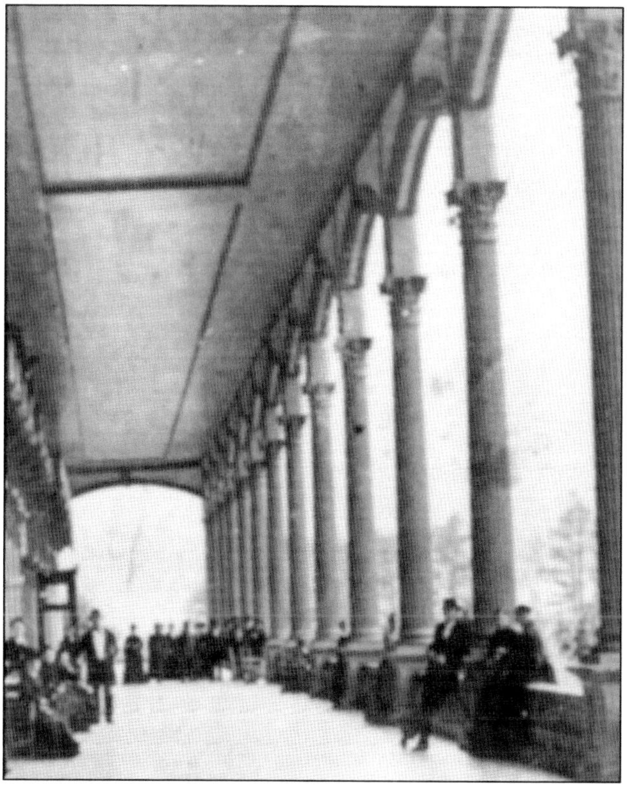

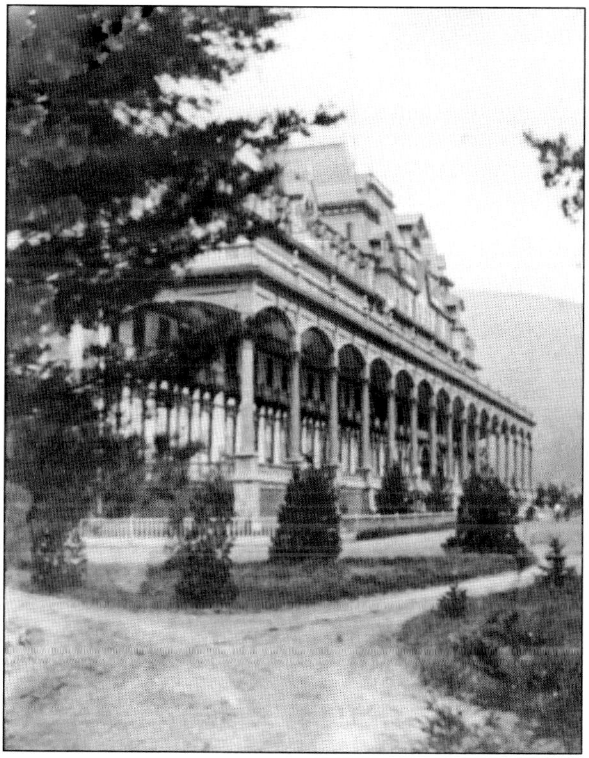

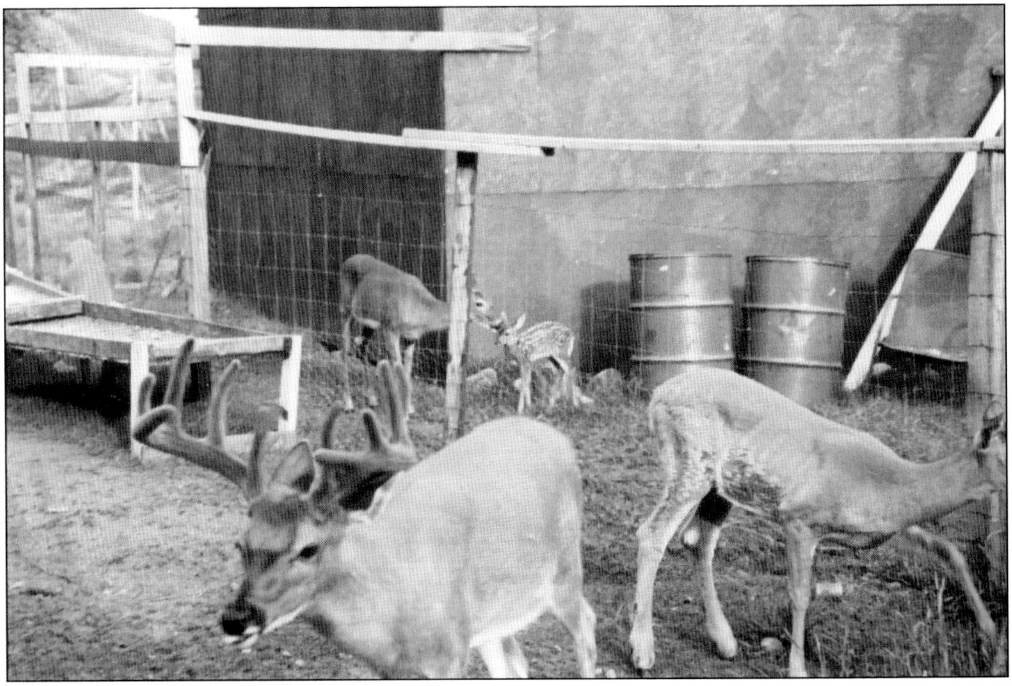

The Averys had a 200-acre enclosure in Arietta where protected deer became a major attraction in the southern Adirondacks. A story is told of an outsider spying the deer while eating breakfast at the Avery restaurant across the street from the enclosure. The outsider ran from the restaurant with his gun, jumped the fence, and shot the deer before anyone could stop him. The deer are no longer kept in the enclosure, and the restaurant is gone.

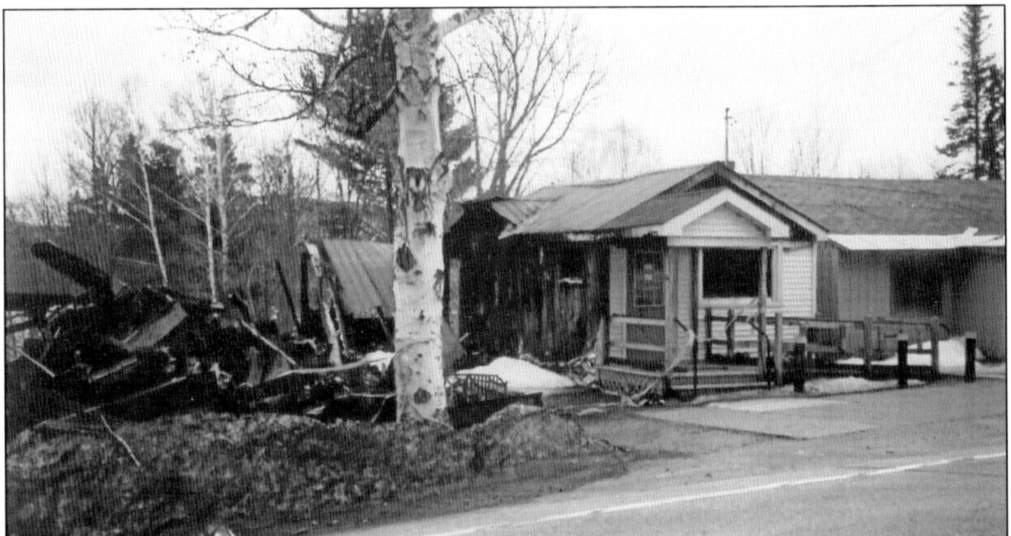

The Sabael Post Office on Route 30 near Indian Lake appears on page 71 in the author's Images of America book *Along The Adirondack Trail.* Since the publication of that book in 2004, the post office was destroyed by fire. Post offices in the Adirondacks have a long history of being the gathering spots of the community. Early post offices were often located in general stores or hotels until separate buildings were required.

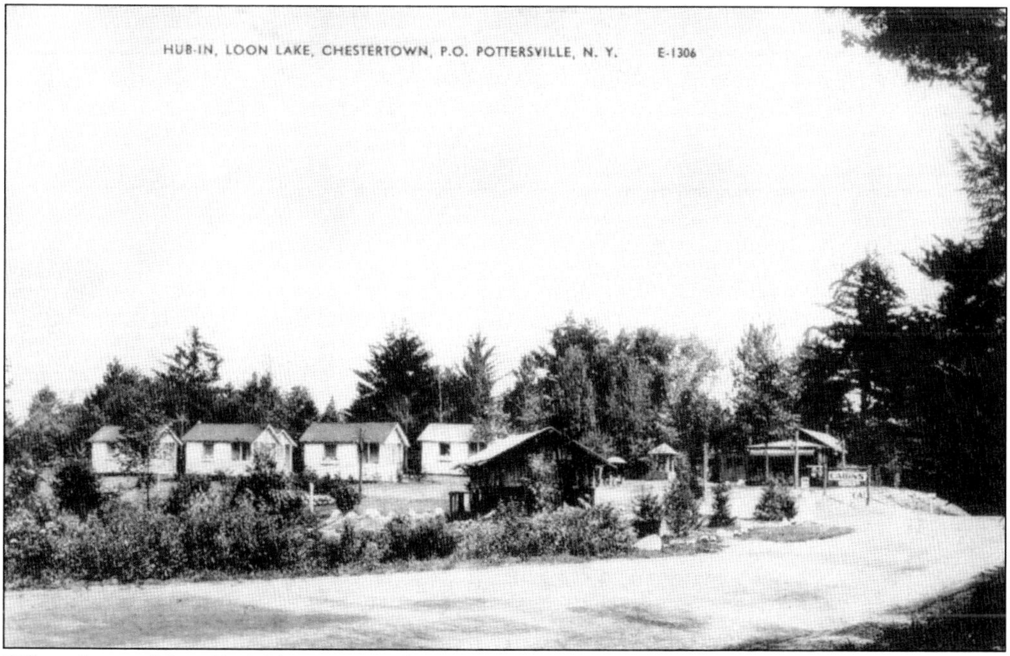

When the need for affordable accommodations became widespread in the Adirondack vacationlands, hundreds of cabins appeared on the scene. Built by local carpenters, they were rustic, with unfinished interiors. The two-by-fours were left exposed, and, in most cases, plumbing did not exist. Hotels added cabins to their properties to handle any overflow. Summer camps housed staff and campers in cabins. Roadside cabins attracted passing motorists, and hunting and fishing camps supplied cabins for sportsmen. In a day when moving a building was more practical than tearing it down, cabin colonies were created by turning small buildings brought from other sites into rental cabins. Cabins located adjacent to the Adirondack waterways were more popular than those along the highways.

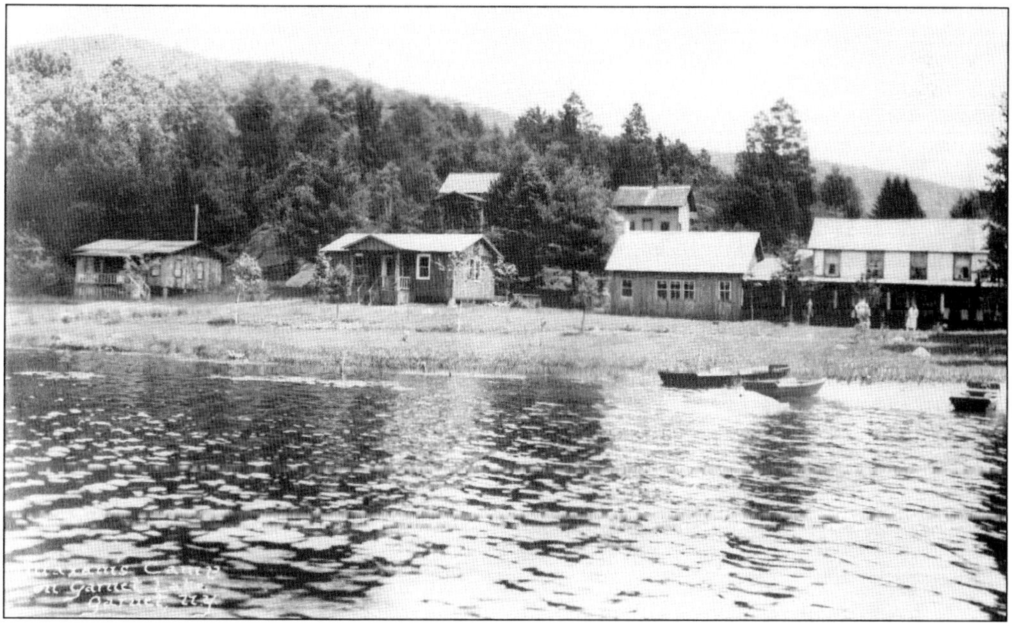

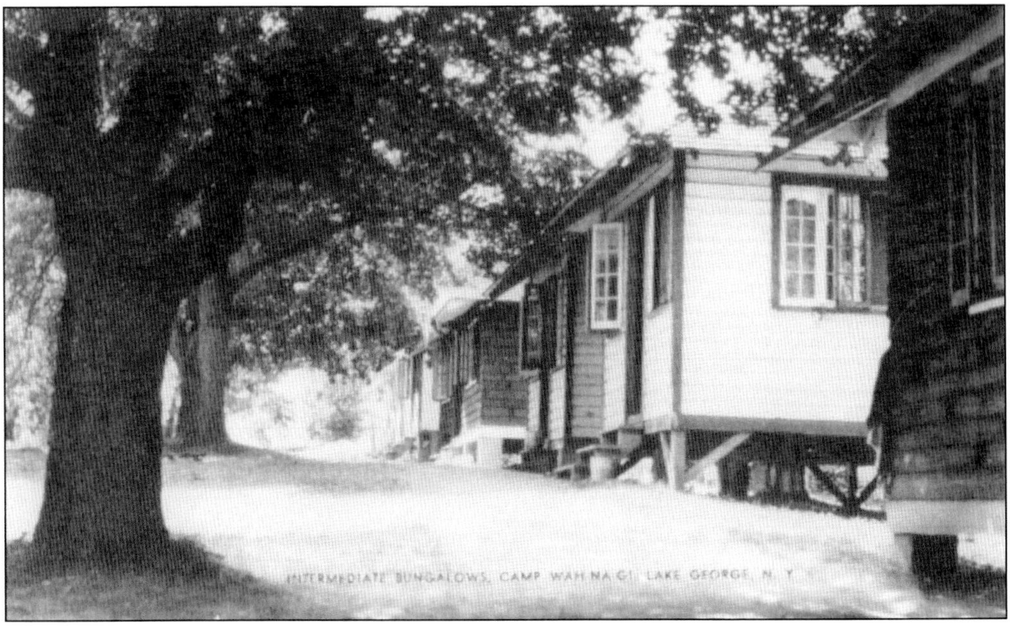

Cottage colonies and rental cabins numbered in the hundreds until the days of modern motels and high-speed highways. Shown here, Camp Wah-na-gi at Lake George advertised "intermediate bungalows." Built without cellars and indoor plumbing, most were only in use during the summer season. The Black Point Camps, also on Lake George, were a good example of larger camps that could house a whole family. Many returned to the same cabin year after year. Repeat visitors often took the next step, which was to buy a camp of their own. Today, a large number of the summer residents of the Adirondacks spend their time at their own place or that of a friend. Some estimates report that the Adirondack region population doubles in the summer months.

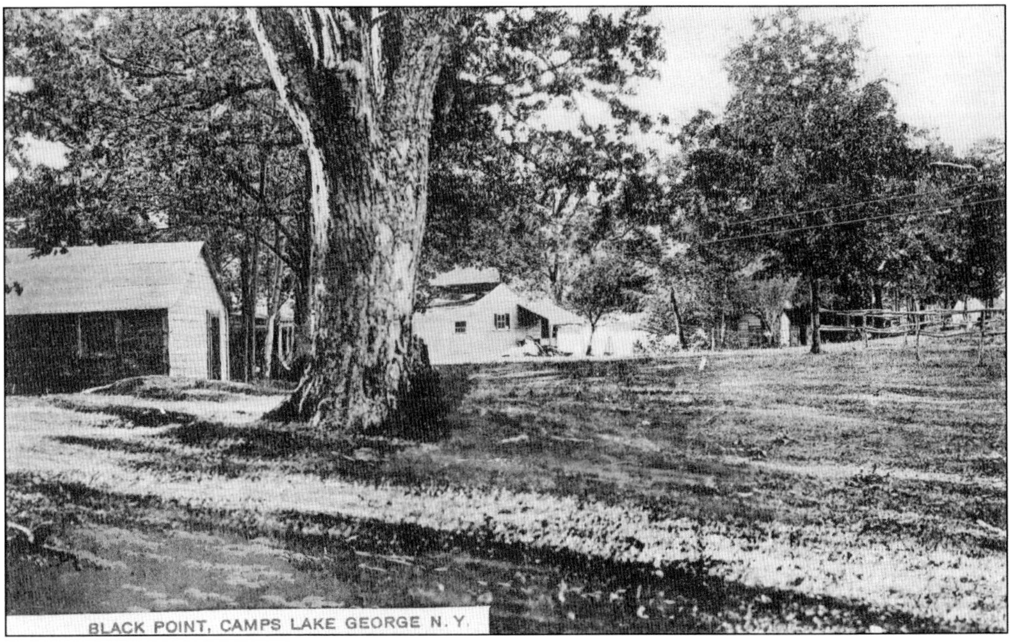

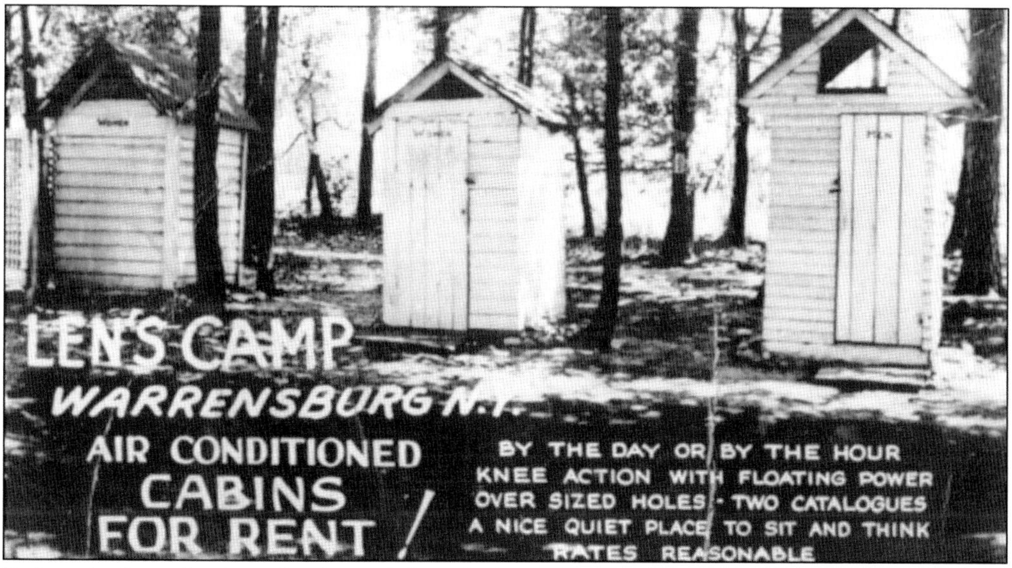

Before the days of indoor plumbing, Adirondack residents and visitors had to go outside to find a restroom. Small buildings called privies, necessaries, or outhouses were constructed within a short walking distance from the house. Catalogs were hung from a rope for use as toilet tissue. During cold weather, hot coals from the kitchen stove were brought to the outhouse for a little warmth.

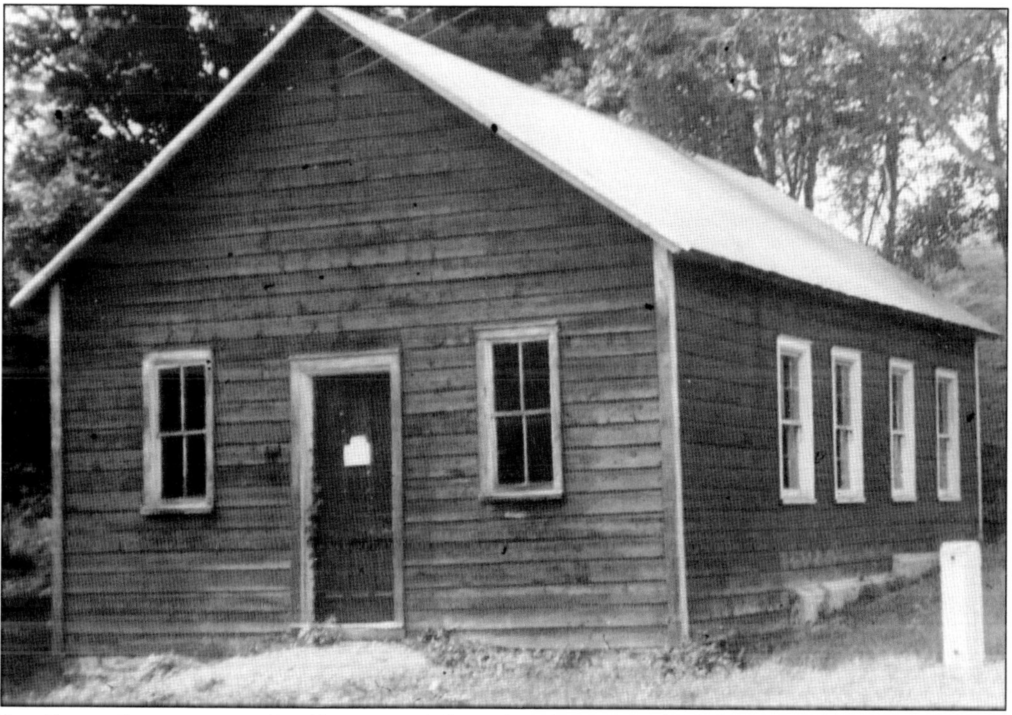

Small, usually one-room schoolhouses proliferated in the Adirondacks. Some of those still standing retain their original look, while others have been remodeled into camps or homes. One of the first places constructed in the settlements was the schoolhouse, which could be used for church and community gatherings as well as for school. The schoolhouse shown here still stands in Hope. A restored schoolhouse can be visited at the Adirondack Museum at Blue Mountain Lake.

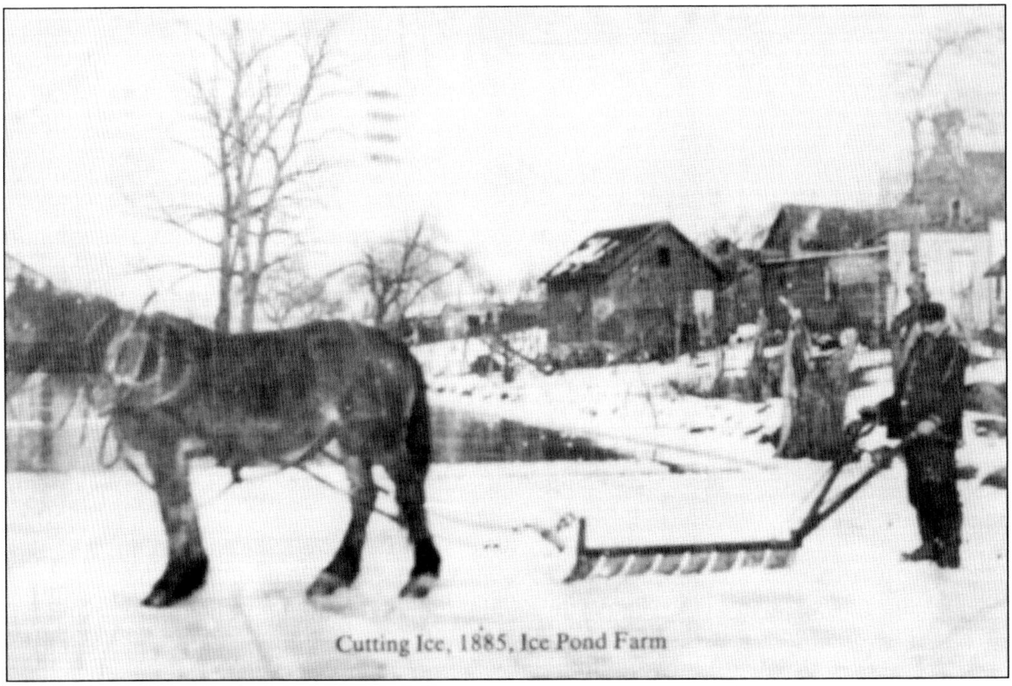

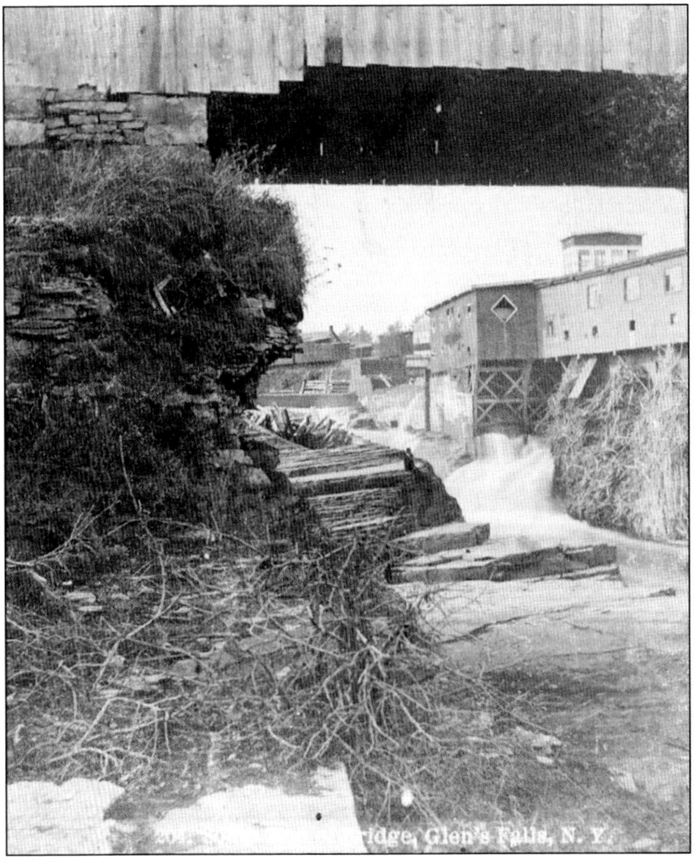

Harvesting ice from the Adirondack lakes and ponds was big business before electric refrigeration. At that time, residents needed fresh blocks of ice for their iceboxes. Ice was preserved in sawdust in special icehouses. Lakes and ponds had to be cleared to allow the ice to freeze thick and solid. It was hard work to saw out the square blocks, pull them from the water, and load them on a sleigh.

Glens Falls was the terminus of some of the major log drives. Erected on the Hudson River in the mid-1800s, the big boom was a log enclosure that caught floating logs. In its day, it caught millions of logs to be used in lumber and paper mills.

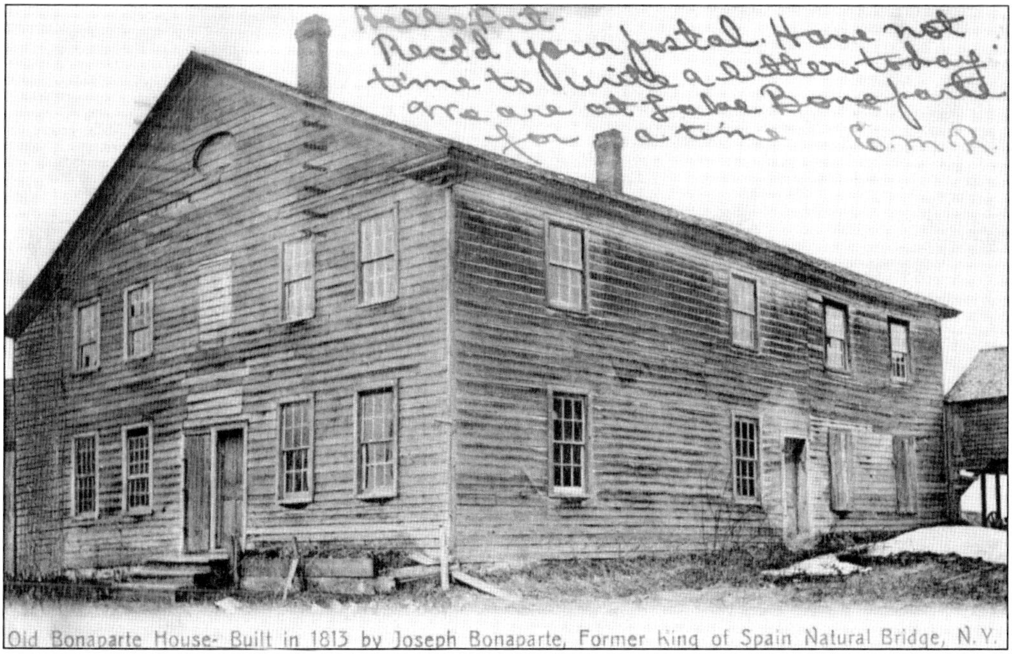

The famous Bonaparte family had an Adirondack connection. Joseph Bonaparte, elder brother of Napoleon, visited America in 1800 to consummate a treaty of friendship with France. In 1815, he returned to America after being driven out as the king of Spain. He arrived with great wealth and prestige and had no trouble making friends. Joseph acquired land in Jefferson County in the western Adirondacks, where he built a lodge.

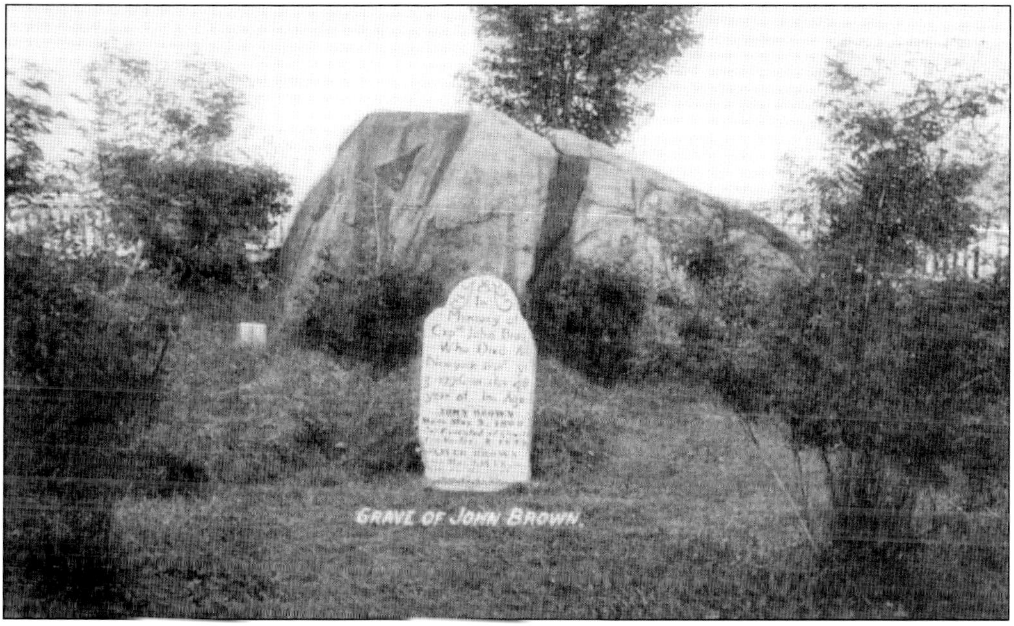

Philanthropist Gerritt Smith offered Adirondack land to black people. Abolitionist John Brown. Brown started a farm in 1849 in North Elba and invited black people to move to the Adirondacks. Ten years later, he was killed leading an arsenal raid at Harper's Ferry, Virginia. His body was brought to the Adirondacks for burial, and his name was added to his grandfather's tombstone.

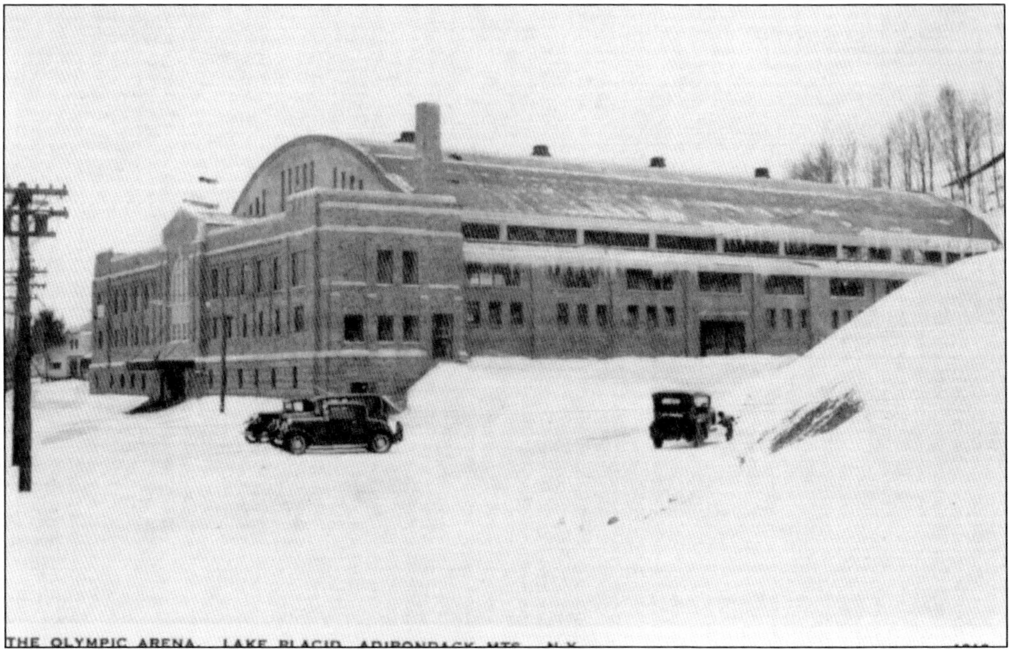

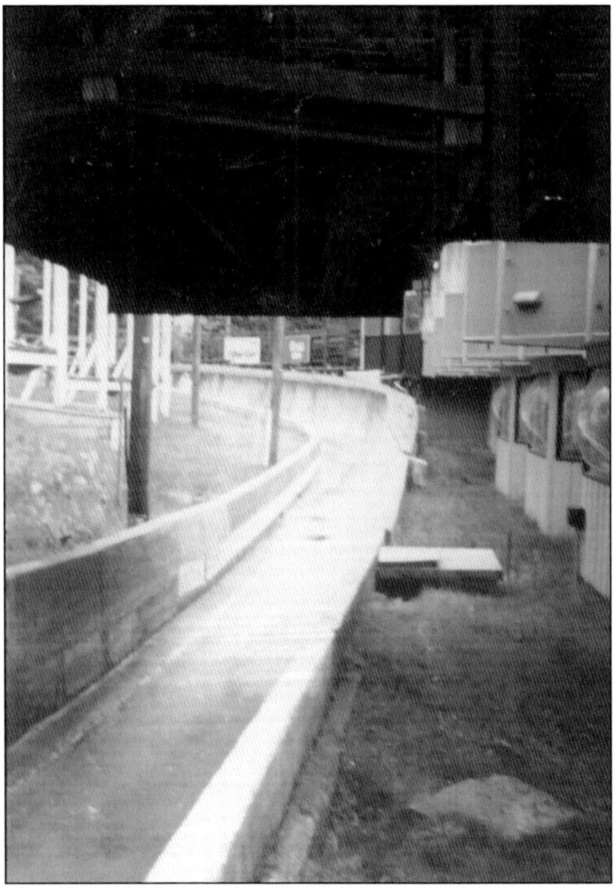

The 1932 Lake Placid Olympic Arena is still in use today. The first two winter games were held in Europe in the 1920s, while the third came to Lake Placid in 1932. The Adirondacks later hosted another Winter Olympics, based in Lake Placid in 1980.

Lake Placid hosted the 1932 and 1980 Olympic bobsled races. Today, it is open for practice runs, championship races, luge races, and general public use. Named after an Adirondack pioneer, the Mount Van Hoevenberg bob run was designed in 1930 by German engineer Stanislaus Zentzytzki. Today, observation decks and stairways provide a view of the 90-miles-per-hour sleds.

Located between Northville and Wells, the gauging station on the Sacandaga River appears on page 12 of the author's Images of America book *Adirondacks 1931–1990*. It had been used to measure water flow since the early 1900s, supplying half of the water entering the Great Sacandaga Lake. Since the publication of the book in 2003, the gauging station has been abandoned. It is now falling into disrepair.

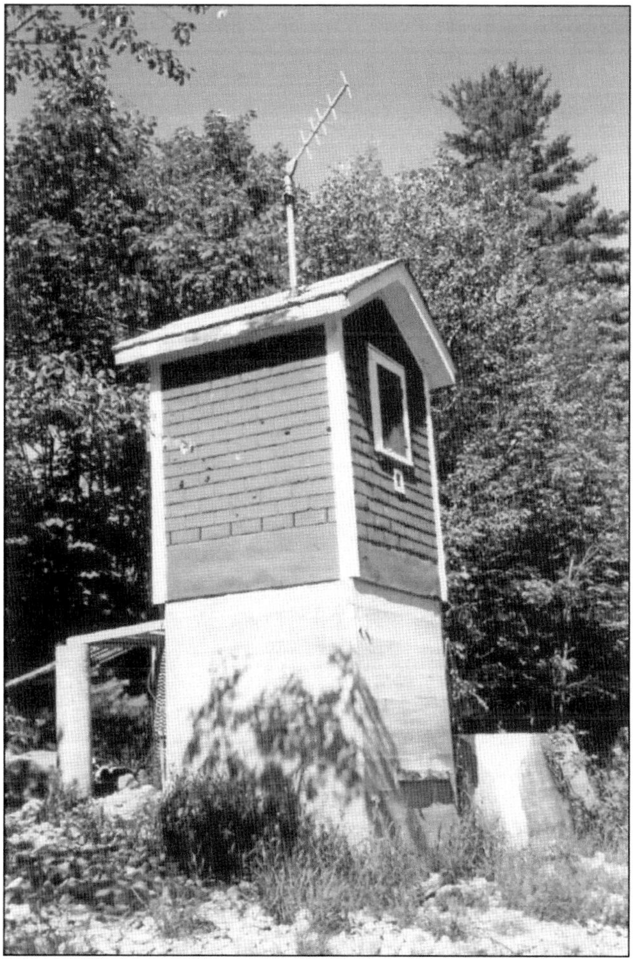

The small hill on the west side of Lake Algonquin at Wells was a good location for an aircraft warning station during World War II. One of thousands located in the eastern United States, the small structure was manned by volunteers 24 hours a day. Each station contained a stove, telephone, desk, chair, and silhouette guidebook. The midnight–six a.m. shift was the most difficult to fill.

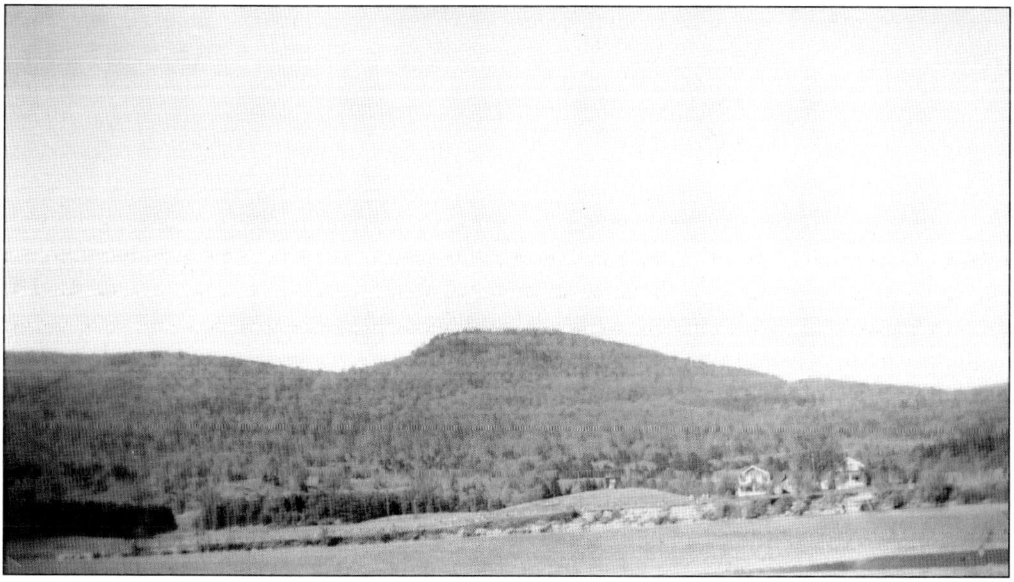

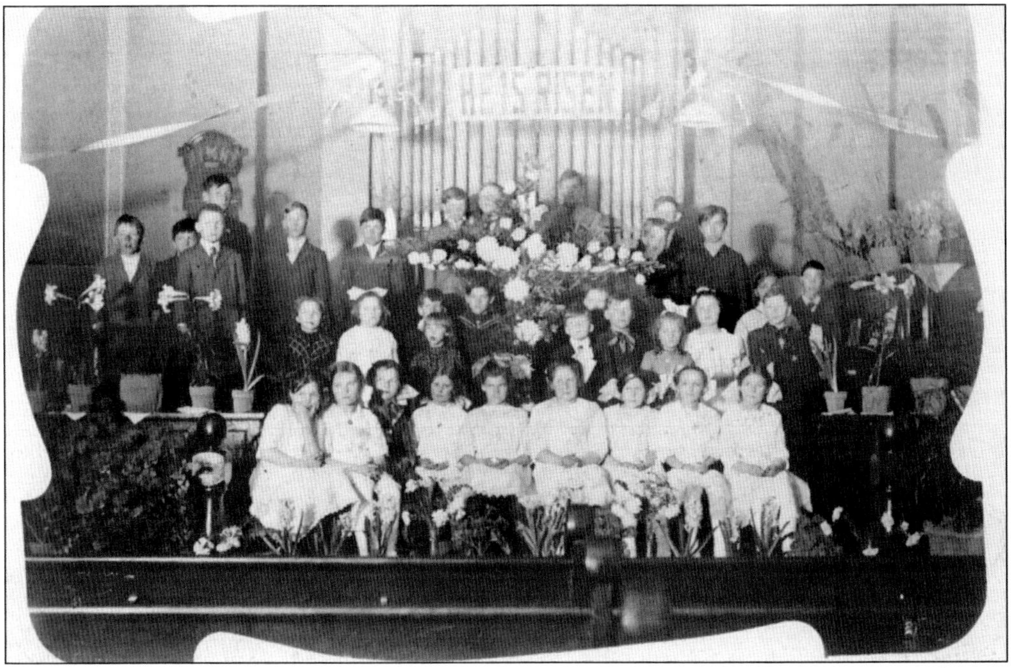

The Mayfield Presbyterian Church traces its roots back to the 1793 Low Dutch Reformed Church. After some splitting, the original church was reorganized as the Central Presbyterian Church of Mayfield by 1826. In 1850, it was rebuilt. Some additional improvements were made in 1920. Unfortunately, on April 28, 2011, the church steeple was struck by lightning, and the building was destroyed. As of early 2012, the church is being rebuilt.

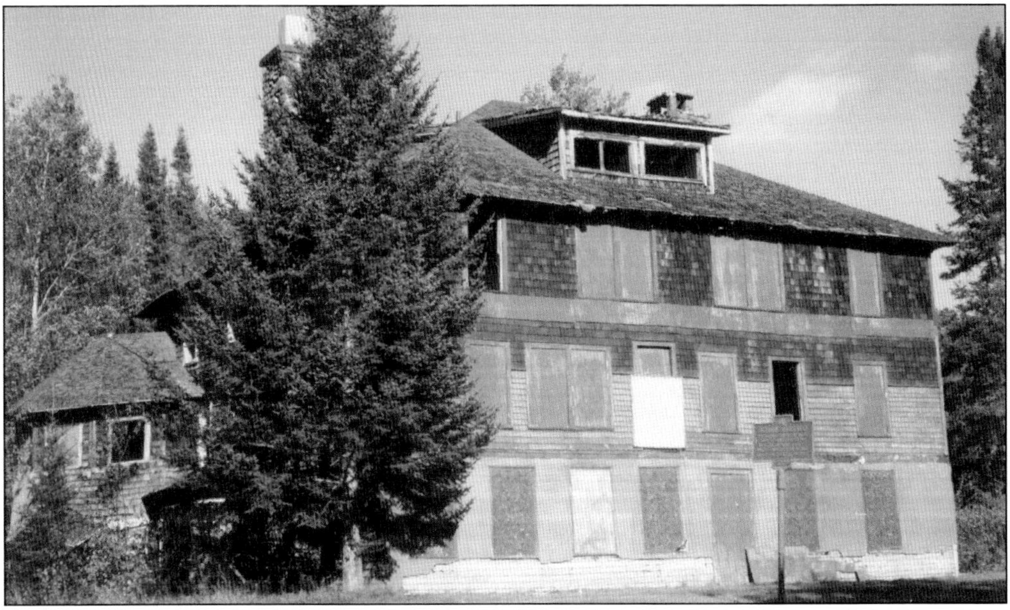

On September 13, 1901, while on a Mount Marcy hike, Theodore Roosevelt heard that President McKinley, recently shot, had taken a turn for the worst. Michael Cronin of Aiden Lair rushed Vice President Roosevelt to the train station. Aiden Lair is now one of the historic Adirondack places in danger of being lost.

Four

THE PURSUITS

At one time, Adirondack maps spoke of the mountains as a place unfit for settlements. In spite of the dire map predictions, however, the human spirit prevailed. The mountains could not hold them back—people came, pursued their dreams, and stayed.

The list of what might be called Adirondack pursuits is long. There were those who came to fish and those who came to hunt and to trap. The mountains and lakes attracted hikers and water-sports enthusiasts. Those seeking relief from the summer heat enjoyed the cool mountain nights and swimming at the beaches. Boaters came to the waterways of the Adirondacks—for lightweight canoes, guide boats, and giant steamboats. Artists, craftsmen, and woodworkers found the Adirondacks an ideal place to pursue their interests.

Engaging in winter activities resulted in the establishment of the world-renowned Olympic Center in the Adirondacks. Piseco Lake attracted a fishing club as early as 1840; the story became important enough to be published in *The Compleat Angler.* Pursuing fish and game called for statewide fish and game management. Taking part in outdoor activities was the basis for the conservation department, and protecting the Adirondacks now remains a natural priority by those who follow Adirondack pursuits.

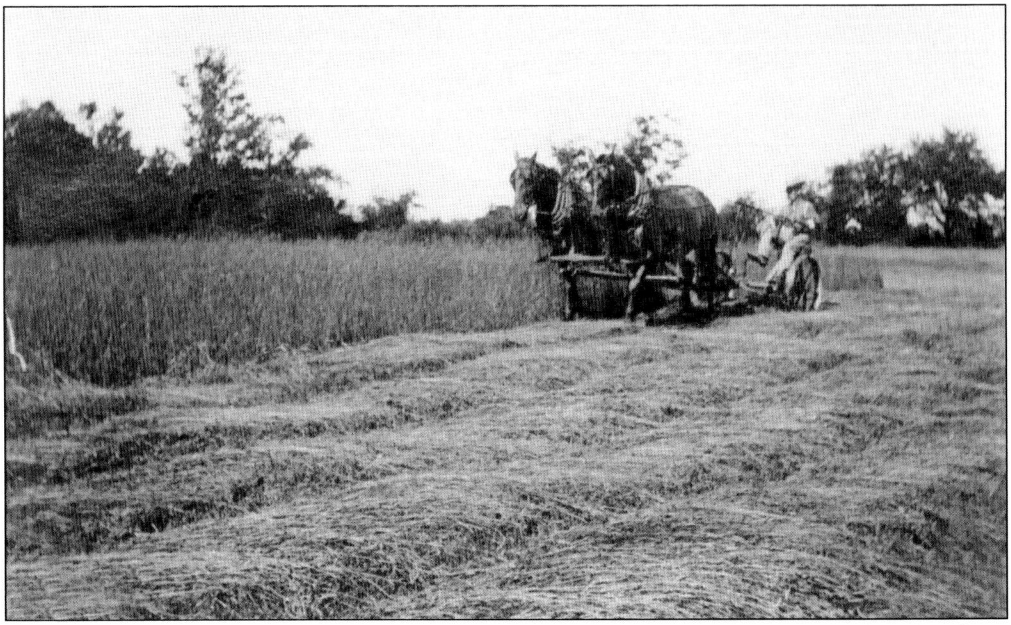

Those who came to the Adirondacks to farm the rugged country took on a difficult task. Those who prevailed had good horses. Horses pulled equipment used to plant and harvest crops. Feed and bedding for the cows, horses, and other farm animals required hay and corn, among other crops. Flax for cloth also had to be sown and harvested. In the 1845 census, almost 90,000 horses are listed in 12 Adirondack counties.

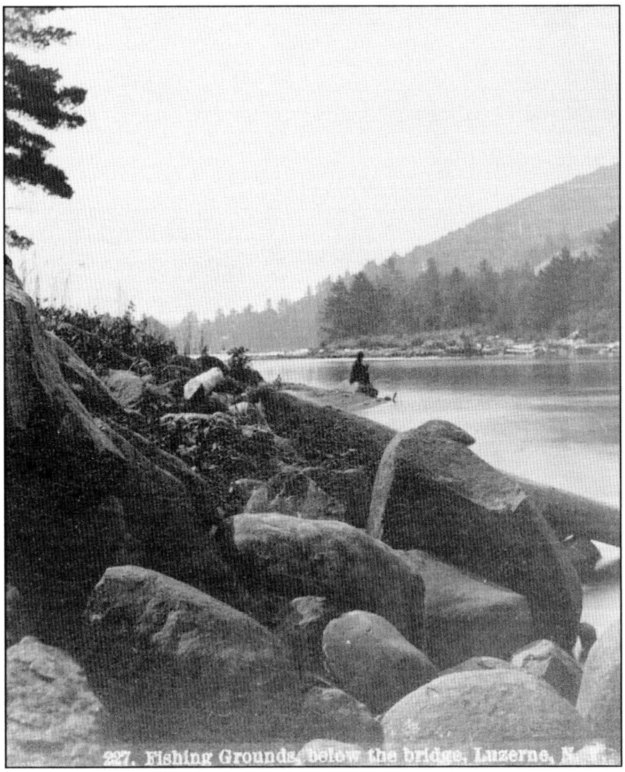

One farmer said that he no longer picked the rocks out of his garden. "We have been doing that for three generations and they keep growing back," he explained. It is true—Adirondack country is full of rocks. The glaciers scattered rocks throughout the mountainous country as well as moving waters and mountainsides. Rockslides still occur on the mountains today.

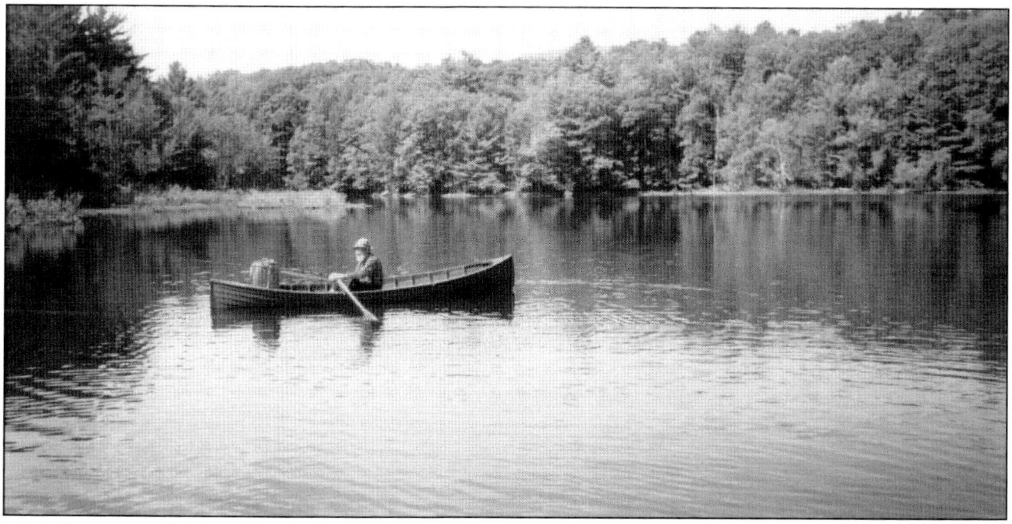

Nick Stoner and John Cheney pursued guiding in the mid-1800s, and by 1923, New York State mandated guiding licenses. Guides needed a license for the New York State Forest Preserve and were given the power of game protectors up until 1944. Each guide made $2.50 to $3.00 per day to equip tourists with axes, cooking utensils, tents, and guide boats, and to carry the gear between the waterways. They cooked the meals at camp and performed other domestic duties. Guides also found the trails, the game, and the fish. New York State counted on these first "tourist directors" of the mountains to keep the forest intact.

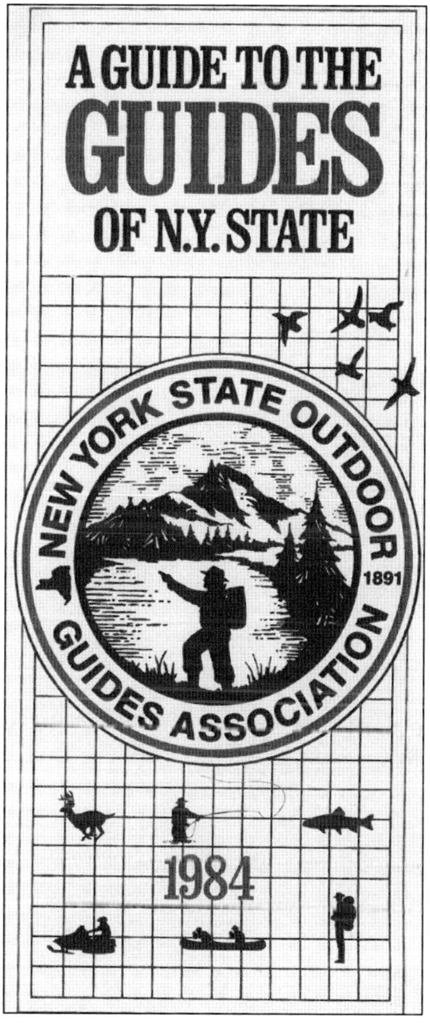

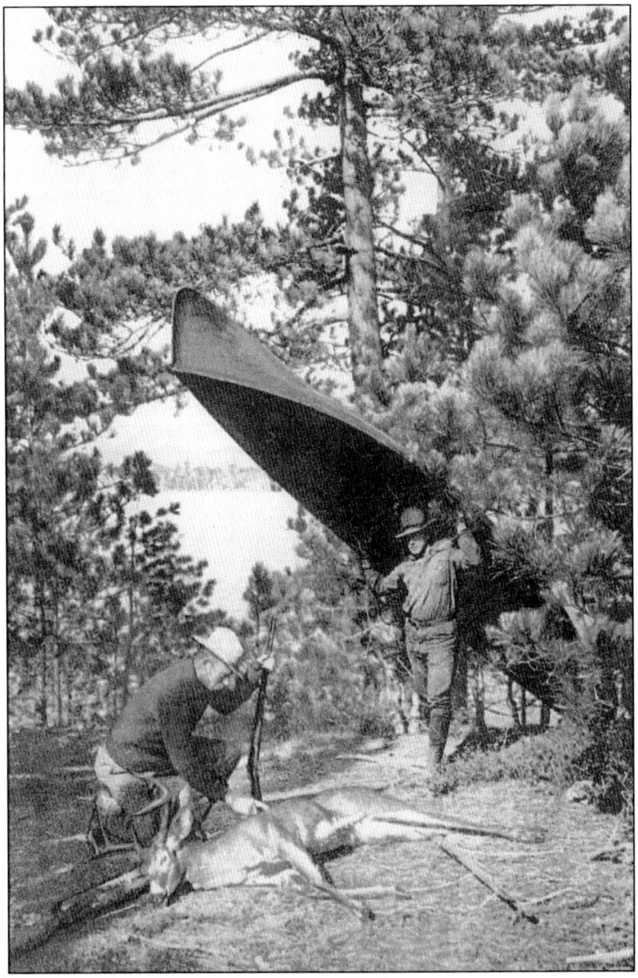

Hunters were among the first to seek the wilds of the Adirondacks in pursuit of game. Hunters coming from cities hired guides to help them find game. Year after year, successful guides were hired by the same clients. Once hotels were built, guides were hired by the hotelkeepers to serve their clientele.

Bear hunting encompasses more than a century of tradition in the Adirondacks. Most hunters have a "bear story" to tell. About a hundred years ago, Charles Dudley Warner's popular narrative *How I Killed A Bear* was required reading by the New York State Regents. Early settlers depended on bear oil, used in medicine, grease, hair tonic, perfume, rugs, and blankets.

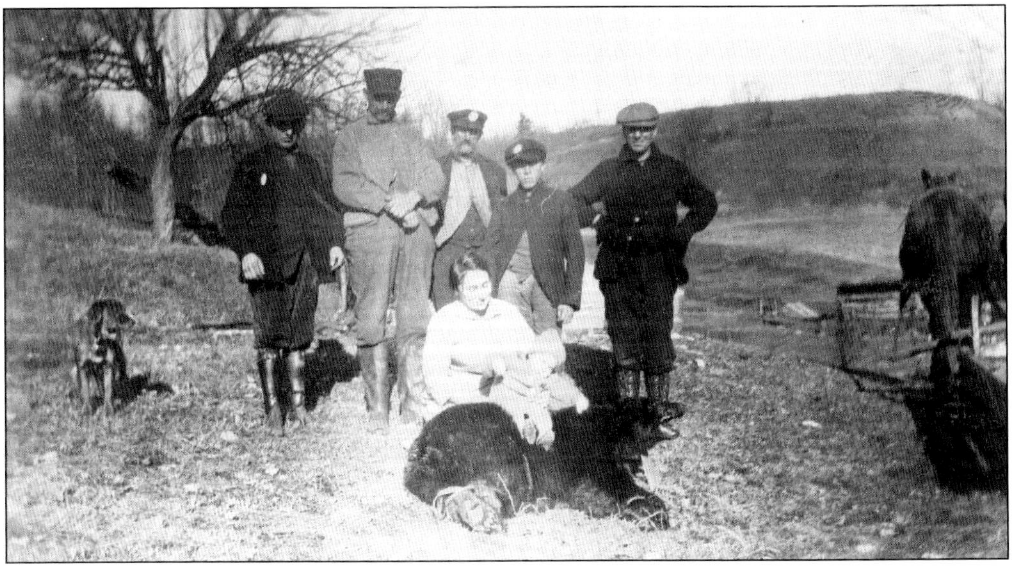

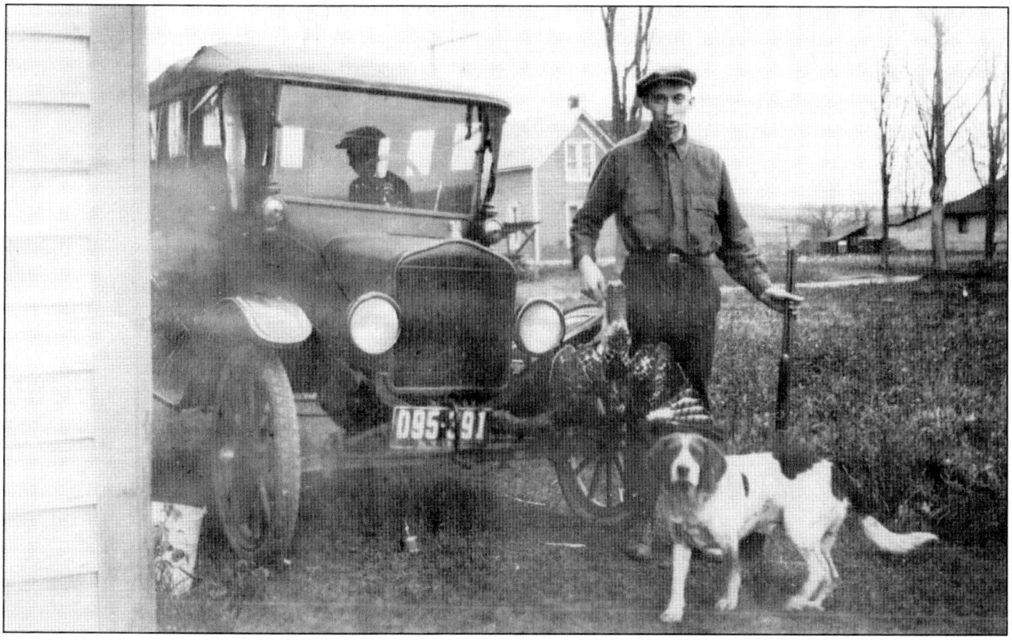

Bird hunters and small-game hunters have made good use of hunting dogs in their pursuits. Time was set aside each fall to train dogs as part of hunting regulations. Ring-necked pheasants, originally from China and England, were raised beginning in 1909 and stocked to maintain the population. An early study found that pheasants could be deprived of all food for at least 10 days without ill effects, thus surviving Adirondack winters.

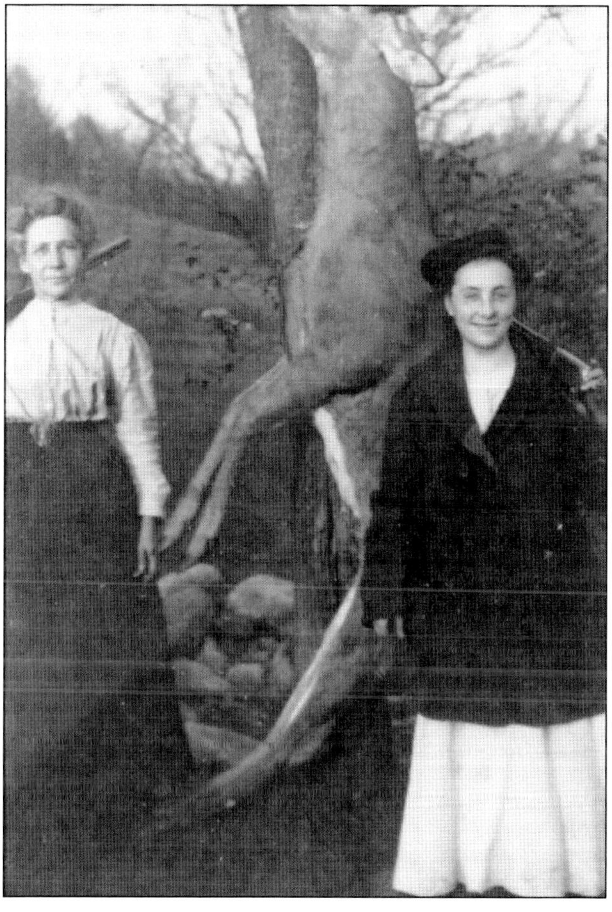

There is a history of female hunters in the Adirondacks. These two women with guns over their shoulders probably account for the deer in the background of this photograph. Adirondack furniture maker Lee Fountain's wife, Ott, was known as "the mighty huntress." Families survived (in part) on wild game in Adirondack winters.

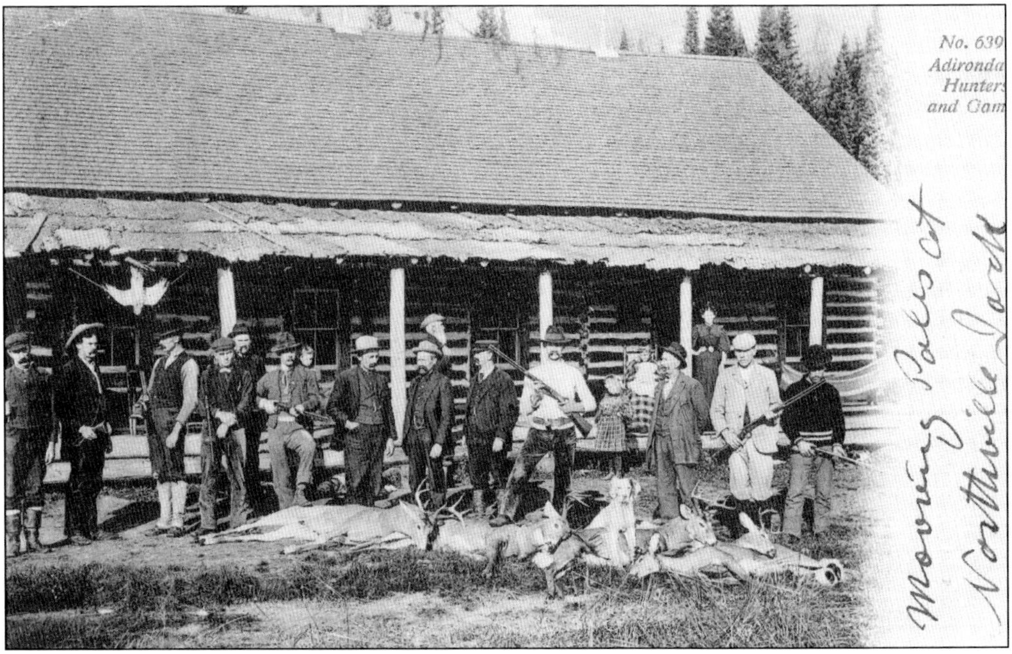

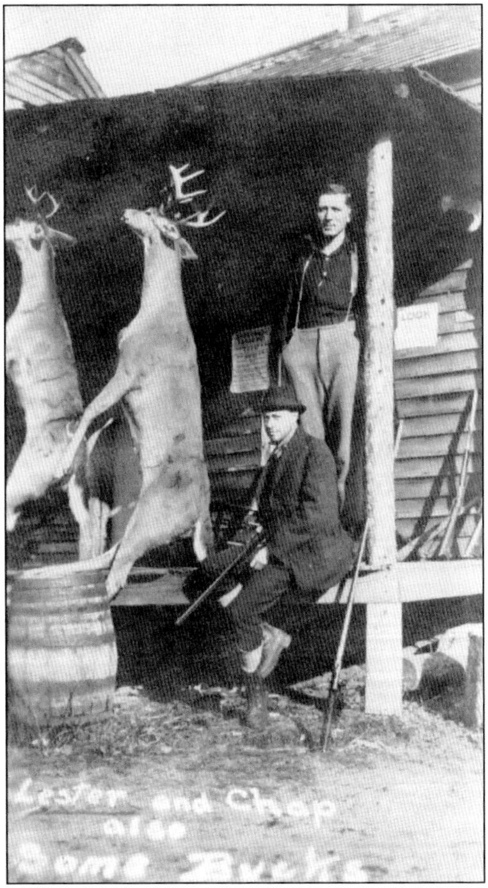

The Adirondacks are well known for their great hunting. The tradition evolved from hunters and trappers who eked out a living, was picked up by settlers who survived on venison, and was finally passed to sportsmen seeking game for meat and trophies. Successful deer hunting once depended upon dogs, water, and jacklights. Deer were driven into the lakes or hunted at night using a light on the front of a guide boat. Great drives that used a large number of hunters became the preferred method. Some talented hunters also preferred lone stalking, or still hunting. Hunting camps and hunting stories took on lives of their own.

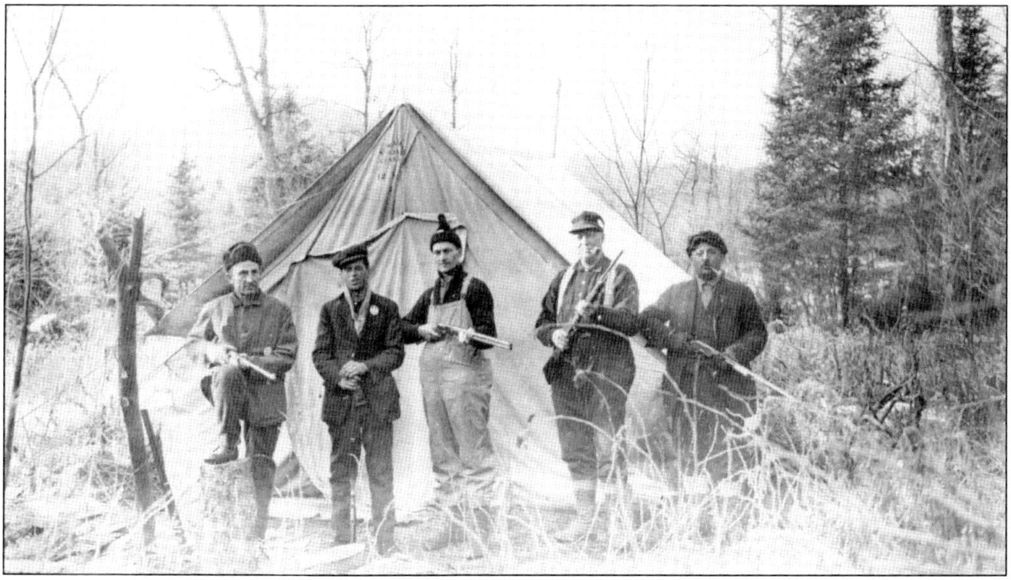

Canvas tents were used not only for summer camping in the Adirondacks but were also put to use by hunting parties during the annual big-game season. Tents could be transported by the hunting guide and set up for the season, often complete with a woodstove and cots. At the end of a day, hunters welcomed dry clothes and boots.

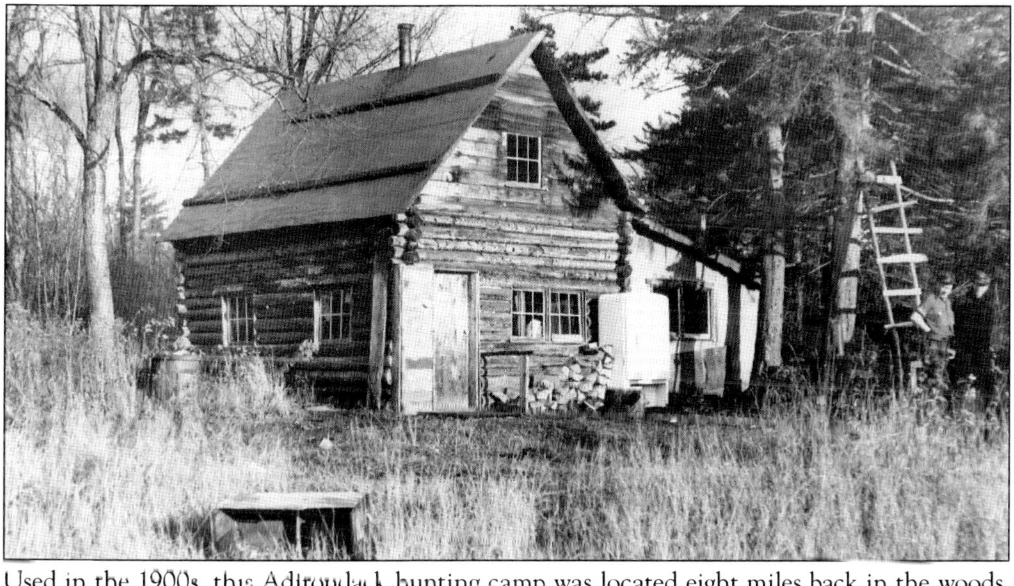

Used in the 1900s, this Adirondack hunting camp was located eight miles back in the woods. Adirondack guides who could afford accommodations in the backwoods could count on loyal clients to return each year. Most camps were made from native logs or rough-cut lumber covered with tar paper. Shingled roofs kept out the rain, and the woodstove with its protruding chimney provided heat. Refrigerators kept the food away from the marauding bears.

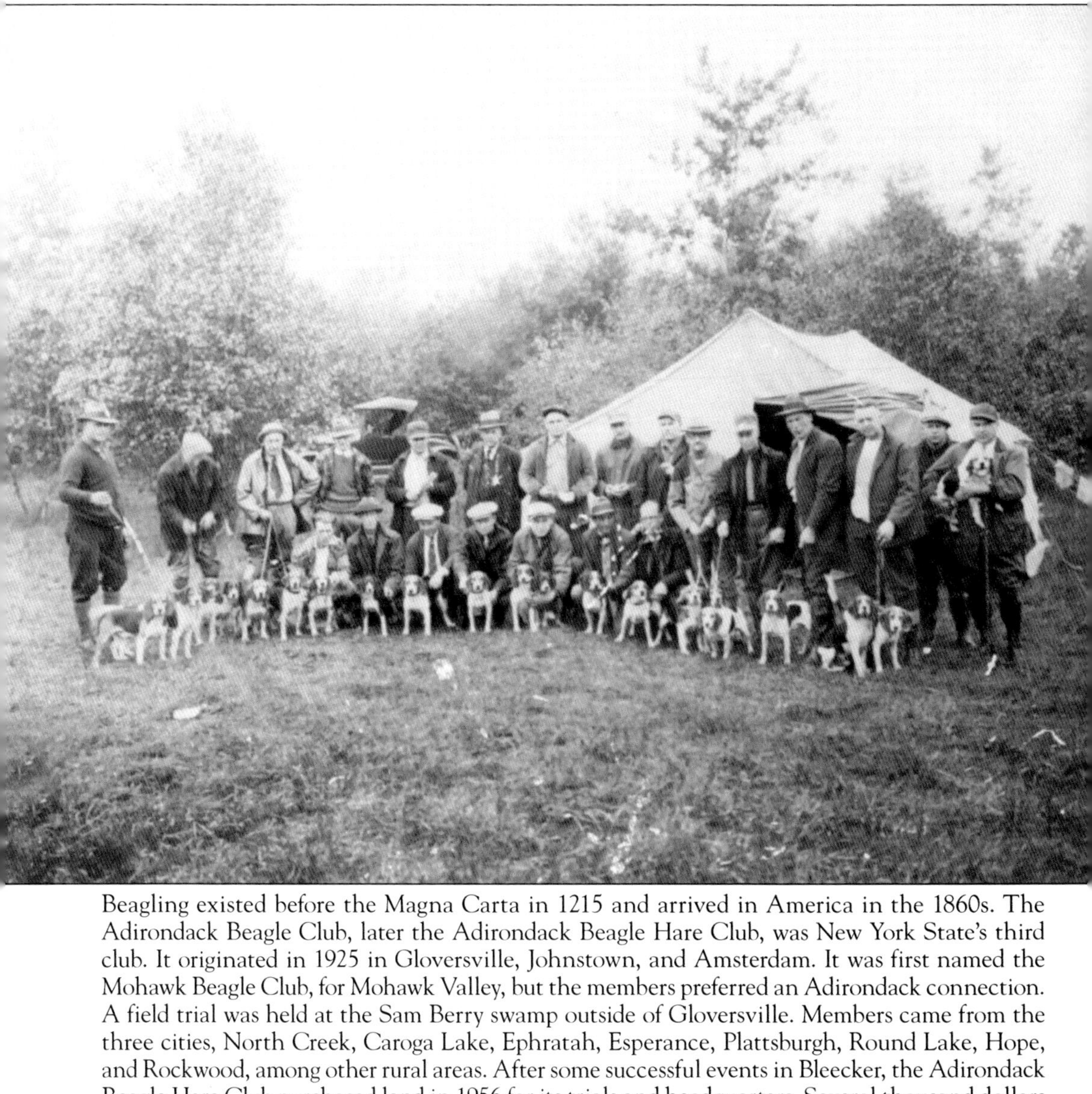

Beagling existed before the Magna Carta in 1215 and arrived in America in the 1860s. The Adirondack Beagle Club, later the Adirondack Beagle Hare Club, was New York State's third club. It originated in 1925 in Gloversville, Johnstown, and Amsterdam. It was first named the Mohawk Beagle Club, for Mohawk Valley, but the members preferred an Adirondack connection. A field trial was held at the Sam Berry swamp outside of Gloversville. Members came from the three cities, North Creek, Caroga Lake, Ephratah, Esperance, Plattsburgh, Round Lake, Hope, and Rockwood, among other rural areas. After some successful events in Bleecker, the Adirondack Beagle Hare Club purchased land in 1956 for its trials and headquarters. Several thousand dollars were spent on fencing, and more acreage was purchased. It has been one of the most successful beagle clubs in America.

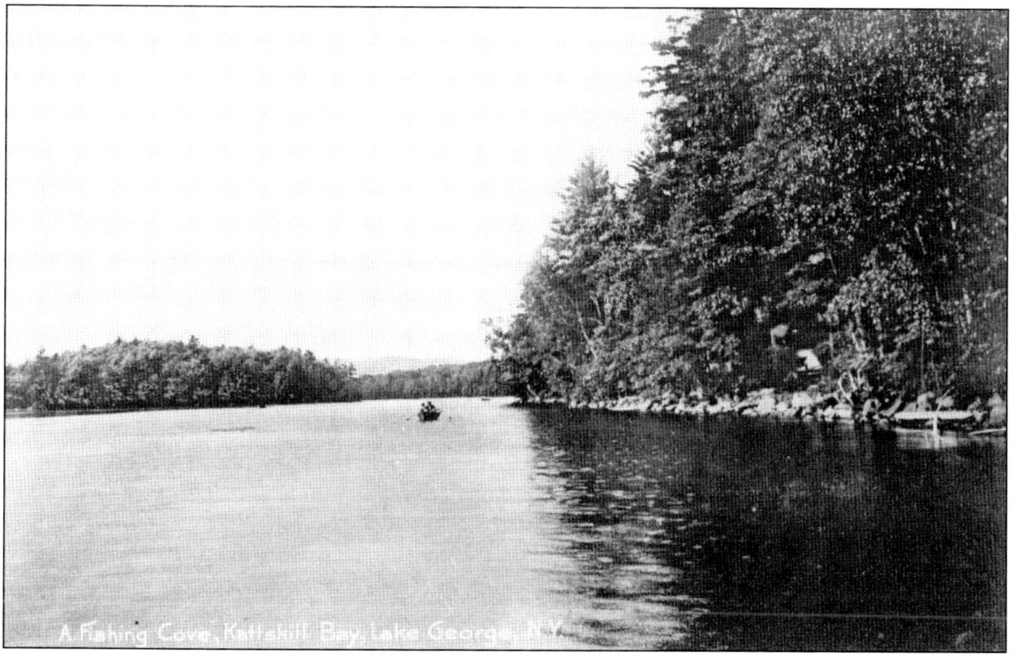

Anglers have been fishing Lake George's coves and bays, shown here, since before white settlers arrived. Father Isaac Jogues passed through in 1642, when Native Americans took him to Lake George, then called Andiartarocte, or "Tail of the Lake." In 1646, Father Jogues renamed the beautiful waters Lac du Saint Sacrement, or "Lake of the Blessed Sacrament." Gen. William Johnson arrived in 1755, during the French and Indian War, and renamed it Lake George for King George II of the United Kingdom. In 1791, Secretary of State Thomas Jefferson and James Madison visited Lake George on a fishing trip, whereupon Jefferson called it "the most beautiful lake I ever saw." Lake George has also been called Queen of the American Lakes.

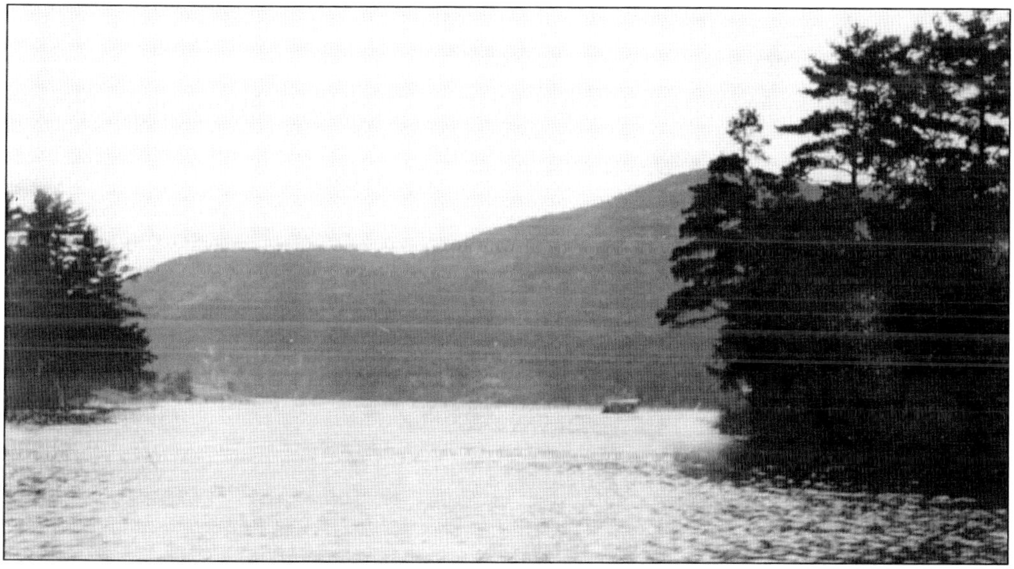

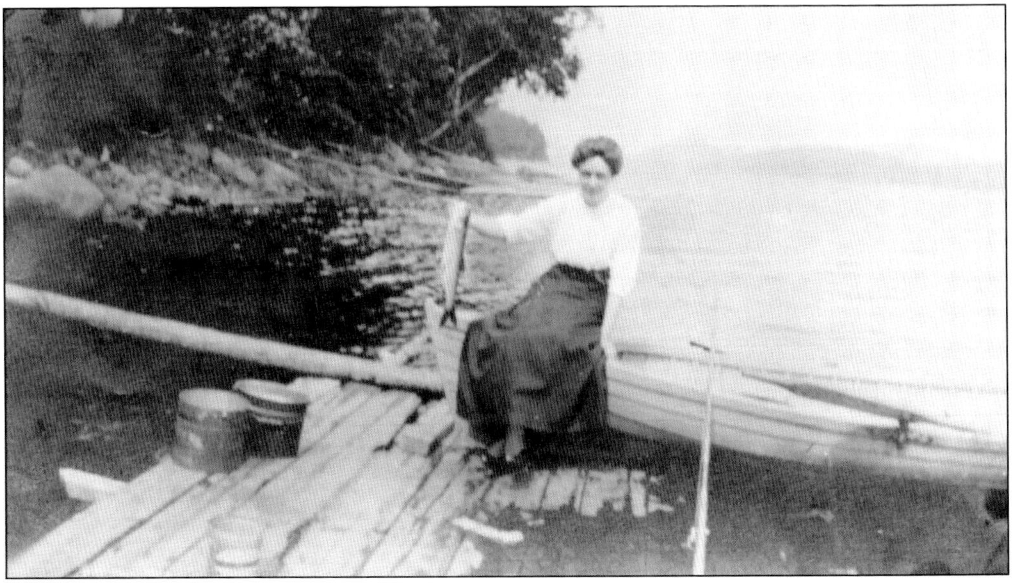

Adirondack fishing continues to be a pursuit for both men and women. There are those hearty Adirondack women who pursued tasty and trophy fish found in the lakes and backcountry waters. Julia Burton Preston hunted and fished with her father for several years. She may be the first licensed female guide in the Adirondacks, having begun her guiding career in 1914.

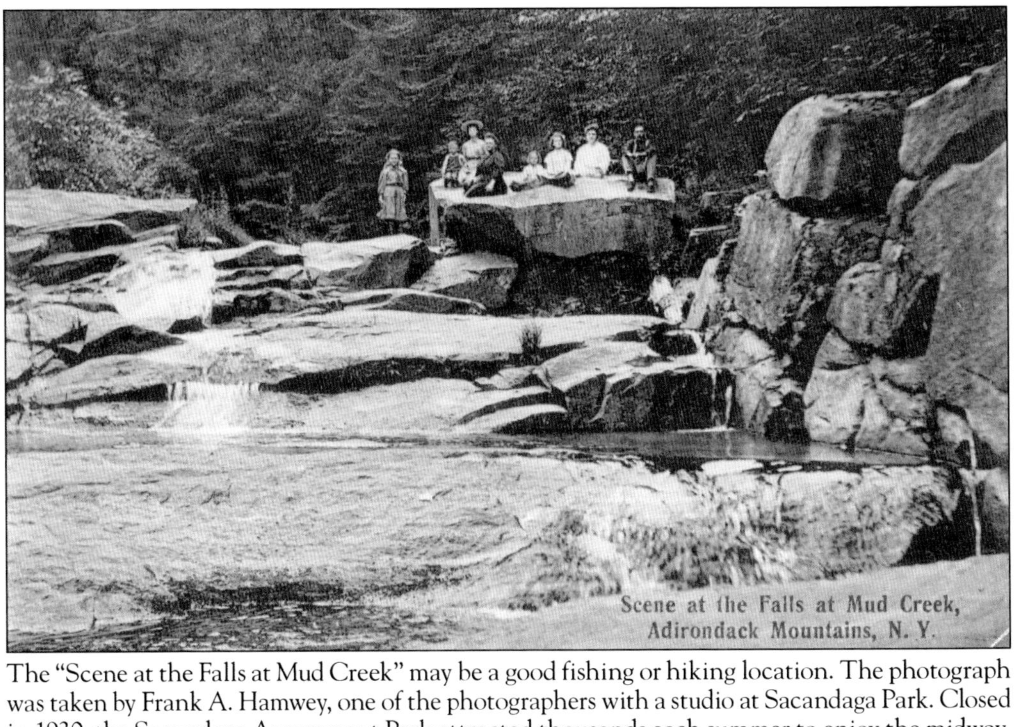

The "Scene at the Falls at Mud Creek" may be a good fishing or hiking location. The photograph was taken by Frank A. Hamwey, one of the photographers with a studio at Sacandaga Park. Closed in 1930, the Sacandaga Amusement Park attracted thousands each summer to enjoy the midway, music, and beach and to get their photographs taken in one of the studios.

Anglers of all ages find Adirondack waters teeming with fish. Founded in 1840, Lake Piseco Trout Club was one of the first sports clubs in America. Club records, published in *The Compleat Angler*, tell of massive catches of some two tons of lake trout in a five-year period. One trout weighed over 26 pounds. By 1851, it was little wonder that the lake was nearly fished out. Today, the Adirondacks offer freshwater fish in 3,000 lakes and ponds and 30,000 miles of streams and rivers. In recent years, acid rain has become a real threat to fishing. Pollution from Midwestern and Canadian power plants is blown across the country to the mountains.

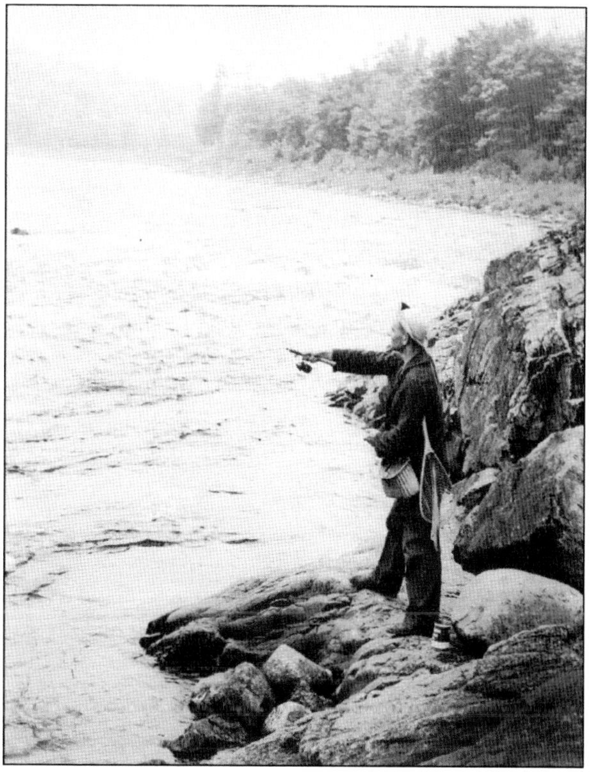

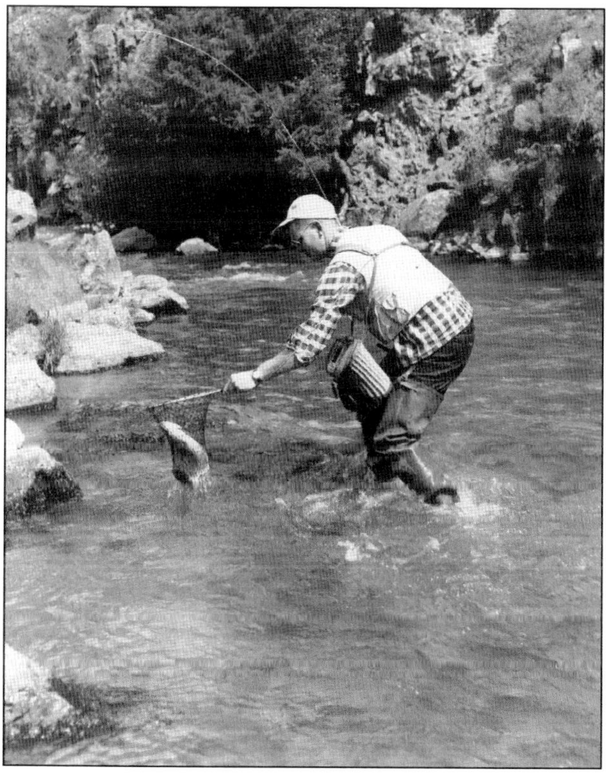

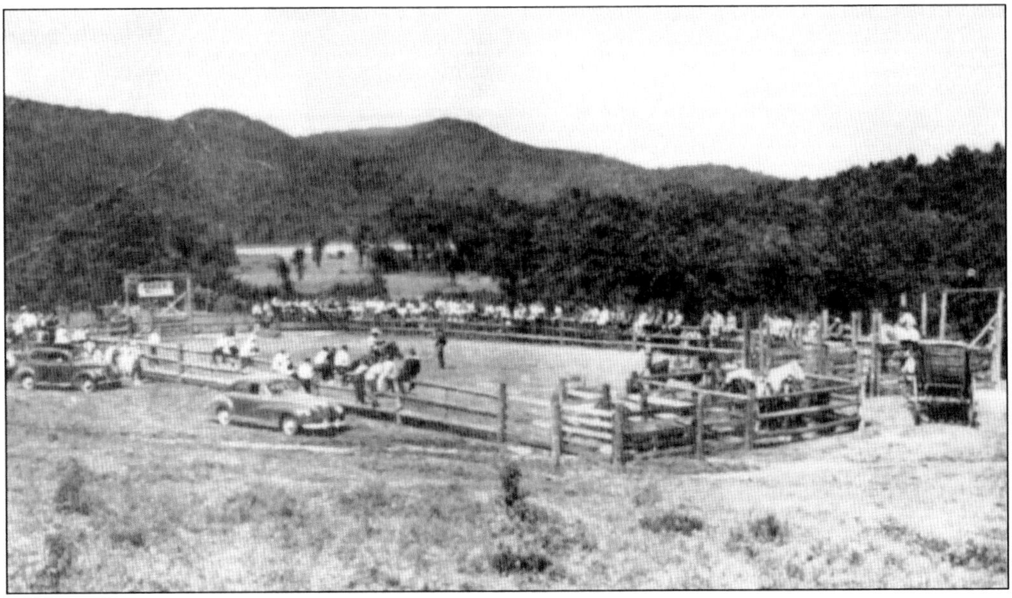

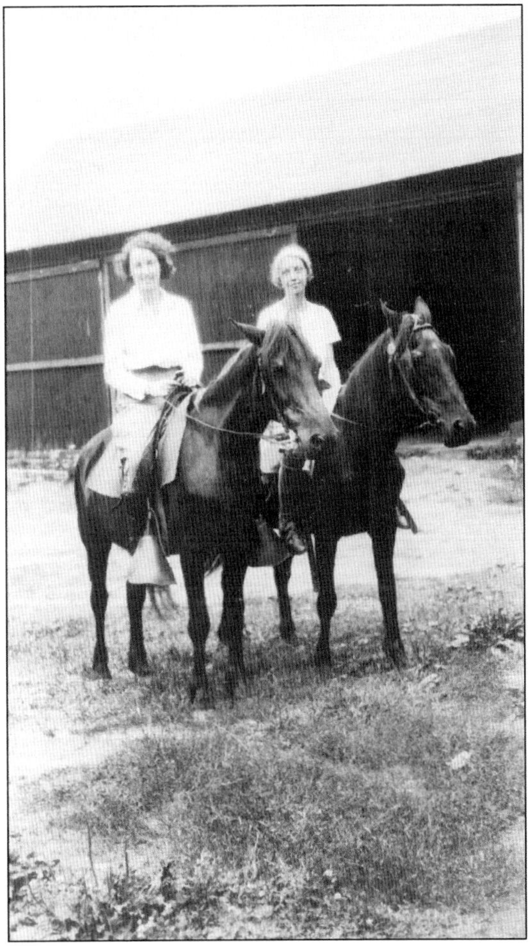

The Sun Canyon in Warrensburg, "America's Famous Dude Ranch," was typical of the dozens of such ranches found in the Adirondacks. They advertised: "romance and color of the true West is experienced in a thrilling rodeo each week." After a week at one of the dude ranch resorts, one visitor wrote, "I'll never enjoy eastern-style riding again." Apparently, the "true West" could be found in the Adirondacks.

The Adirondacks transitioned from a horse-driven economy to a motorized economy sometime after 1900, but horses remained. They were privately owned, and horse trails were privately developed. Dude ranches became a regular part of the growing tourist industry in the Adirondacks, and hundreds of horses were housed on the ranches for the enjoyment of summer "cowboys" and "cowgirls." Warren County had some 20 dude ranches in the 1940s.

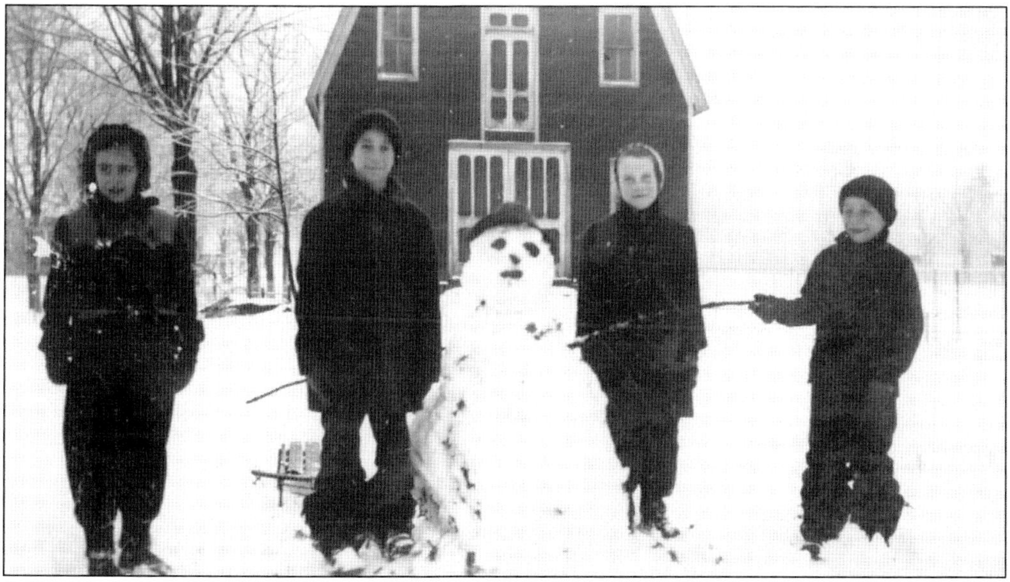

Adirondack winters were known for deep snows and long cold spells, but winter activities were pursued that made it a welcome season. Winter sports clubs organized in the hamlets. Skating, skiing, sleigh and toboggan riding filled many winter hours. Making snowmen and snow angels was also a popular pastime.

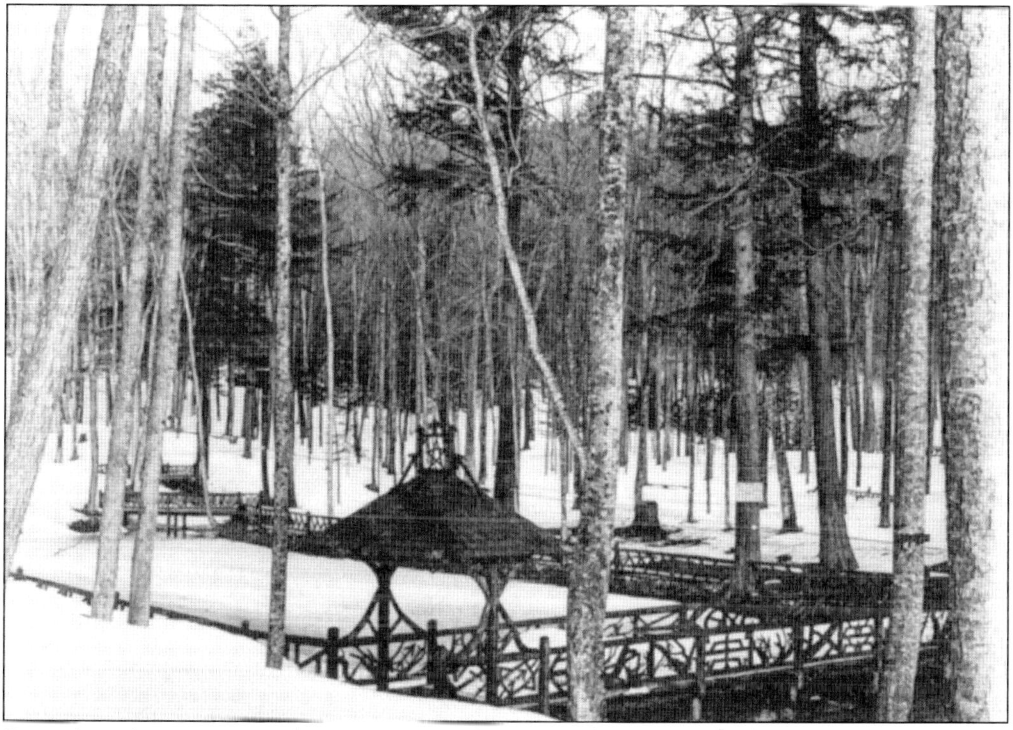

Sacandaga Amusement Park was not a popular winter destination. In first three decades of the 20th century, at the height of its popularity, thousands took the train each day to Sacandaga Park to enjoy the midway of concession stands and rides, the shows, the ballgames, the picnics, and the rustic park during the summers.

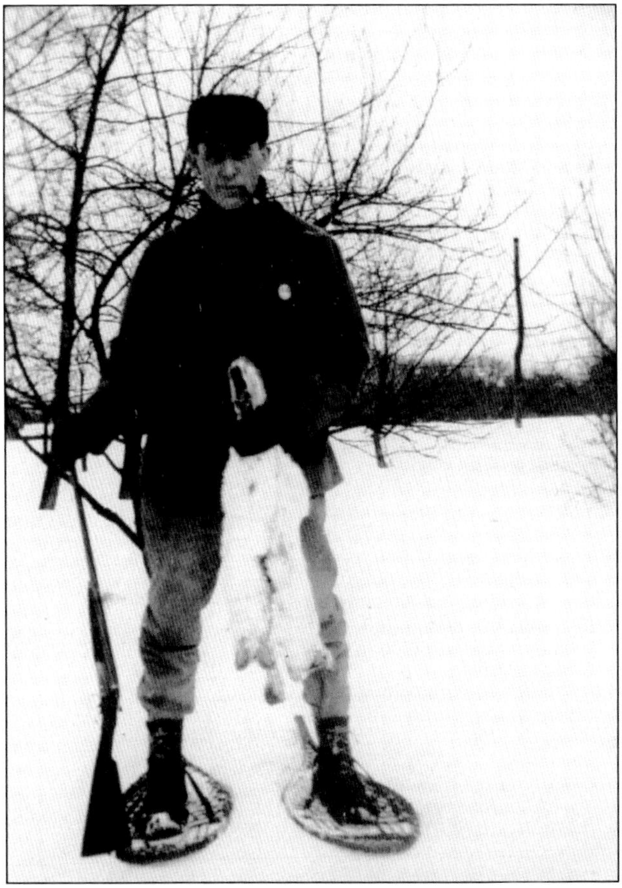

Survival in the Adirondacks at the time of the early settlements depended on outdoor skills—learning to live off the land. Simply farming the lands would lead to failure; it became necessary to develop a relationship with the wilderness. Hunting, fishing, and trapping (sometimes on snowshoes) was essential to life in the mountains. Oliver Whitman's late-1800s Adirondack journals recorded large numbers of animals that were killed for survival.

Snowshoeing was not just for the Native Americans and trappers in the Adirondacks; men and women of all ages found snowshoes were the best way to traverse the snowy trails. Note the heavy fur coat.

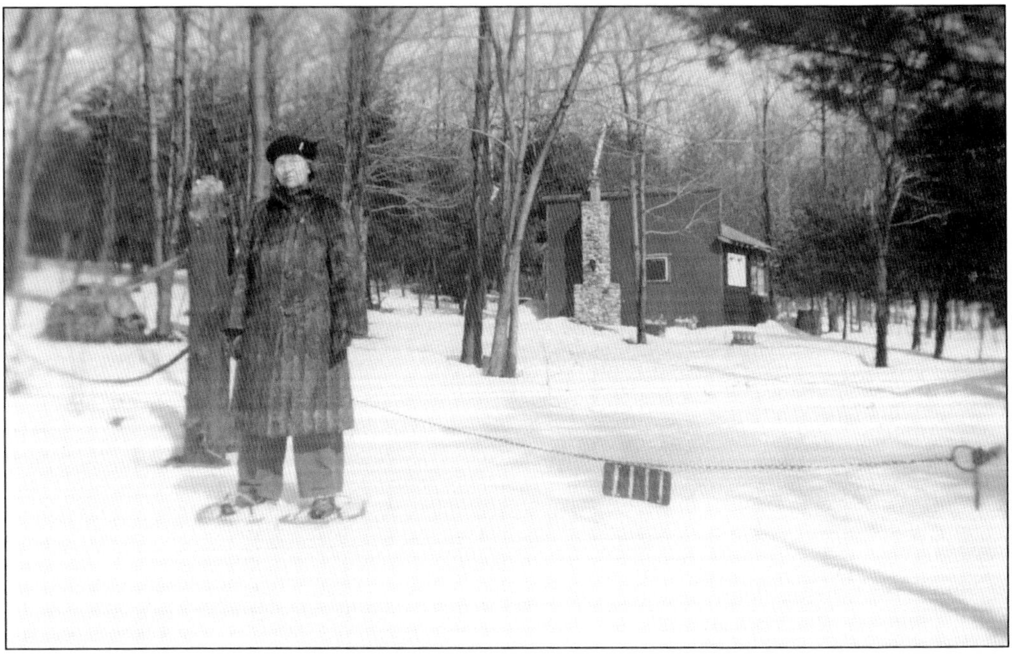

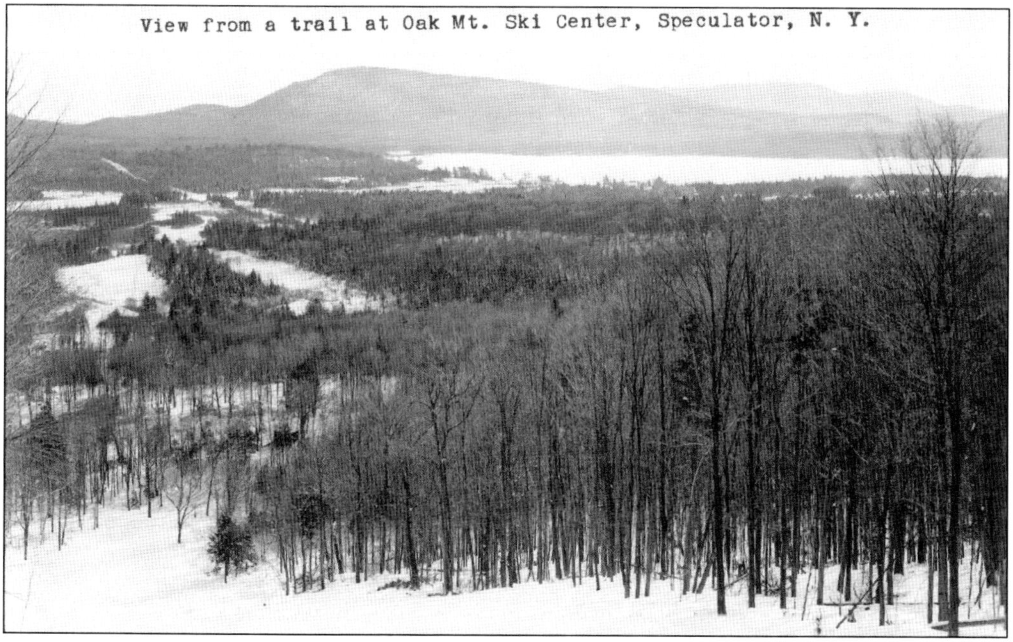

Those who pursue skiing and ride the ski tows enjoy a view of the mountainous and lake country not shared by those below. Tefft's Adirondack Studio took these 1940s photographs from the ski trails on the Oak Mountain Ski Center in Speculator. Winter sports had been formalized in Speculator in the early 1900s with the advent of the Winter Sports Club. Around 1927, the town toboggan slide with its seven-second ride was in full use along with the town skating rink. The Oak Mountain Ski Center, with seven trails, was built in 1946 and was operated and leased by the town until 1967. The Novosel family purchased the center and doubled the size, adding a chairlift. Recently, the town has been operating the center again.

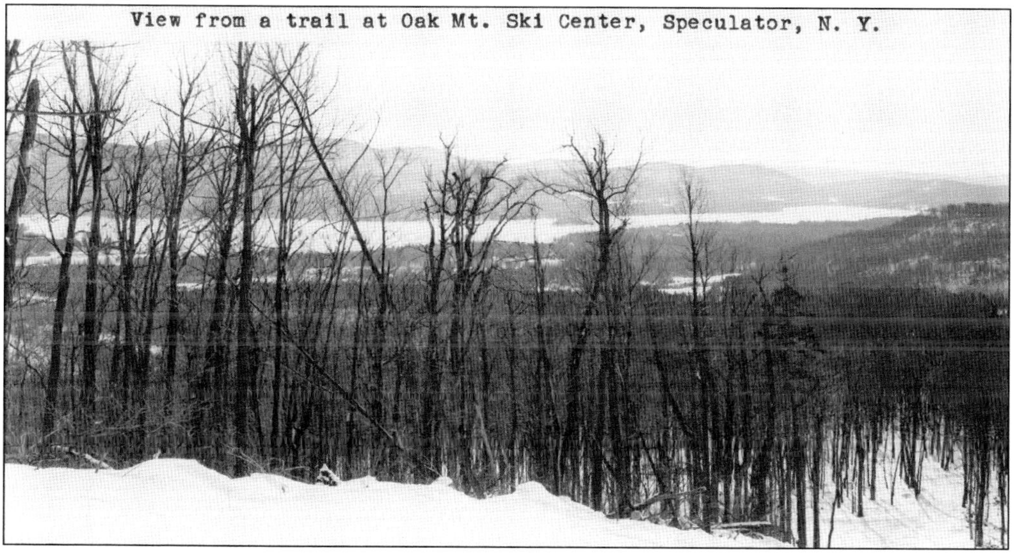

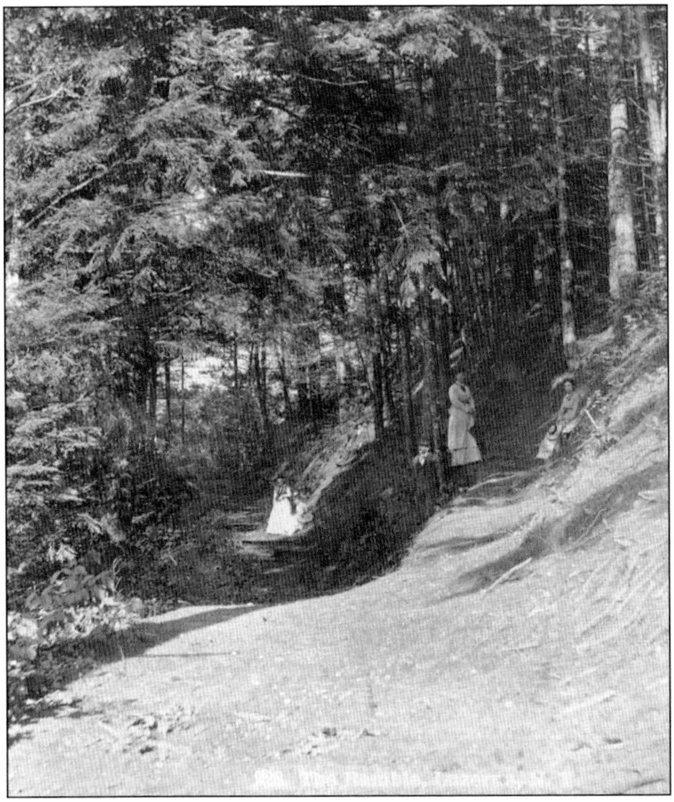

It would not be the Adirondacks without 3,000 miles of hiking trails to pursue. State trails are marked with colored markers that are attached to trees to keep hikers from getting lost. There are trails for horses, bikes, and snowmobiles, as well as pedestrians. Handicap-accessible trails enjoy regular use. The 133-mile Northville–Lake Placid Trail traverses the Adirondacks from south to north through the woodlands.

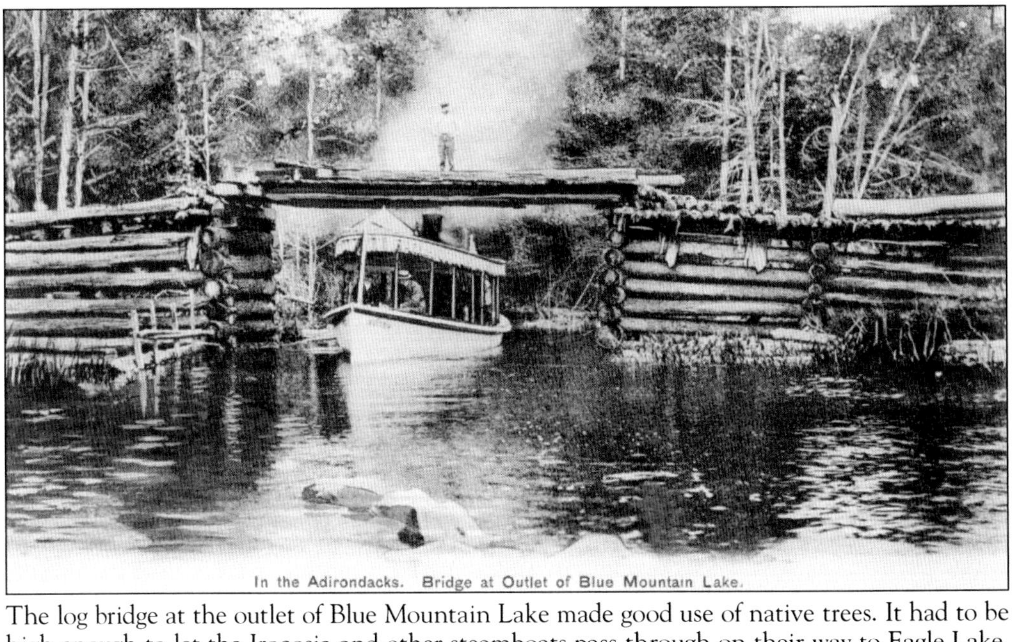

The log bridge at the outlet of Blue Mountain Lake made good use of native trees. It had to be high enough to let the Irocosia and other steamboats pass through on their way to Eagle Lake, to Utowana down the Marion River, and finally to Raquette Lake. The bridge was used in the 1880s and was replaced by W.W. Durant in 1891. The Blue Mountain Lake had a fleet of more than a dozen steamboats.

Once the Adirondack waterways were "public highways" for timber rafting, it was a common sight to see logs moving en masse on the rushing springtime waters, scattered up and down the river, or caught along the shores. This Hudson River logging scene is located above Palmer Falls.

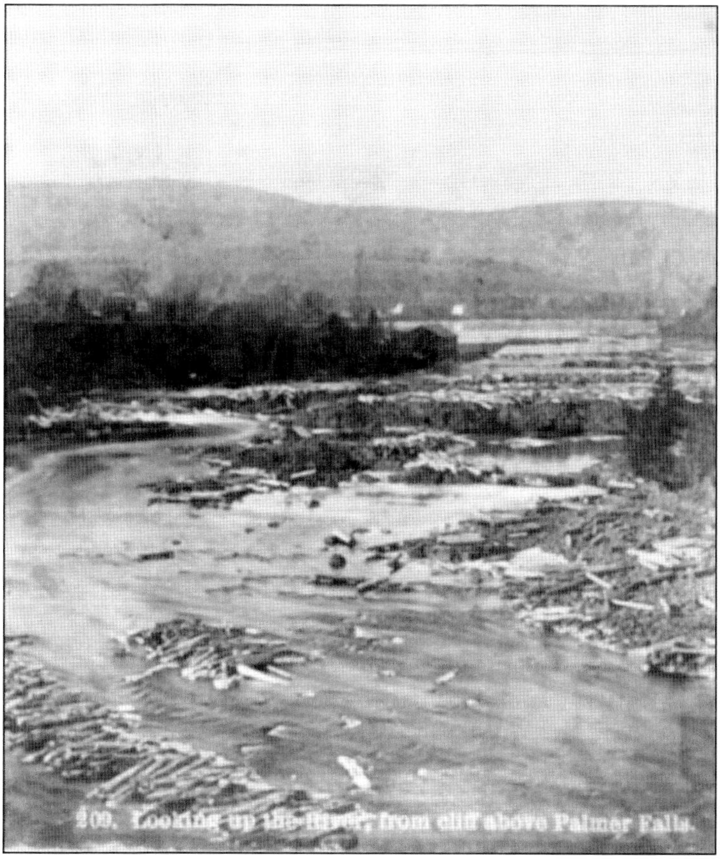

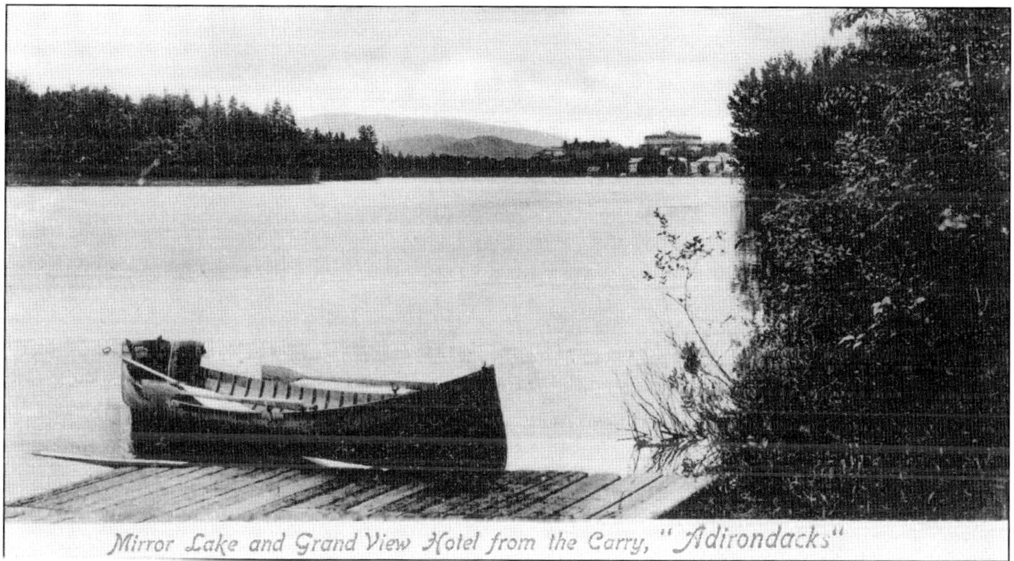

This Adirondack photograph of Mirror Lake and the Grand View Hotel notes that it was taken from the carry. There were several carries in the Adirondacks in the days of widespread water transportation. In the early days, most travel was by water. Portages became known as carries because, obviously, everything including guide boats and gear had to be carried overland.

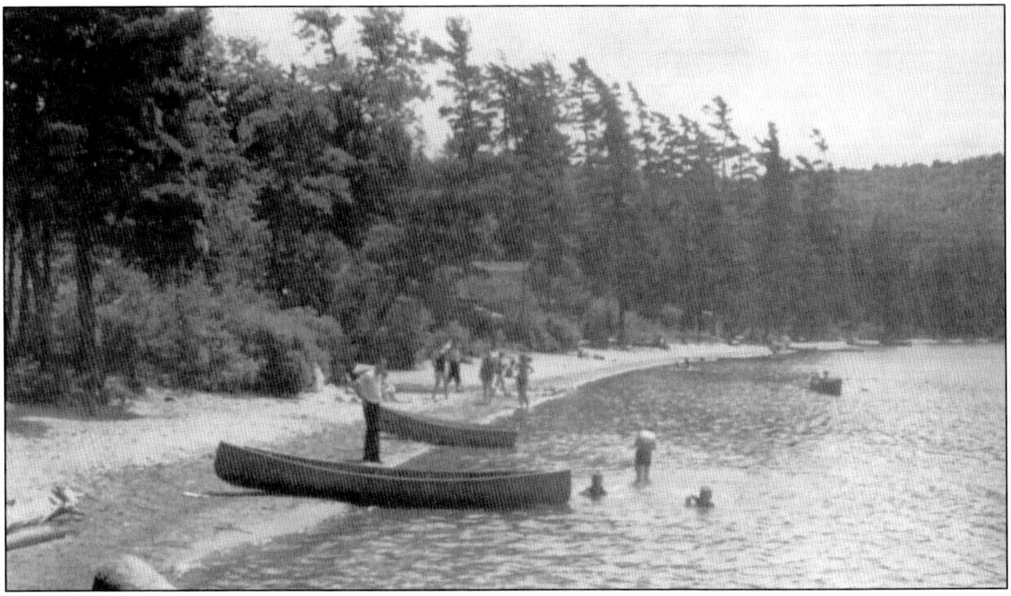

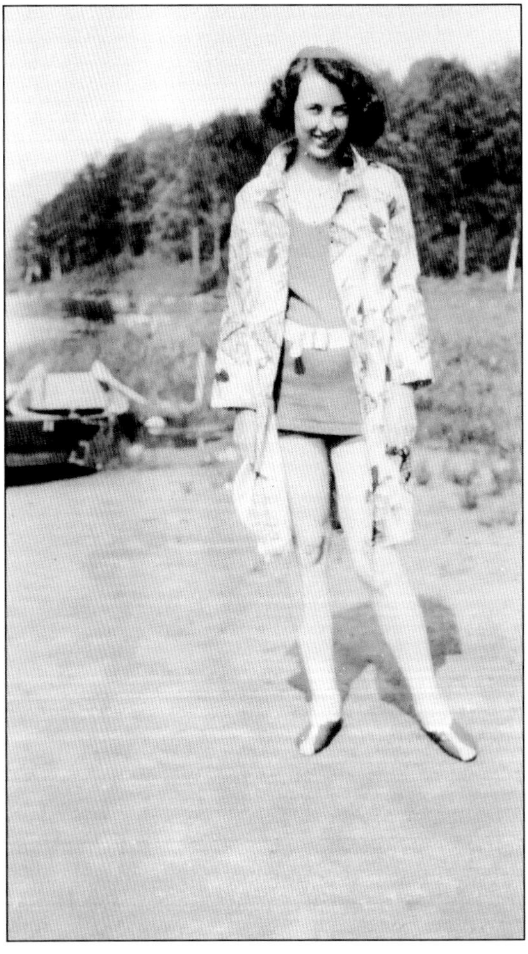

Limekiln Lake State Campground, located in Hamilton County near Inlet, offers over 200 sites for tents and trailers, a boat launch, and a swimming beach. It is typical of the 40-plus public campgrounds located within the Adirondack State Park. Once only accessible by water, the campground was developed by Civilian Conservation Corps (CCC) workers in 1935. Utica lumber-and-rail tycoon Lewis H. Lawrence built a hunting lodge in Limekiln in 1870.

There was a time when swimmers on Adirondack beaches wore heavy wool bathing suits that covered most of their bodies. Men were required to have bathing suit tops as well as bottoms. Styles changed by the 1920s, when sunbathing dictated less coverage. This "bathing beauty" is dressed for a day at the beach with one of the new suits and flapper belts. Her outfit is complete with beach jacket and beach shoes.

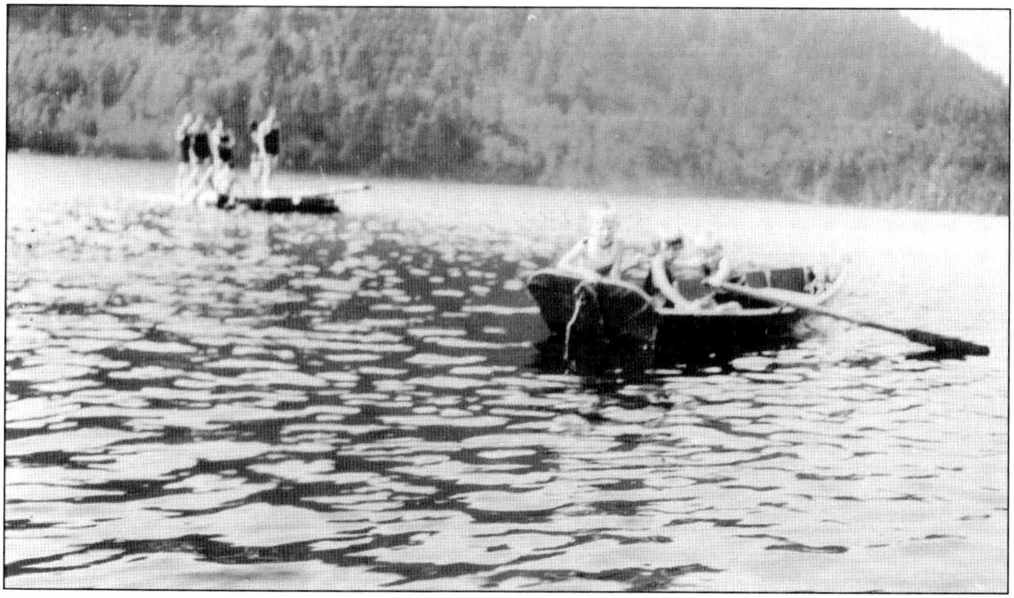

Children who grew up in the mountains had an Adirondack playground to enjoy—especially during the summer months. Boating and swimming occupied most of their sunny summertime. Going to the public beach, riding logs in a remote pond, or splashing in a cool mountain stream provided hours of outdoor water fun without cost. Note the swimming dock and diving board in the background.

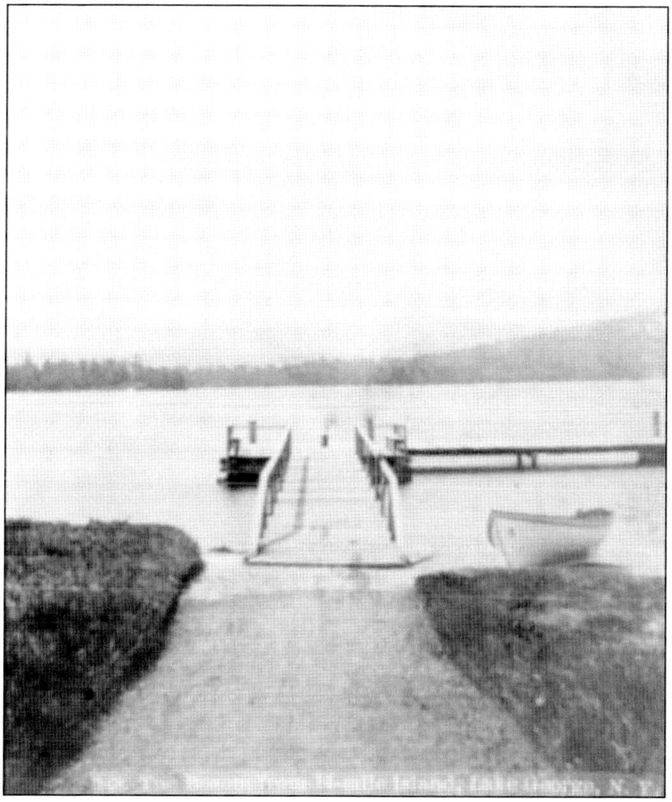

Homes and camps on Adirondack lakes and ponds would be incomplete without a dock. Docks were constructed for swimming, boating, and simply relaxing. Speedboats, rowboats, canoes, and guide boats could be harbored at the docks during the warm season. In the winter, most docks were pulled onto the land to avoid ice damage. Today, docks must meet special building requirements.

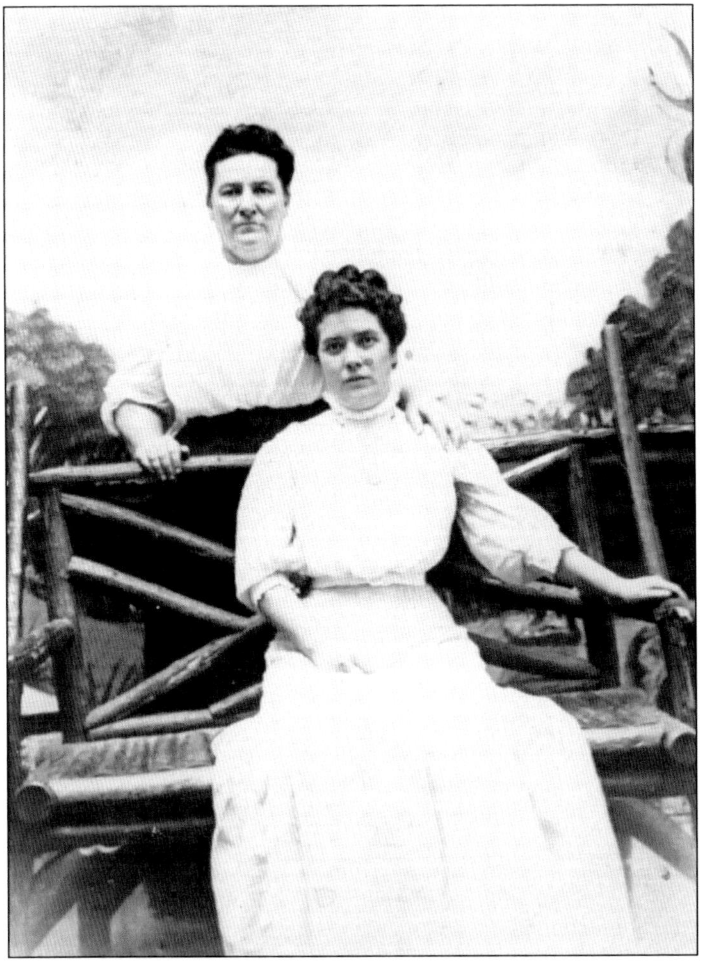

Using native materials to construct bridges, walkways, and docks is a practice that started with the "corduroy roads," constructed of logs placed in the muddy roadways by logging companies. Craftsmen soon learned how to use logs and twigs to fashion bridges, benches, porches, railings, gateways, and decorative trims. Studio photographers tapped into a fad of that day and used twig furniture and backgrounds for their formal photographs, much like the bench shown here with two ladies. The footbridge in the photograph is made entirely from small Adirondack logs. Building Adirondack furniture from native materials, especially for the wealthy camp owners, turned into a large industry that has experienced a resurgence today.

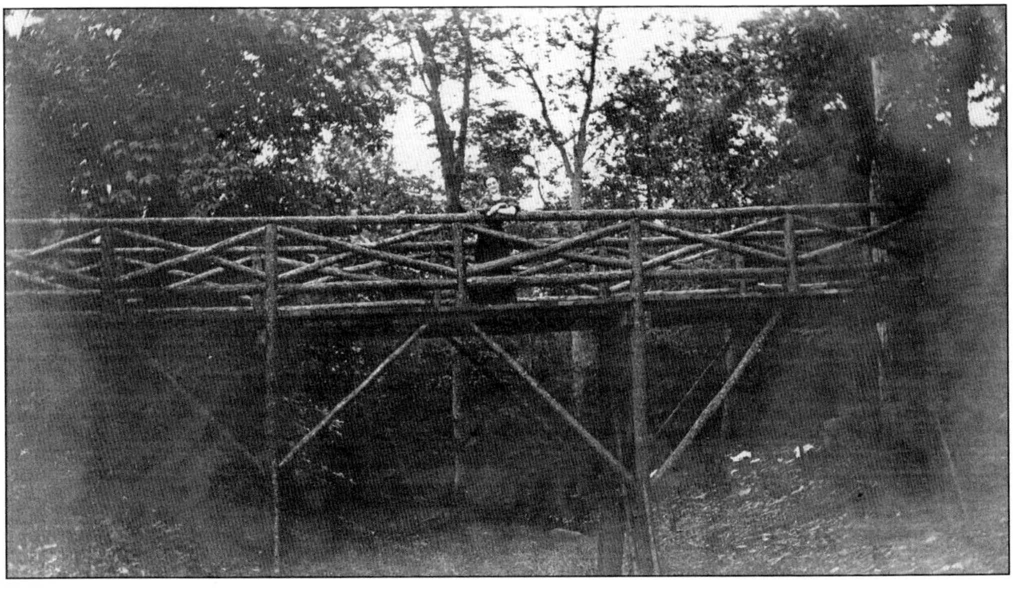

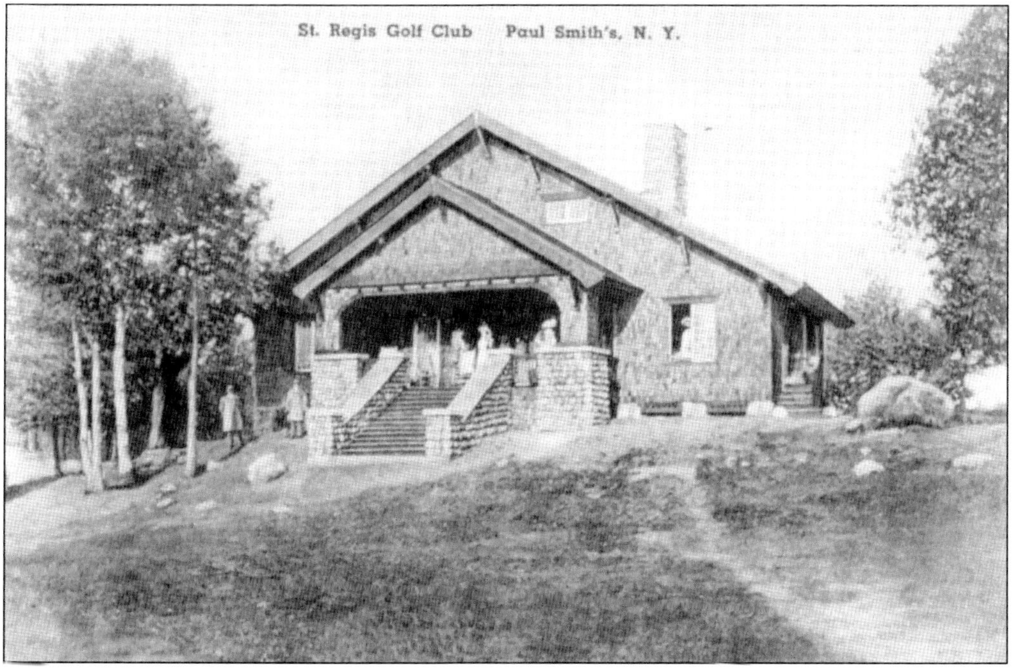

Adirondack country has attracted golf courses since the first influx of summer residents and tourists. Sacandaga Park had a golf course in 1878 that is still in use today. Great camp builder W.W. Durant constructed a golf course at Eagle Nest near Blue Mountain Lake in 1899. Many of the big luxury hotels had private golf courses. Other businesses cleared the forests and rolling hills to establish private and public courses.

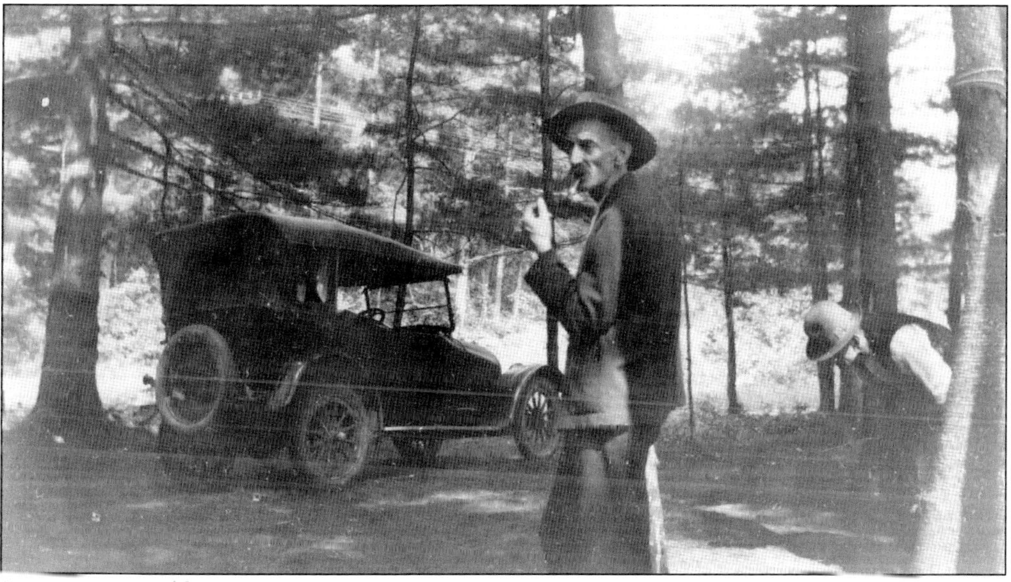

Soon it was possible to jump in a Model T and seek out what the Adirondacks had to offer. Roadside accommodations sprang up along the way, developed by private owners seeking to cash in on the growing craze. Camping was a pursuit enjoyed by young and old, and, in some cases, could be free—except for the food to eat and the gas to get there. The photograph shows Coulumbe's campsite once on the Sacandaga River near Wells.

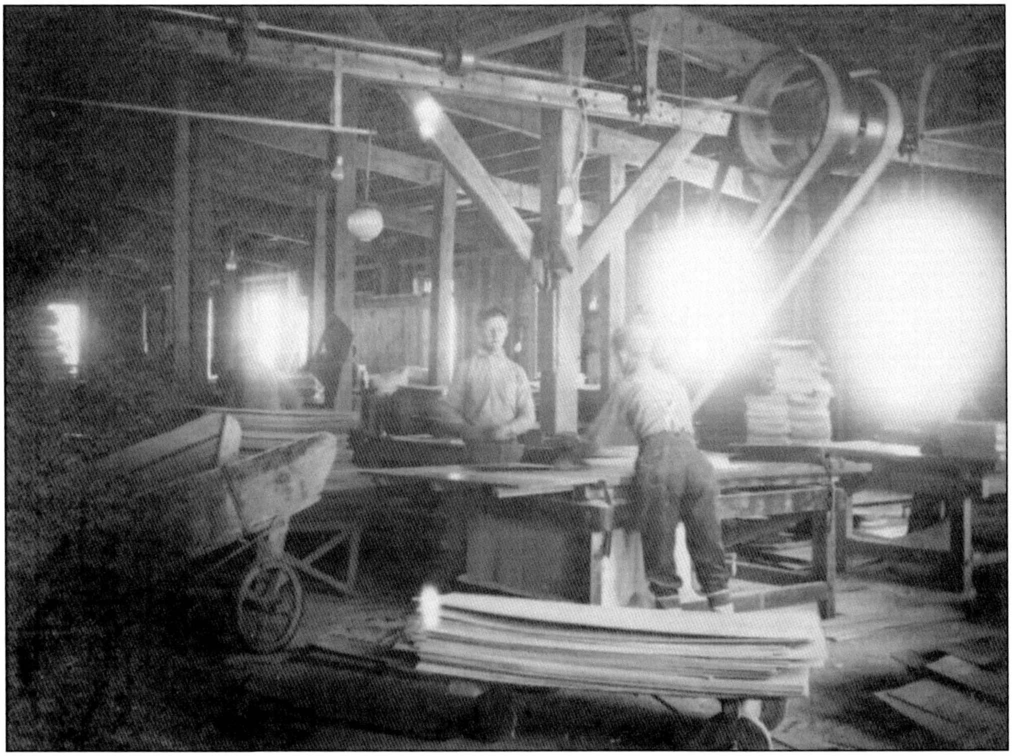

There were those who pursued wood-related manufacturing, most of which was tied to the availability of natural products in the Adirondacks. Lumber mills, veneer mills, pulp mills, furniture mills, tanneries, and wood novelty enterprises sprang up. Waterpower from the rushing mountain streams or dams on the lakes provided cheap power for production. Giant pulleys and belts, shown here, ran throughout the factory buildings to provide power.

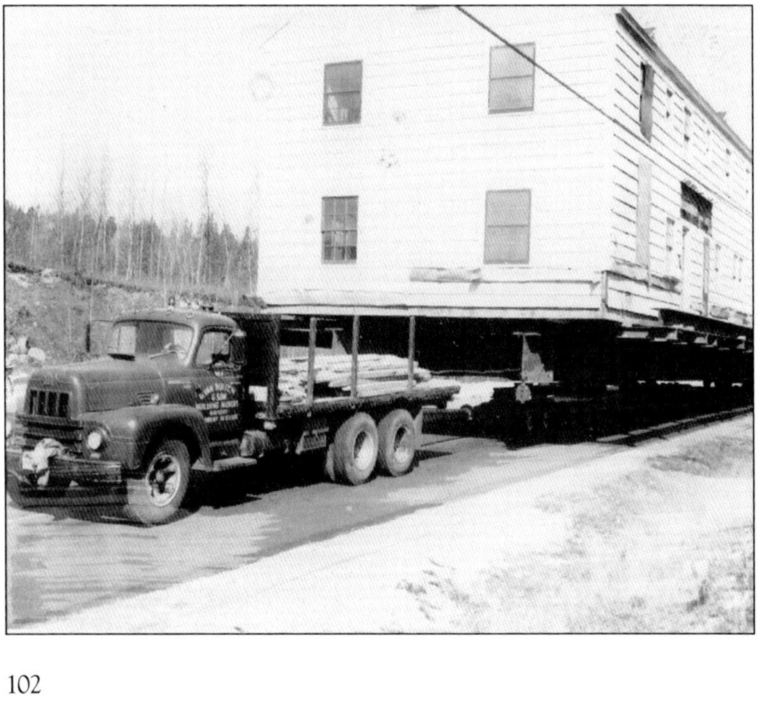

Industry in the Adirondacks has had its strange twists and turns. One industrial event required the moving of an entire town. In 1961, the mining town of Tahawus, site of the 1832 MacIntyre iron mine, was moved to dig another pit of titanium and magnetite, which was located below the settlement. The town was dismantled and moved to the neighboring village of Newcomb.

Five

The Pastimes

How did they pass the time in the remote Adirondack country of yesteryear? Some brought city practices to the wilderness. Etiquette author Emily Post wrote a chapter on how to dress and act at a great-camp gathering. Others passed the time with the popular parlor games, and playing 78-revolutions-per-minute records on windup phonographs.

Much of life in the Adirondacks revolved around winter sports, pioneered at the Lake Placid Club in the 1920s. Skiing and skating topped the list in many communities. Toboggan slides were constructed, and winter events were scheduled. The 1932 and 1980 Winter Olympics came to the Adirondacks, providing a great spectacle for thousands.

The natural attractions of the forested mountains of New York provided a much needed pastime for growing America. Camping and hiking, some connected to summer youth camps, opened up the Adirondacks for many who otherwise may have never experienced the out-of-doors. Hiking the high peaks and searching out the waterfalls, caves, and virgin timber motivated outdoor lovers.

Hunting became one of the greatest pastimes in America, beginning with the first settlers. The hunting tradition ran deep in the nation's families, and the wilds of the Adirondacks became the place to go. Hunting camps served, and still serve, generations of hunting families. To this day, diehard hunters manage to get time off from work during every hunting season.

And much can be said about spending some quiet time fishing from a wooden boat on an Adirondack lake, lying in the sun on an Adirondack beach, sitting in a grotto above a rushing waterfall, or enjoying the view from a mountaintop. It is a good time when someone passes the time in the Adirondacks.

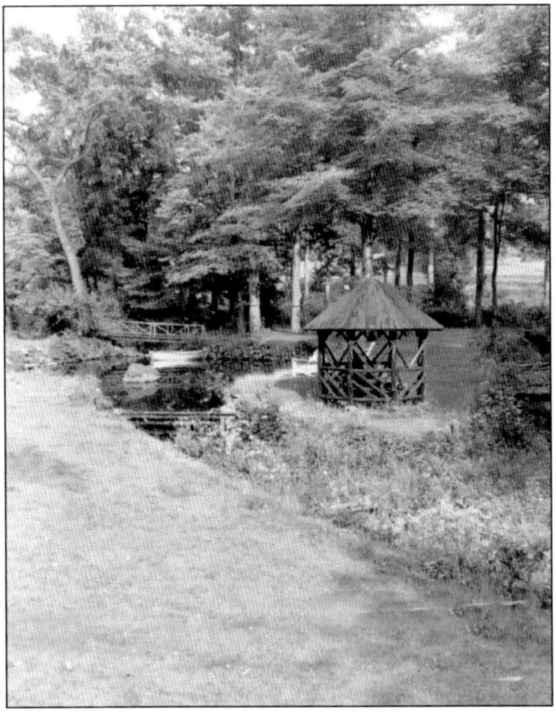

Rustic gazebos and bridges adorn Adirondack parks and village greens. Native logs and twigs create a rustic motif that fits well with the woodland country. Craftsmen developed their skills along with the native materials, creating ideal places to spend time. A whole industry based on rustic materials developed in the Adirondacks. Prize pieces of rustic furniture can be found in museums today.

During the first half of the 20th century, lawn swings were seen in Adirondack yards. Almost every family had to have one of the bench-style swings. Old folks enjoyed them on sunny afternoons or cool Adirondack evenings, especially when joined by a neighbor. Loving couples whiled away hours courting in swings. Young children spent their free time swinging and climbing on the large wooden structures.

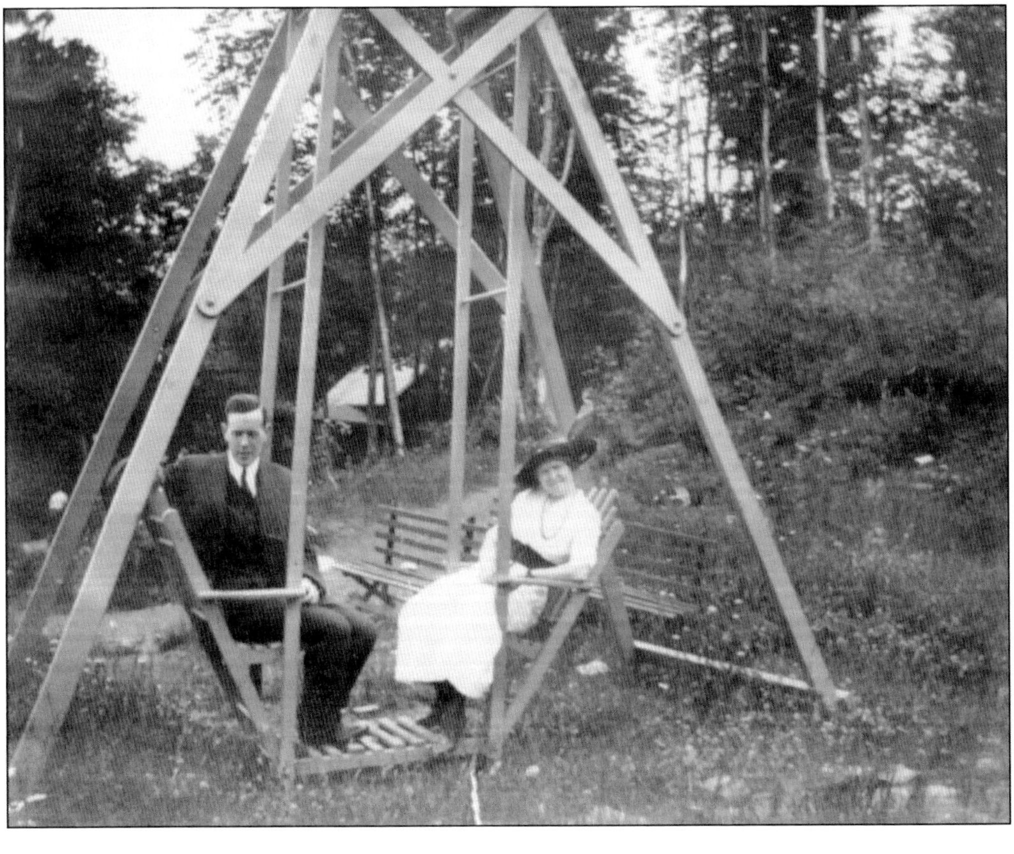

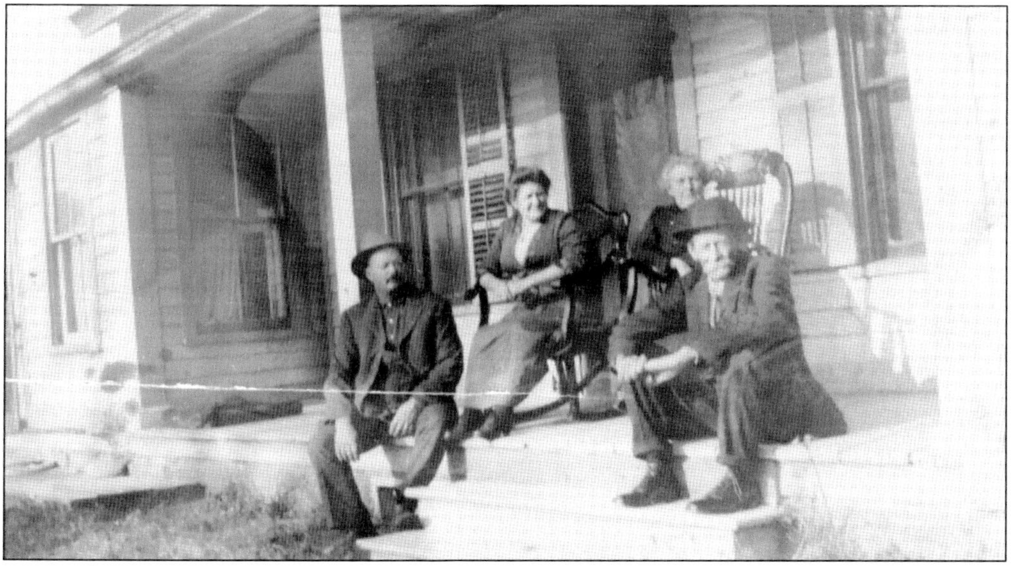

Most Adirondack homes had a place where everyone enjoyed passing the time away. It could be the front porch, the back porch, the side porch, or the sun porch. Porches were also known as a piazza or a veranda. Old-timers called it the stoop. The high porches were porticos. Household furniture, as seen in the photograph, was used before porch-specific furniture came into use.

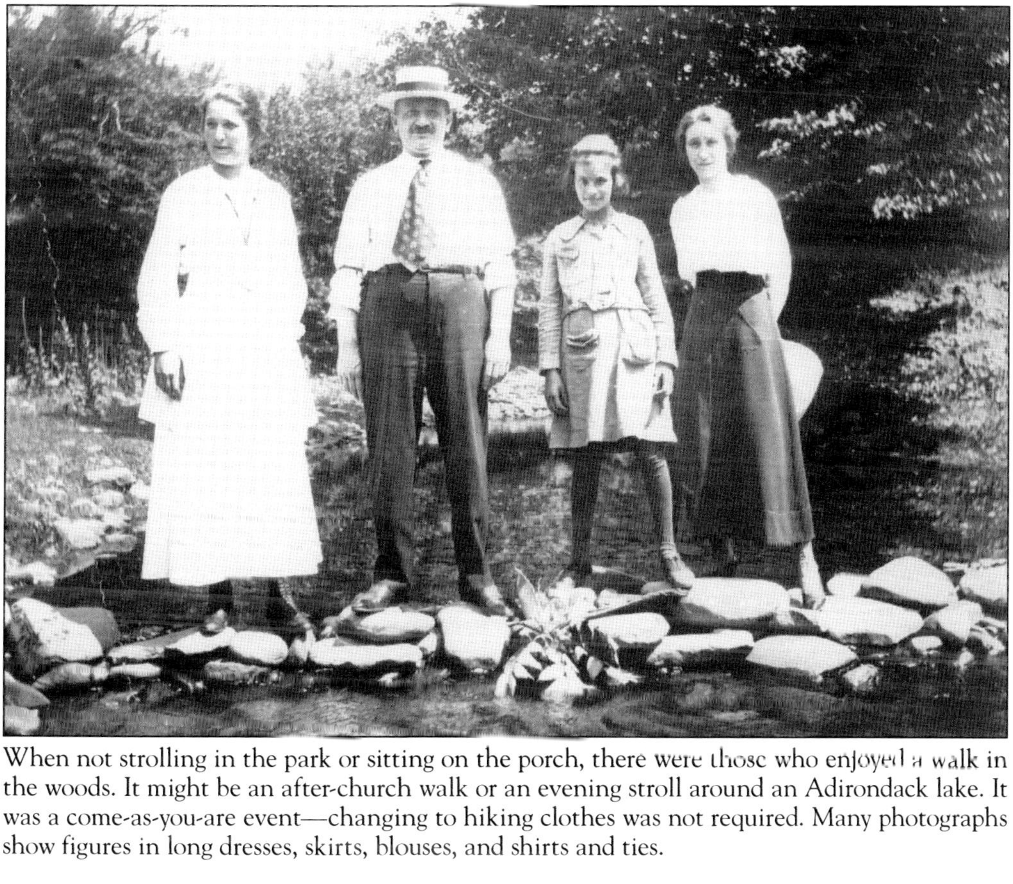

When not strolling in the park or sitting on the porch, there were those who enjoyed a walk in the woods. It might be an after-church walk or an evening stroll around an Adirondack lake. It was a come-as-you-are event—changing to hiking clothes was not required. Many photographs show figures in long dresses, skirts, blouses, and shirts and ties.

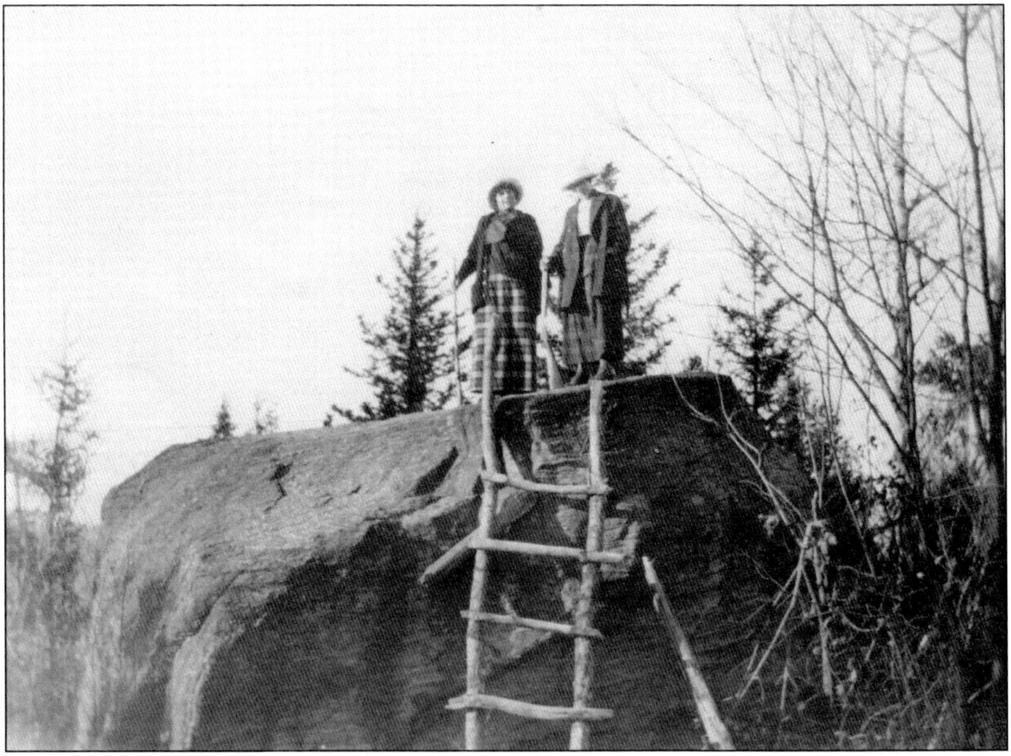

The glaciers of geological history moved and dropped rocks of all sizes throughout the Adirondack mountains. Erratics, or rocks dropped on other rocks, can be found on the mountainsides. This huge rock was part of a great pastime for the schoolchildren in Wells; the school custodian took them up to see a "footprint of Bigfoot" on the top of the rock.

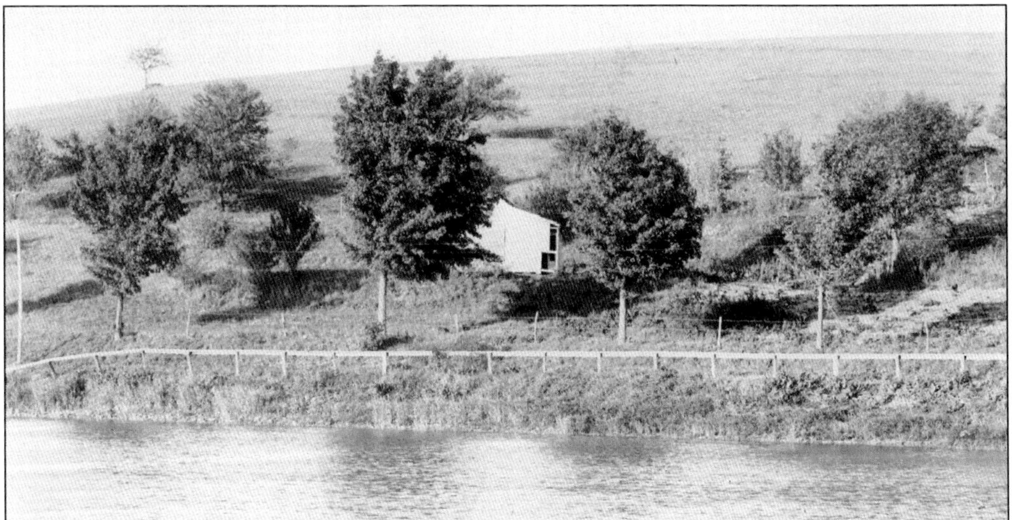

Emily Chubback lived in Eaton in Madison County and also had Underhill Cottage in the Adirondack Park at Alder Brook in Franklin County. Born in 1817, she became one of America's great poets, writing under the pseudonym Fanny Forrester. Married to a missionary who died at sea, she wrote a two-volume collection of short stories titled *Alderbrook*.

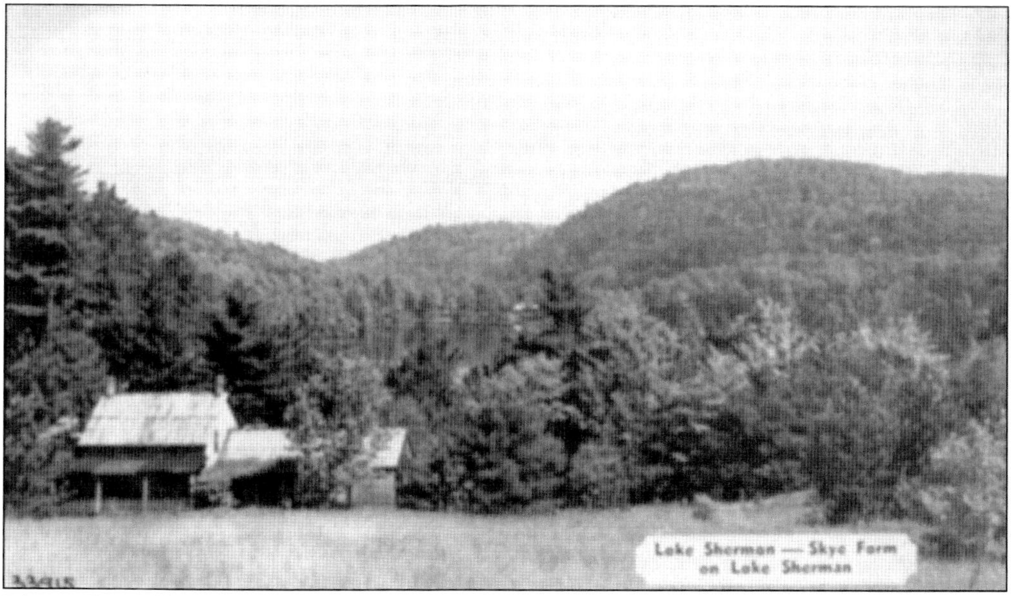

Those who walk through the woodlands at Lake Sherman near Warrensburg will find rambling stone walls and remnants of farm equipment. The now forested acres were once cleared farmland, an occurrence often found in the Adirondacks. A farmhouse, barn, and other buildings dotted the hillside when three Methodist ministers saw the potential for a religious camp on Lake Sherman. Since 1940, the Skye Farm Camp and Retreat Center has grown into a year-round Adirondack facility.

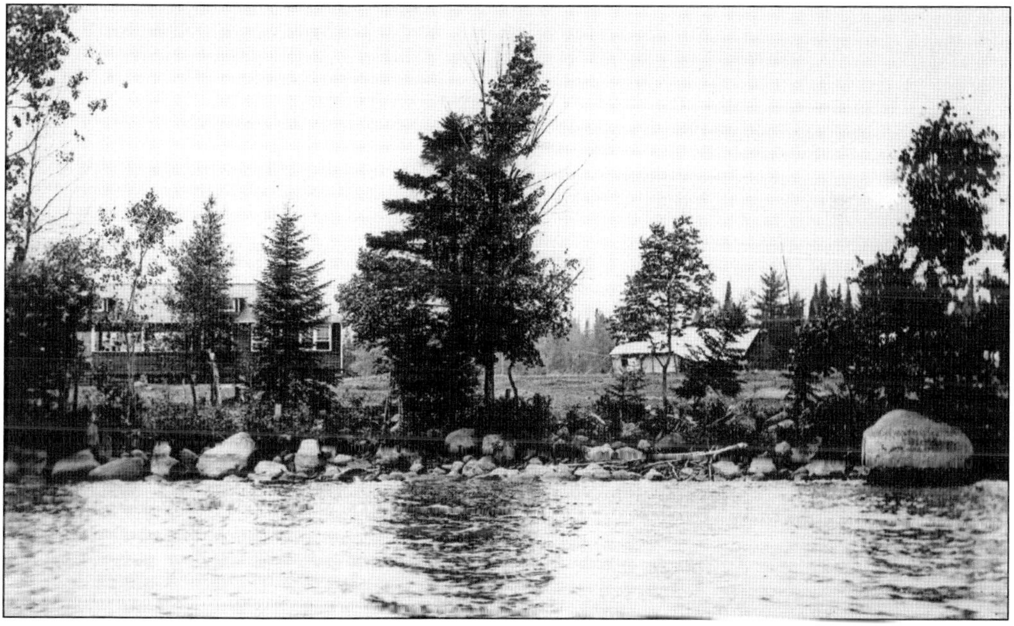

The YMCA has a long history of establishing Adirondack camps. It opened a facility on Lake Pleasant in 1923 named Camp Agaming, meaning "on the shore." The Gloversville YMCA constructed the cabin-style camp that housed some 200 boys each summer. Lack of attendance (a modern malady) and rising expenses forced the camp to close—the fate of numbers of Adirondack youth camps.

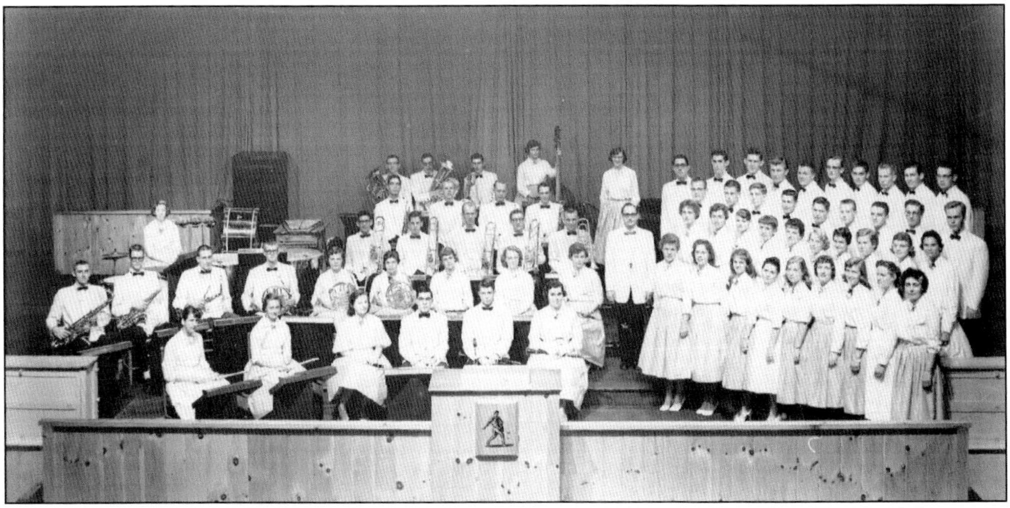

CAMP-of-the-WOODS Testimonials

CAMP-of-the-WOODS has been a delight to me, far surpassing expectations. It combines sane, cheery, wholesome, spiritual atmosphere with unusual natural beauties and physical advantages.

HOMER C. RENTON, Pastor,
First Methodist Episcopal Church,
Tarentum, Pa.

CAMP-of-the-WOODS is a good place to relax and strengthen threadbare nerves; to awaken and quicken a dormant spiritual life; and to absorb and retain a helpful friendly atmosphere.

A vacation here helps to give us a new lease on life, makes our daily tasks more effective, and broadens our Christian experiences.

OLIVE WILDER, Waterbury, Conn.

Just as a man may be judged by the company he keeps, so a vacation resort may be judged by its activities and ideals.

All that CAMP-of-the-WOODS stands for: Christian character, physical and mental health, spiritual vision, and sincerity of worship—is welcomed by its guests. Such a vacation place is of the greatest value.

FRED J. VOIGHT, Staten Island, N. Y.

Our family consider it one of our greatest blessings that we may be members of your Great Camp Family. Each summer we get together a few plain clothes, some blankets, etc., and start out for CAMP-of-the-WOODS, where we know that we shall have all one could desire of spiritual uplift, rest, recreation, entertainment, good fellowship, and nourishing food.

MR. and MRS. H. N. EDMONDS,
Brooklyn, New York.

I wish to express my deepest appreciation to the man of vision who was able to foresee the physical and spiritual benefits of a place such as CAMP-of-the-WOODS. The wholesome friendliness, the charm of youthful directors, and the opportunity for bathing on the famous beach all become so much a part of one that it is an increasing pleasure to return again and again.

MARJORIE DICKERSON, Fayetteville, N. Y.

Seven vacations at CAMP-of-the-WOODS make us feel that this camp is almost an answer to the wise man who said: "Where there is not vision, the people perish."

"Pop" Tibbitts had such a vision thirty-three years ago. Since then, hosts of young and older people have come and gone, thoroughly appreciating having found a place where congenial Christian people practice the Golden Rule.

H. A. MARSHALL, Summit, N. J.

Are you looking for an ideal vacation place where you will have delightful fellowship and an opportunity to build strength and happiness?

For over ten years I have been searching for such a place. At last I have found it at CAMP-of-the-WOODS. Two weeks here make it much easier to go through the remaining fifty weeks without a break. I am already eagerly looking forward to coming back again next summer.

"BILL" TEMPLETON, JR.,
Amsterdam, New York.

For over nine decades, Camp-of-the-Woods at Speculator has been welcoming summer campers and visitors to pass time in the Adirondacks. Founded by former YMCA director George "Pop" Tibbitts, the camp on Lake Pleasant in the Adirondack Park was established "to bring congenial people together for a safe and uplifting fellowship." The 1934 brochure, shown here, promises "tent, room, or cabin camping at reasonable rates." The camp provided auto rentals, parking, blanket rental, boat and canoe rentals, a photography studio, camp store, golf, grocery supplies, an Indian museum and store, a laundry, and beaches. The camp is well known for its large auditorium and music program. The public is still invited during the summer season. However, as one patron cautioned, "Do not mistake Camp-of-the-Woods for a hotel!"

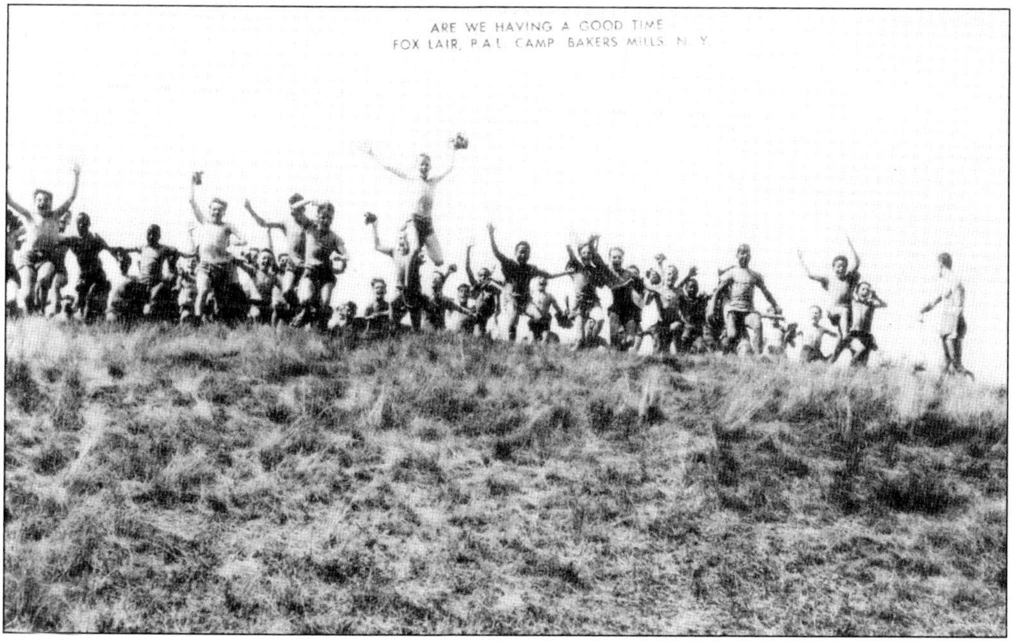

Summer camps abound in the woodlands to this day. Hundreds of our youth continue to enjoy the Adirondack out-of-doors at these camps, while others find summer jobs. Churches, Scouts, YMCA organizations, and private owners run Adirondack youth camps. Specialty camps for the arts, sports, environment, and computers are among those offered. The camp shown here is on Route 8 at a place called Fox Lair, a former Hudnut estate. Today, it is part of the forest preserve and is returning to wilderness.

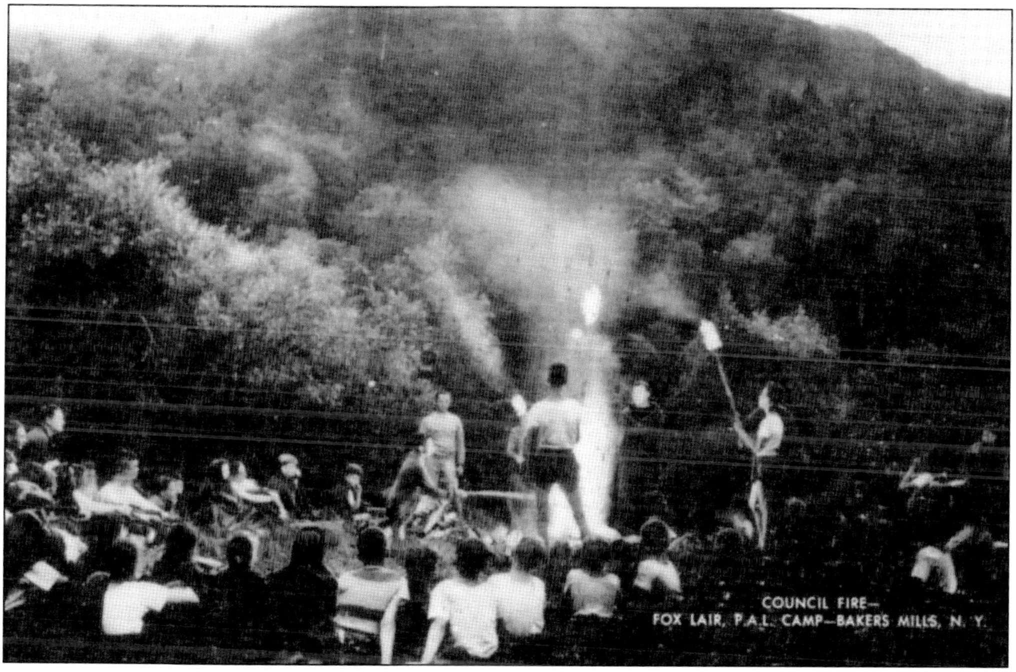

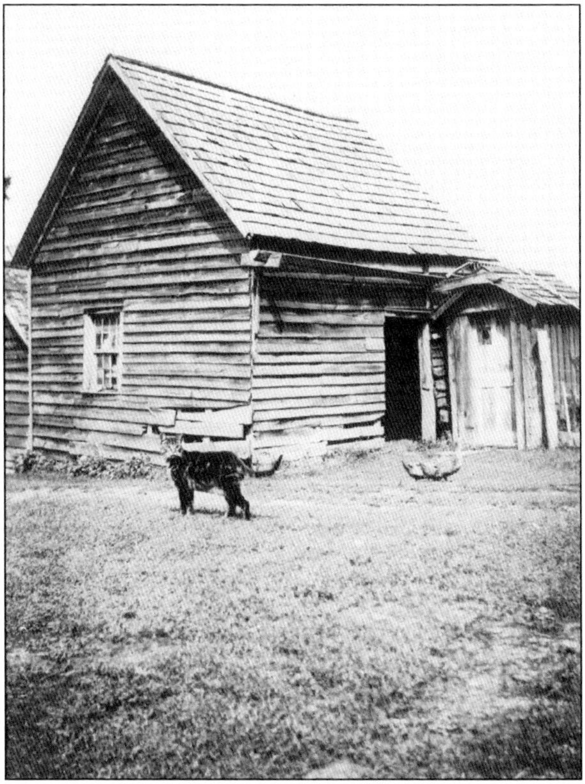

Cats were necessary to keep rodents away in Adirondack barns. Pests were attracted to the grain and hay, which provided them with food and a place to live. The barn cats required little care. Some learned to catch the milk stream sprayed to them from milking cows. Note the ducks running loose in the barnyard and the privy near the barn door.

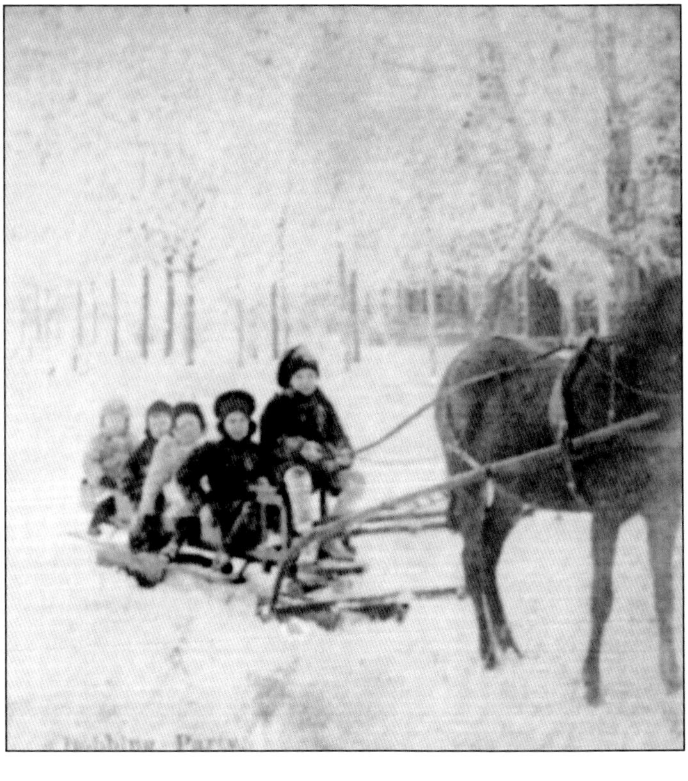

Hitching the six-man bobsled to the old mare brought joy to the children of yesteryear. Other multi-passenger bobsleds were filled with some dozen or so children and sent down an icy roadway or hill, with the strongest boy doing the steering. Adirondack towns owned some big bobsleds, and riding bobsleds was called "a bobbing party."

The photograph of the ladies wading in the lake water is titled "Water Lilies at Luzerne Lake, NY." Modesty prevented them from donning a revealing bathing suit for swimming, so wading was the next best way to pass the time in cool Adirondack lake waters. Hats kept the sun off their faces. Note the apparently bored father watching over his girls from his guide boat.

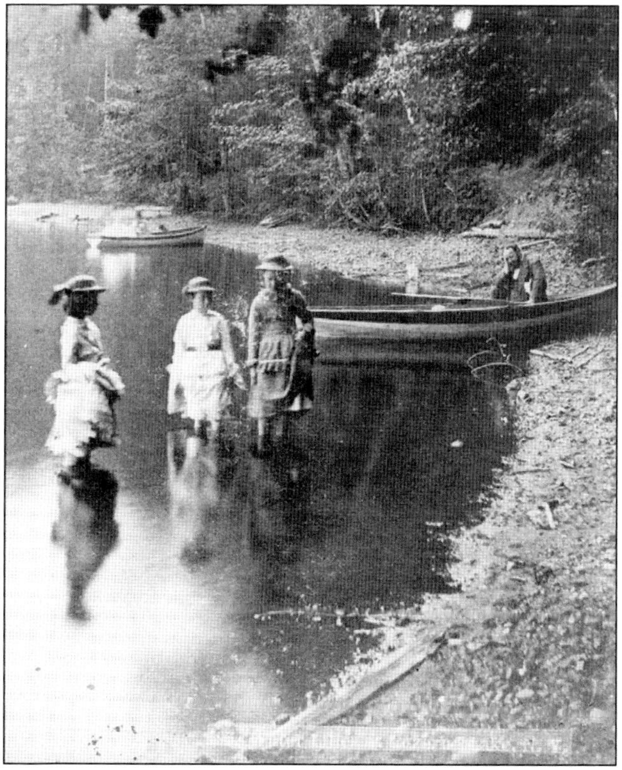

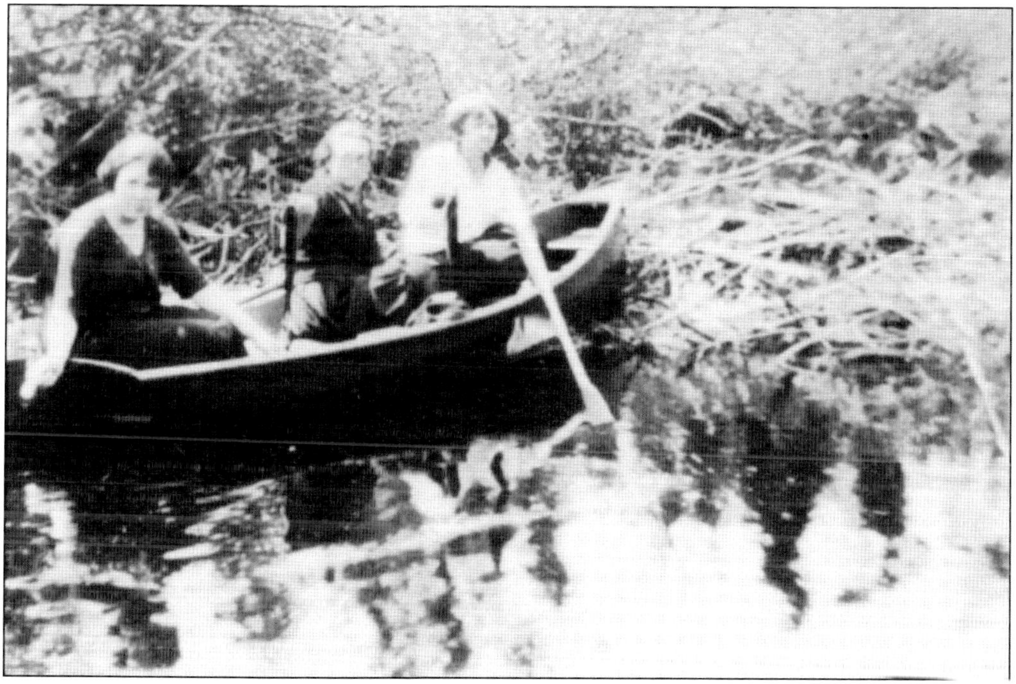

Some 30,000 miles of rivers and streams were a boaters' playground. Paddling the glittering waters brought relief from summer heat and stress and opened up the Adirondack wilderness. Beaver dams, such as the one shown here, had to be forded on the way up the waterways.

A view of a luxurious hotel from across this lake reveals the pristine setting of most Adirondack accommodations. Patrons came from far and wide to enjoy the clean air and water, the surrounding forests and waters, and the best in hotels. Lake Placid Inn, also known as Lake Placid House or Brewsters, was located between Lake Placid Lake and Mirror Lake. It was built in 1874 and burned down some time before 1940.

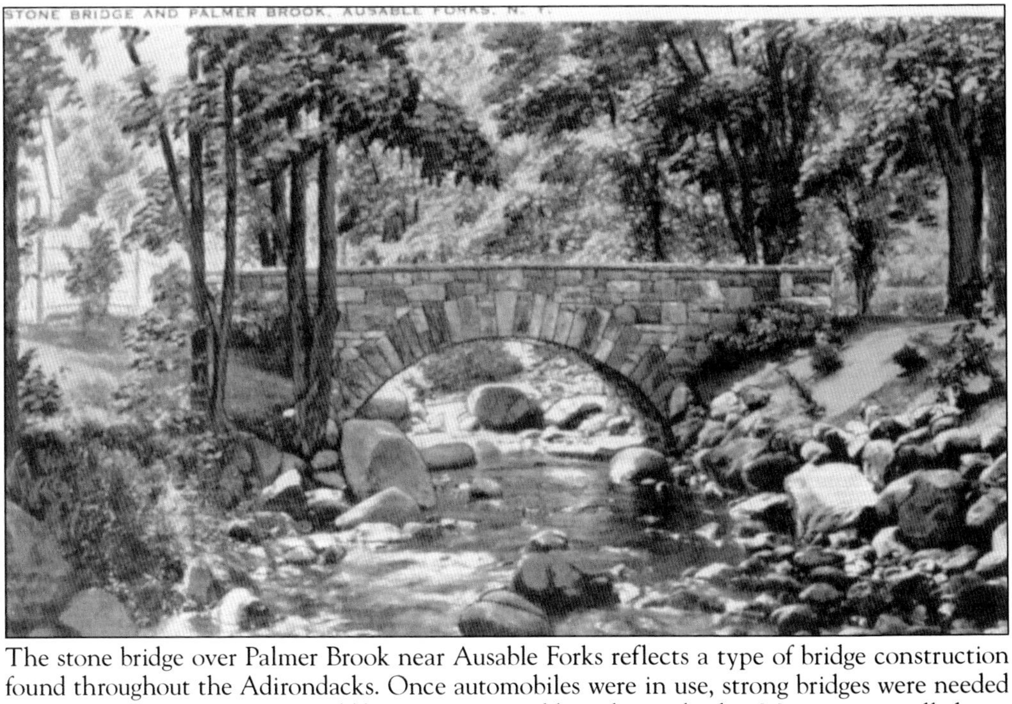

The stone bridge over Palmer Brook near Ausable Forks reflects a type of bridge construction found throughout the Adirondacks. Once automobiles were in use, strong bridges were needed over waterways. Most towns would become inaccessible without a bridge. Masons were called into service to meet the need to make substantial spans, some of which are still in use today.

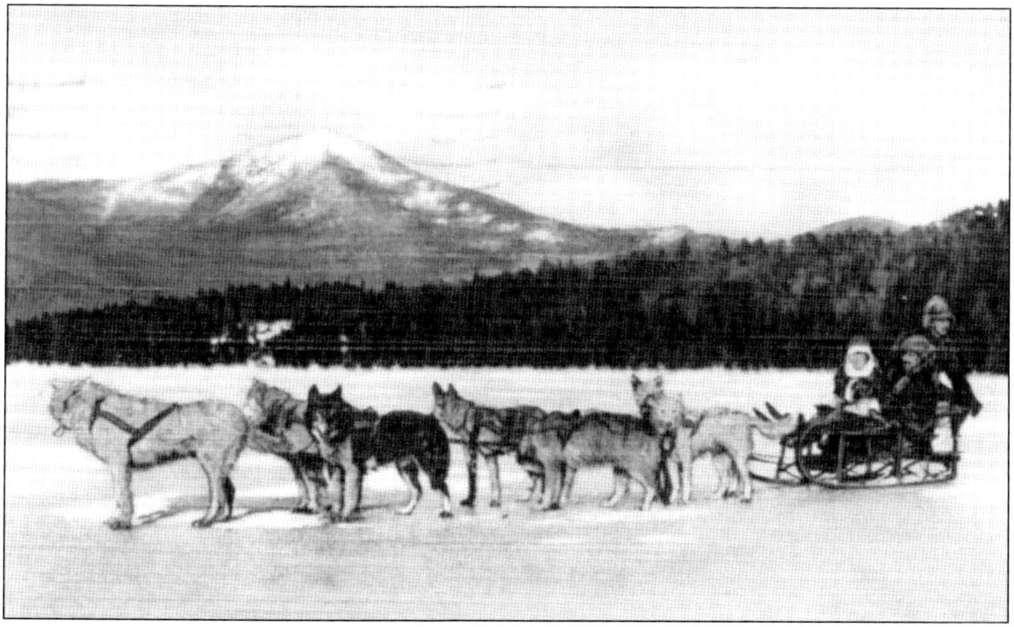

Shown here in 1949, passengers enjoy a dogsled ride on Mirror Lake at Lake Placid. Offering a welcome pastime in the cold season, dog teams can still be found on the Adirondack frozen lakes. Competitive events for the dog teams are still held in the Adirondacks. Observing dog teams from an overlooking lounge window is also a pleasant pastime.

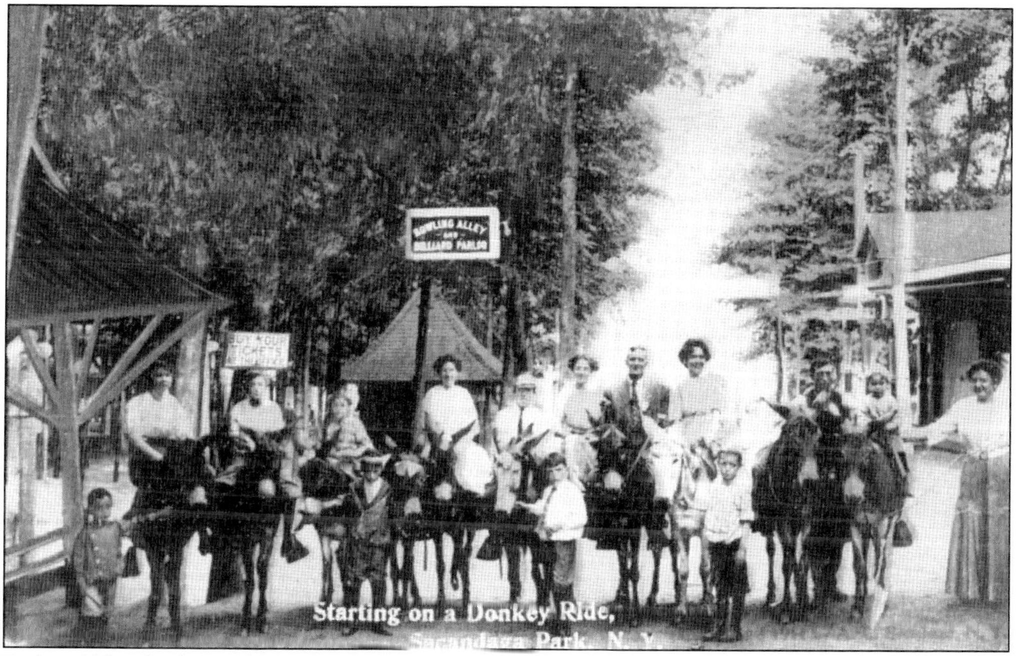

Before 1930, donkey rides were offered at the Sacandaga Amusement Park. One ride on a donkey or burro cost 10¢. The animals were kept in a pasture behind the grandstand on Sport Island in the Sacandaga River. They were turned loose at the end of the day, and they were cared for by "donkey man" Hollis Johnson. Today, Sport Island Pub looks out at the former site.

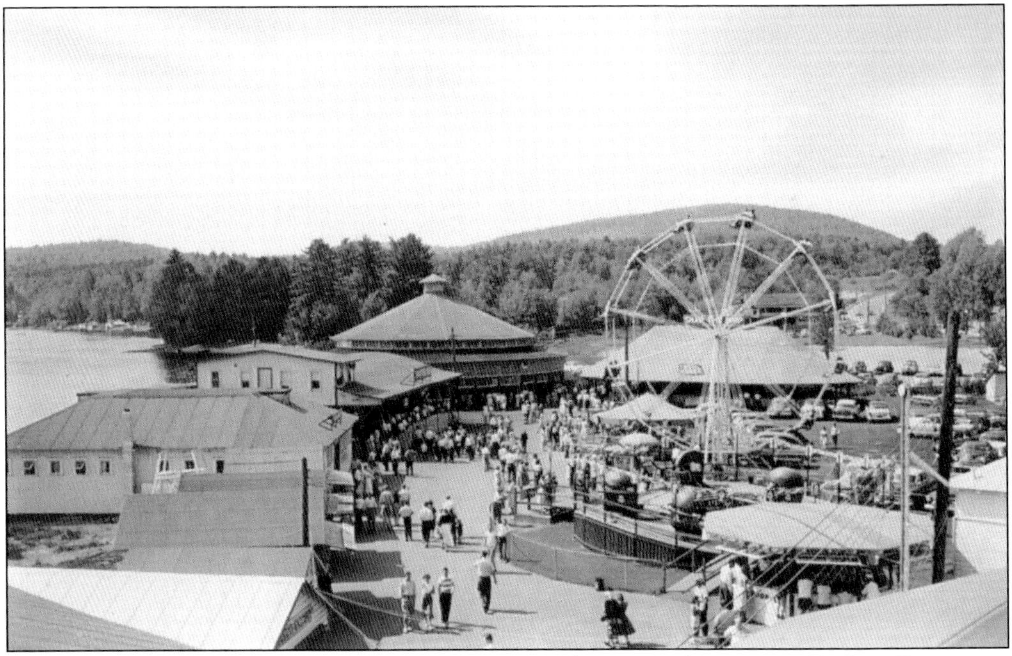

Sherman's Amusement Park at Caroga Lake ceased operation after some 90 years of an on-and-off operation. The park was a popular Adirondack place for big bands and dancing. The midway featured bumper cars, Ferris wheel, a roller coaster, and a merry-go-round. The merry-go-round was refurbished in recent years, but it has only been used for special occasions.

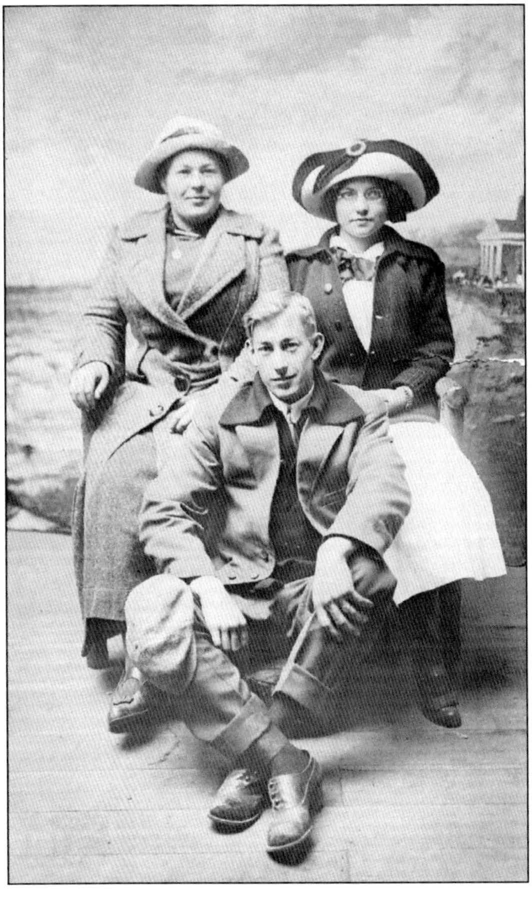

Picture taking was a favorite pastime in the Adirondacks. Residents often went to the amusement parks to visit the photography studios. These three Wells residents got dressed up and went to one of the Sacandaga Park studios. Note the backdrop behind them and the typical rustic bench on which they are sitting.

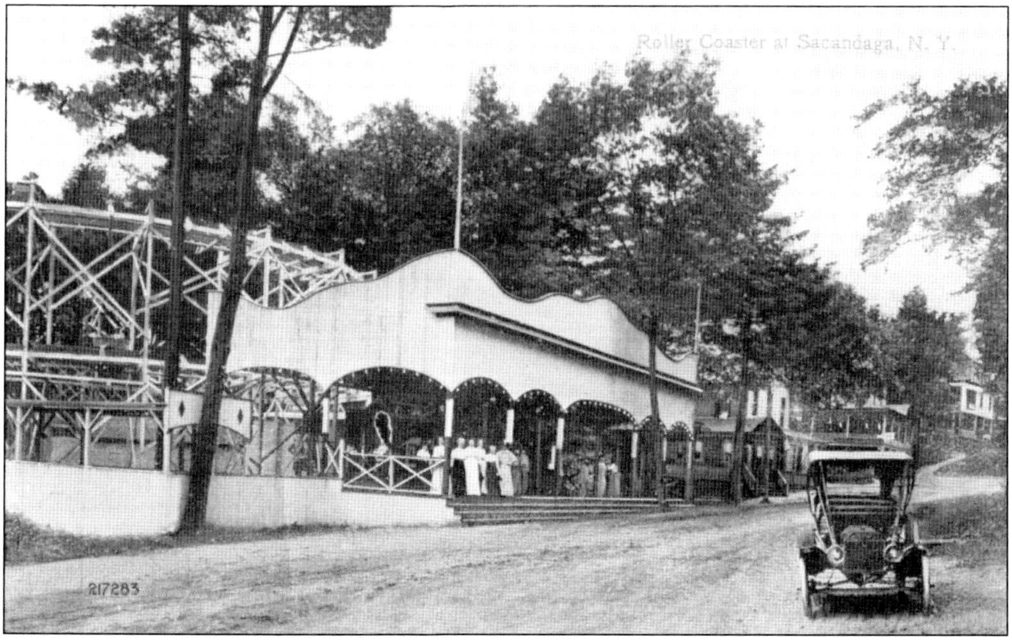

Roller coasters, highly popular today, got their start in small amusement parks—some in the Adirondacks. Sherman's at Caroga Lake had a small roller coaster, while a larger one (shown here) was found at Sacandaga Park. It was one of the main attractions of the park, where thousands came by train each summer to enjoy the midway and other offerings.

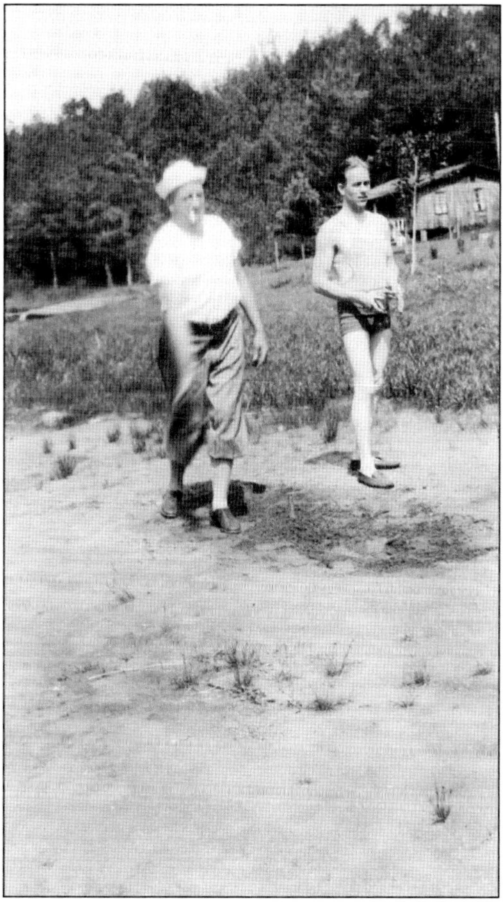

The game of horseshoes was a popular activity at camps, summer homes, clubhouses, and picnics. Still played today, the object of the game is to throw a horseshoe around a small pipe pounded into the ground. According to some, horseshoe pitching dates back to around 150 AD and was played by Greeks and Romans. Colonists brought it to America, and Revolutionary and Civil War soldiers played it. Rules were standardized in 1921.

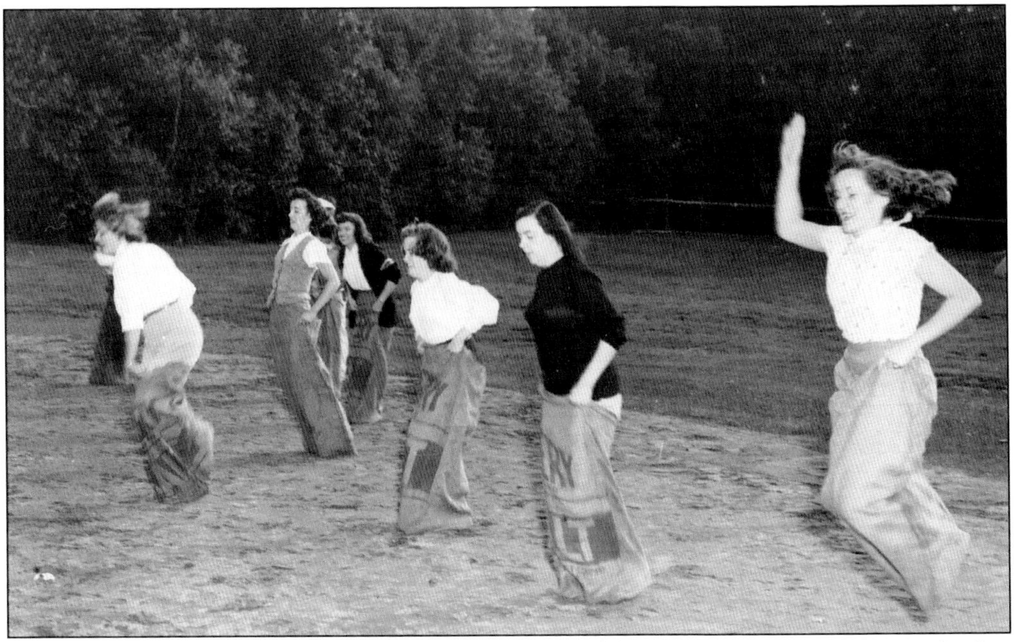

Burlap bags, made from locally harvested flax and used for storing grain, potatoes, and other bulky items, also became part of a popular game. Children's camps found them useful for sack races. Participants climbed into the bags and hopped toward the finish line. Adirondack camps and other groups also used the bags for wallpaper and insulation.

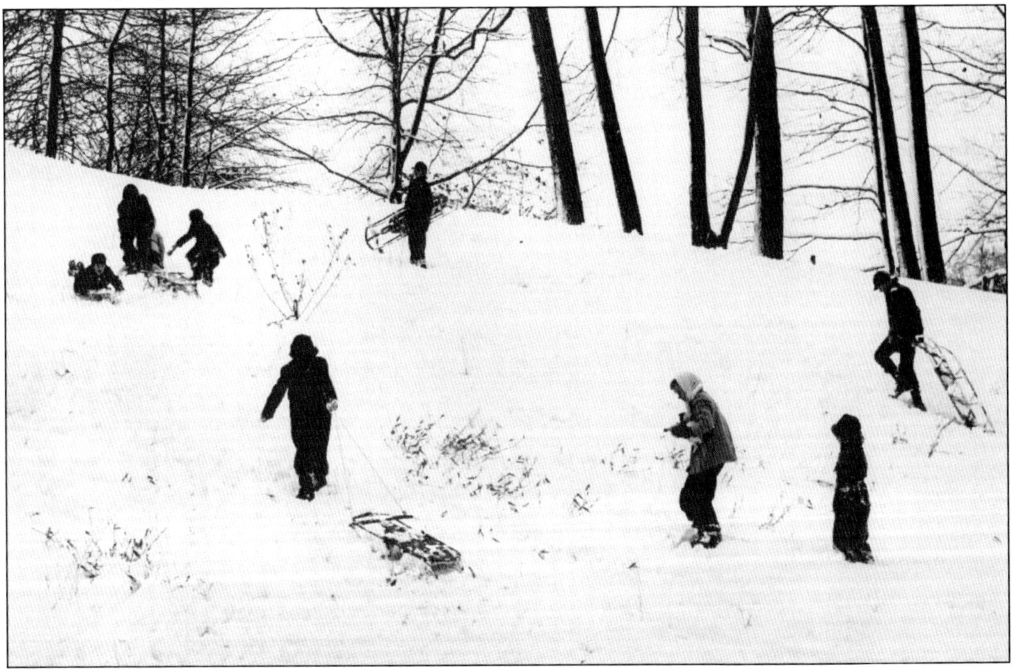

Wintertime in the 20th century Adirondacks was not passed indoors. Bundling up in long underwear, snowsuits, heavy socks, and boots, then getting out one's favorite sled to join friends on the nearest hilltop was an activity that sometimes took all day. Breaking the trail, piling up snow to make a jump, and getting a running start resulted in a thrilling ride to the bottom.

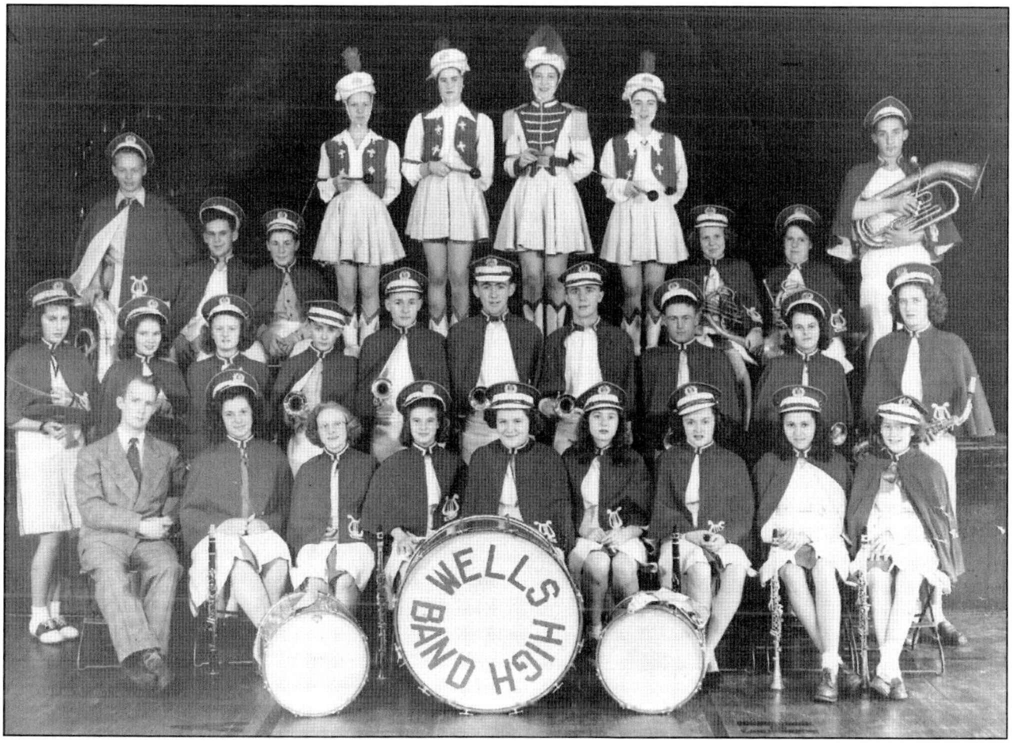

The small Adirondack towns traditionally celebrated Memorial Day, Fourth of July, and Old Home Day with a parade. The local high school band with majorettes was an important part of a good parade and, therefore, well supported by the taxpayers. Uniforms were purchased, and musical instruments were made available for all who wanted to take lessons and practice music. Junior bands often became training grounds for the senior bands.

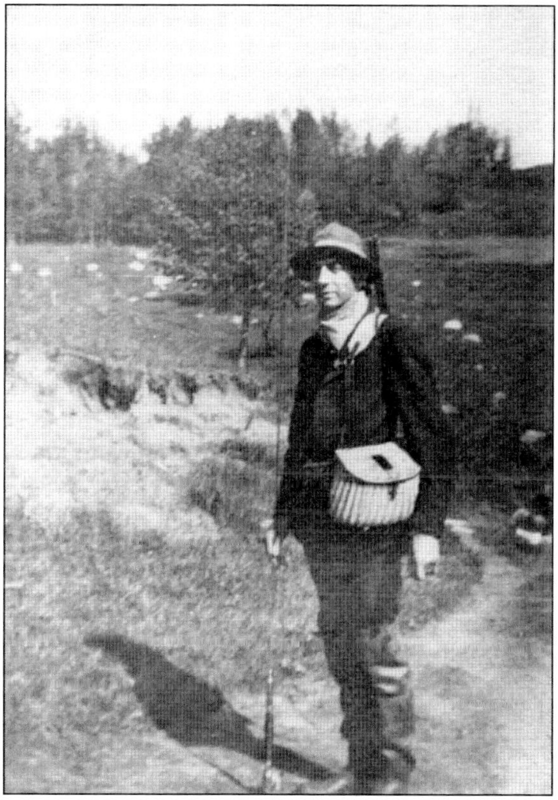

Hiking and fishing are still among the top pastimes in the Adirondacks. Hikers soon learned to take survival gear with them, sometimes hanging a pair of pants around their necks and filling the legs of the pants with gear. Fishermen turned to high boots so that they could wade the streams.

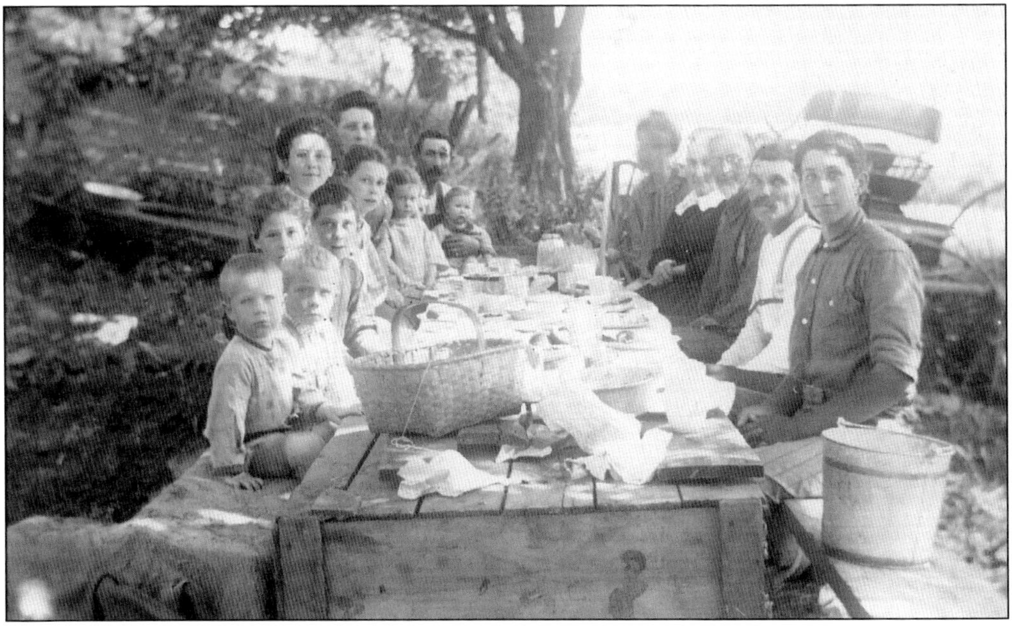

Family reunions and picnics brought extended families and friends together for summer outings in the Adirondacks. Makeshift picnic tables were put together with boards, boxes, and sawhorses. Plank seats were covered with blankets so all could sit down together. Food and drinks were shared along with news of the family. Horse-and-buggy transportation brought picnickers to woodland campgrounds, back pastures, or lakefront beaches for gatherings. Horseshoes, volleyball, and other games became part of the fun at picnics. One of the big events involved a giant watermelon—a real treat in early days. Often, a seed-spitting contest soon followed. Family reunions were also appropriate events to celebrate the birthdays of the oldest family members.

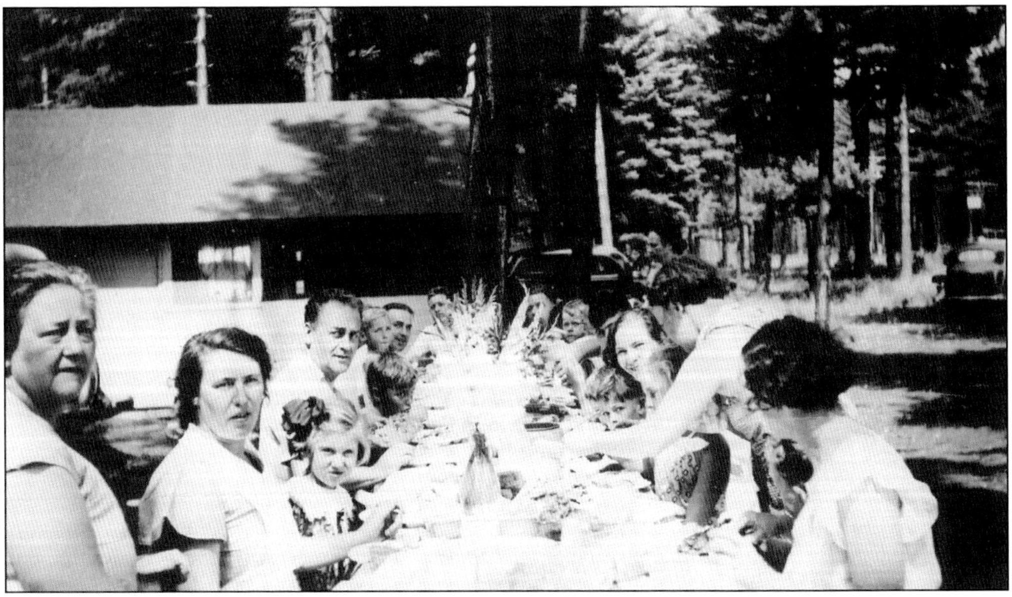

Visitors to the Adirondacks who stayed in big hotels spent many hours in lobbies. Hotels offered newspapers and telephone lines keepers to keep businessmen connected with the outside world. Writing desks were lined up where tourists could compose letters and send postcards to all their friends and relatives back home.

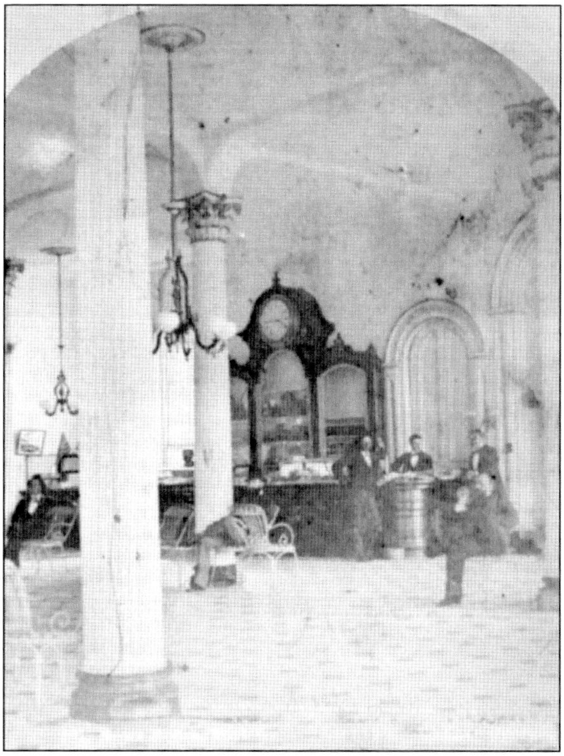

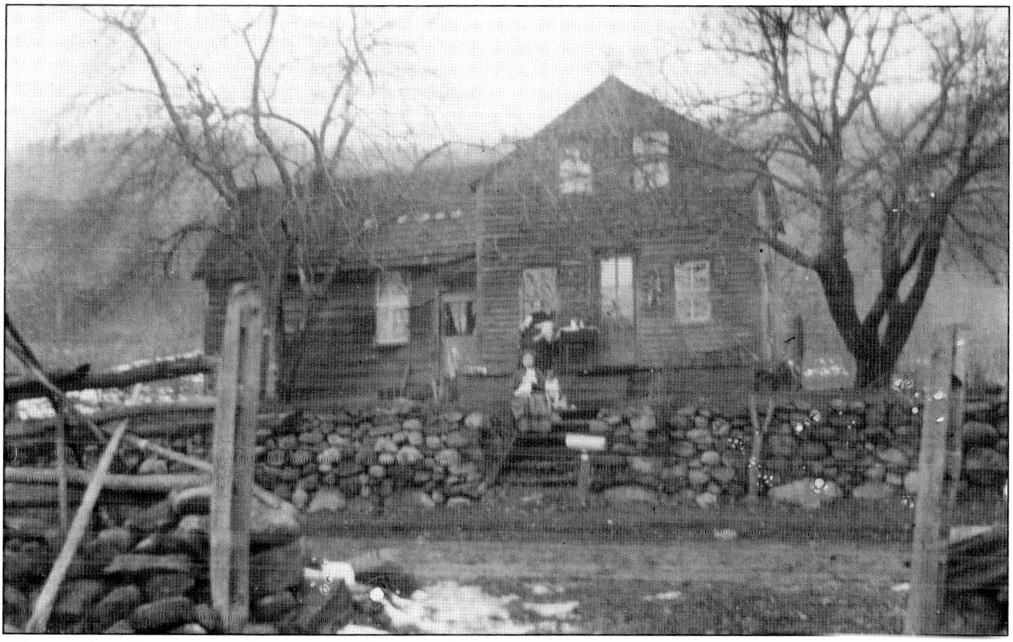

Those who chose to settle in the Adirondacks after the first wave of the log cabins built substantial, yet simple, clapboarded houses. Lumber sawed in the local sawmill and shingles banged out of local log chunks with a froe and mallet were readily available construction materials. The owner of the home shown here called it "our old hut!" Later, some Adirondackers purchased ready-made homes from Sears, Roebuck and Company.

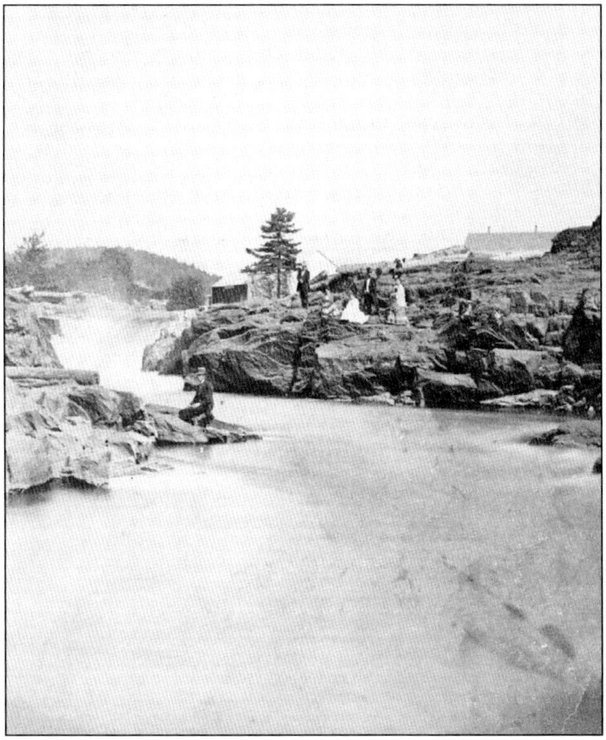

Communing with nature was a part of life before the days of radio, television, and other distractions that kept people indoors. The well-dressed men and women in the photograph are spending the afternoon at Luzerne Falls, one of the many dams in the area.

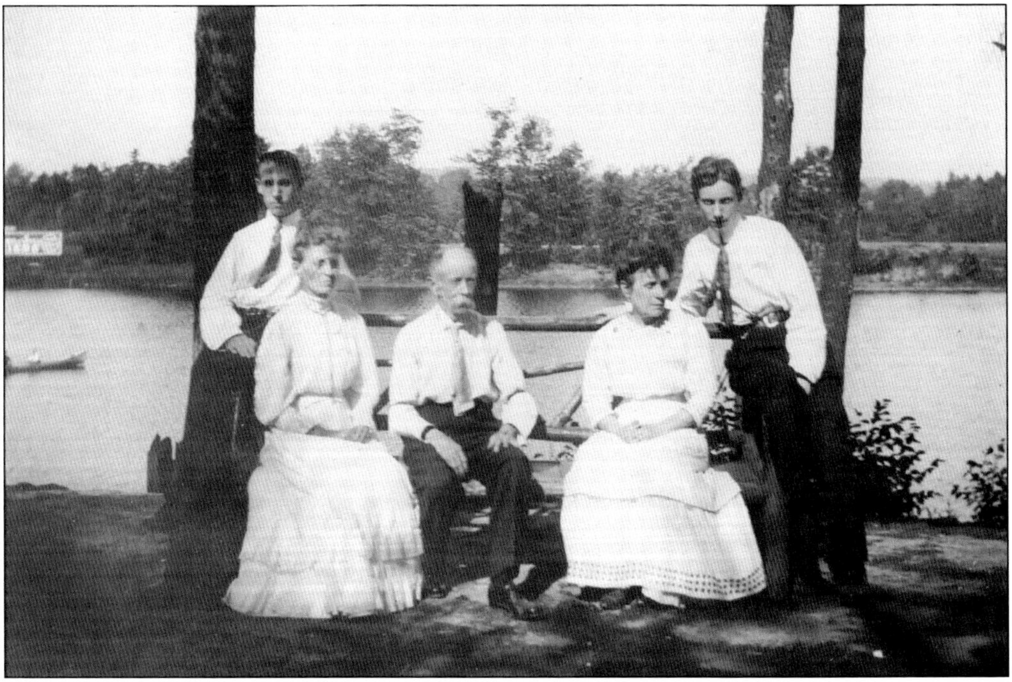

Another pastime, especially enjoyed by the elderly in the Adirondacks, was to spend an afternoon relaxing on a lakeshore. The breezes from the lake and good conversation with friends and relatives tapped into the "health-giving" features of the Adirondacks. Some believed that the pine-scented air had curative powers.

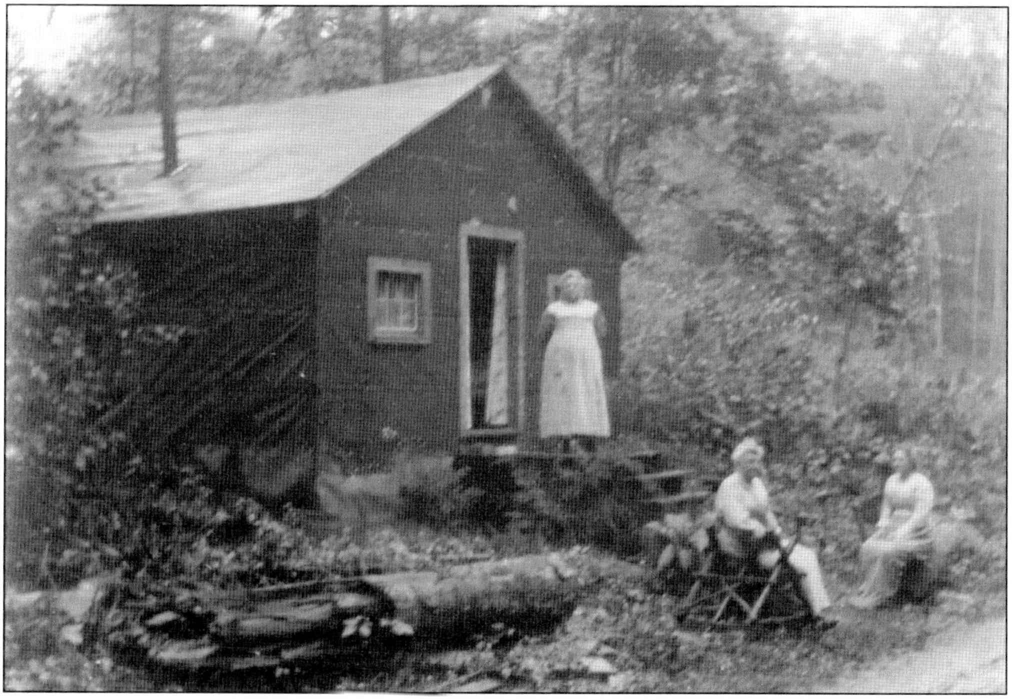

Those who wanted to "get away from it all" could rent or build a remote cabin in Adirondack backcountry. The folks shown here are enjoying some time at a non-pretentious cabin without a lawn to mow or garden a to weed. The stovepipe protruding from the tar-papered roof indicates a small stove for cooking and heating.

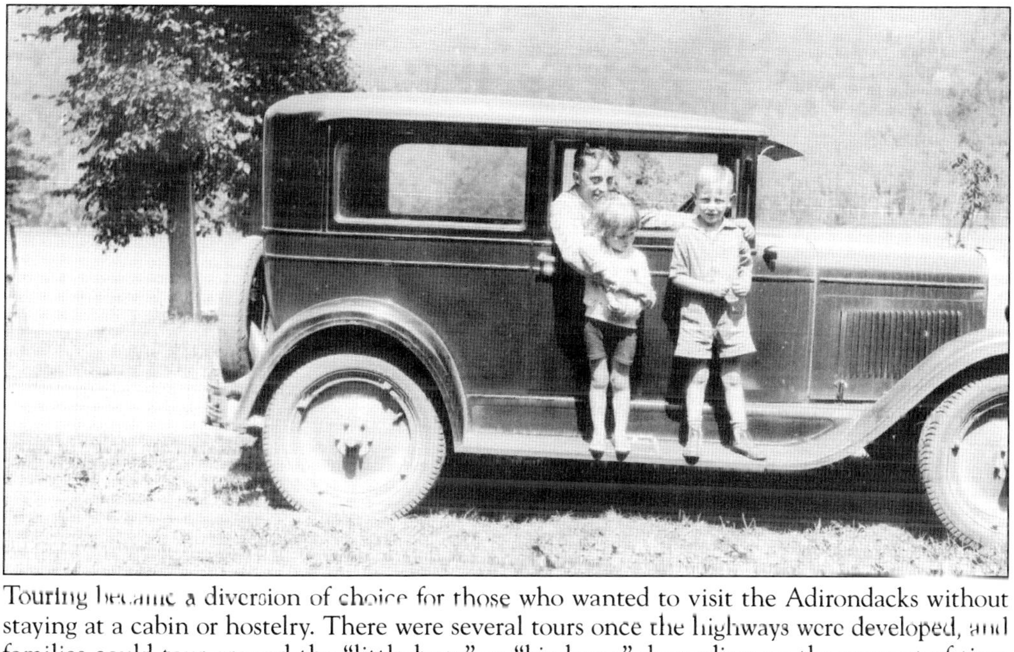

Touring became a diversion of choice for those who wanted to visit the Adirondacks without staying at a cabin or hostelry. There were several tours once the highways were developed, and families could tour around the "little horn" or "big horn," depending on the amount of time available. Auto associations were organized, books were printed, and touring became big business in the Adirondacks.

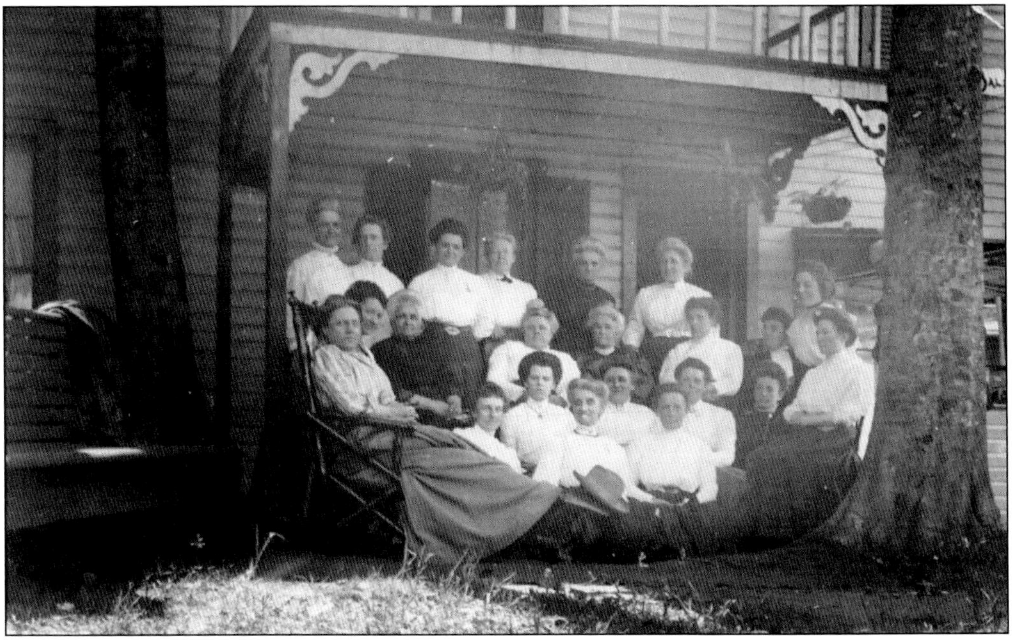

Ladies clubs and organizations could be found throughout the Adirondacks, providing good service and activities for many. Daughters of the American Revolution (DAR), Order of the Eastern Star, women in the foresters, women's groups in all the churches, auxiliaries of the volunteer fire companies and other men's groups, Girl Scout leaders, and others kept the remote communities together.

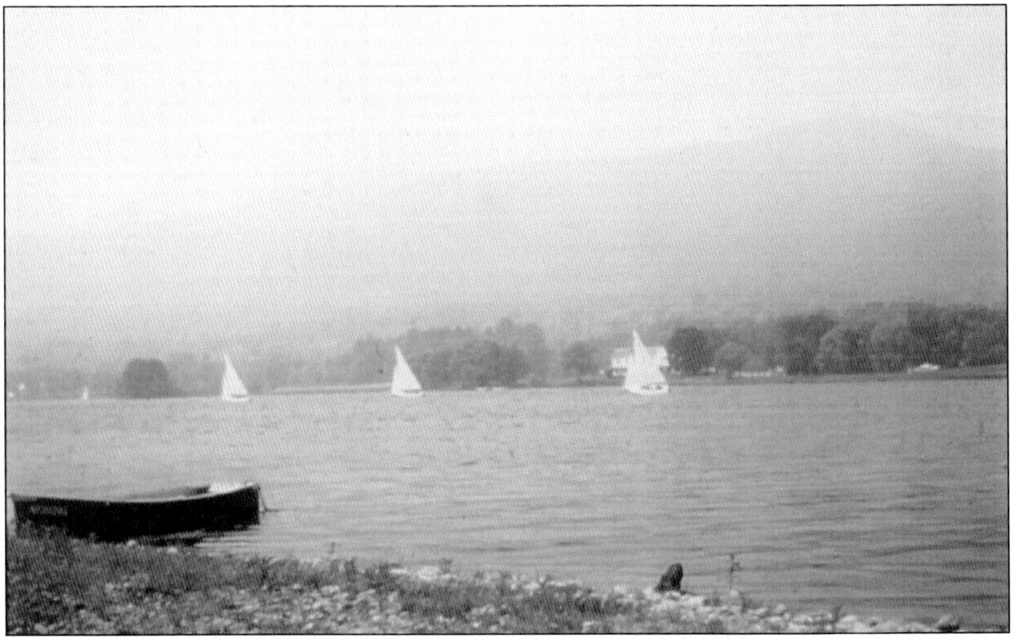

Sailors welcomed the Adirondacks, with their calm waters and gentle breezes. Sailing clubs spent good weather on the lakes. Several sailing events are scheduled throughout the summer. St. Regis has a long history of sailing races, and other lakes hold yearly regattas. Some lakes do not allow motorized boats and make for particularly good sailing.

When young Adirondack boys are not playing marbles or mumblety-peg with their jackknives, they are riding three-wheeled bicycles or tricycles. Highways and village streets were not busy with crowded traffic, making it a safe activity for young children. Peddling the bicycles of that day was good exercise. Some surely enjoyed ringing the bell that was typically fastened on the handlebars.

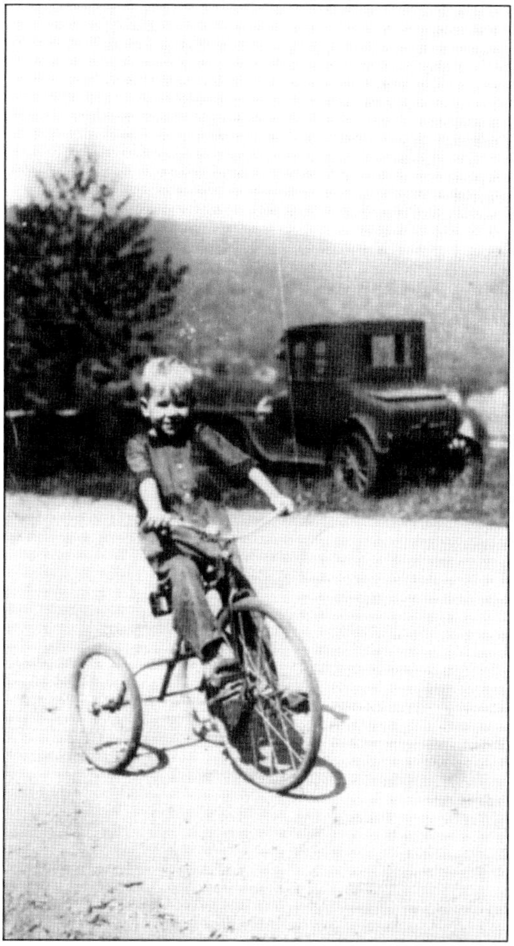

The Adirondacks were a great place for horse lovers. Most families had horses, and young children spent many hours traversing Adirondack country on horseback. One young trapper used his horse to travel his trapline, saving time and a long walk.

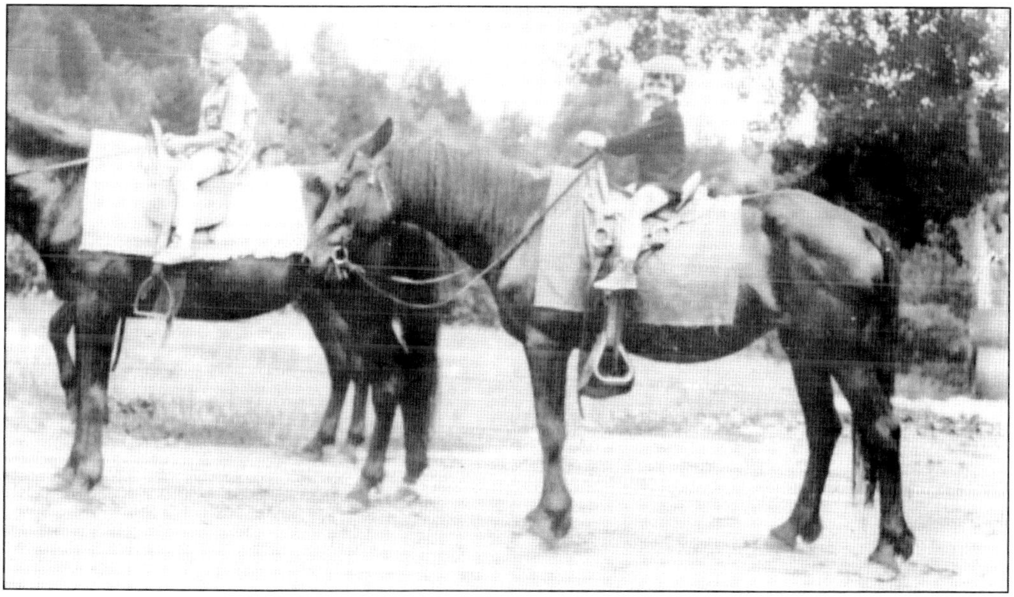

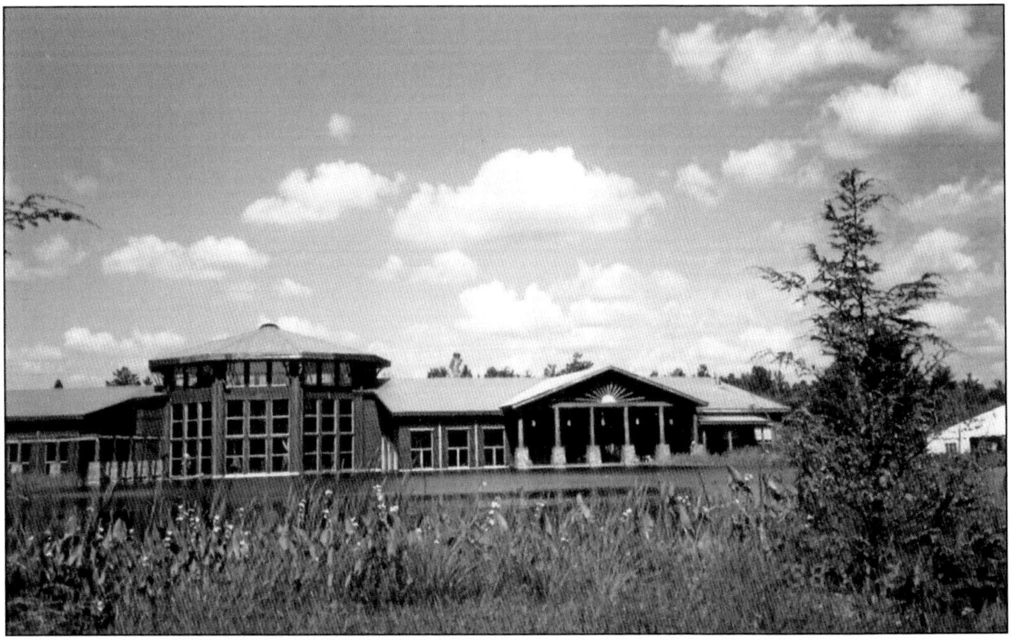

The Wild Center Museum of Natural History at Tupper Lake is a place to return to time and time again. The live animals, historical exhibits, programs, and lectures combine to bring the Adirondacks to life. Open year-round, it is a warm place to be on winter Fridays, Saturdays, and Sundays and offers a full schedule in the summer.

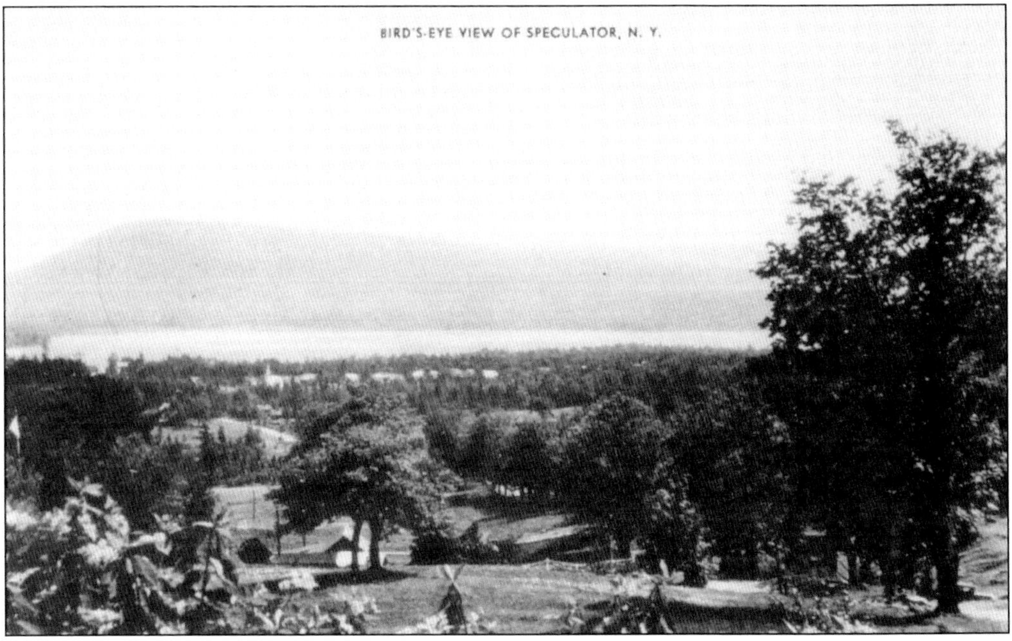

Times have changed in the Adirondacks, and the old ways are mostly gone. The original view of Speculator from Old Page Hill was similar to the view in this photograph; today, the trees have grown and have blocked the vista once again. Hunters returning from the hunt on the dirt road to Indian Lake often joked about not being able to see a caterpillar crawling up that church steeple, but they could hear him walking!

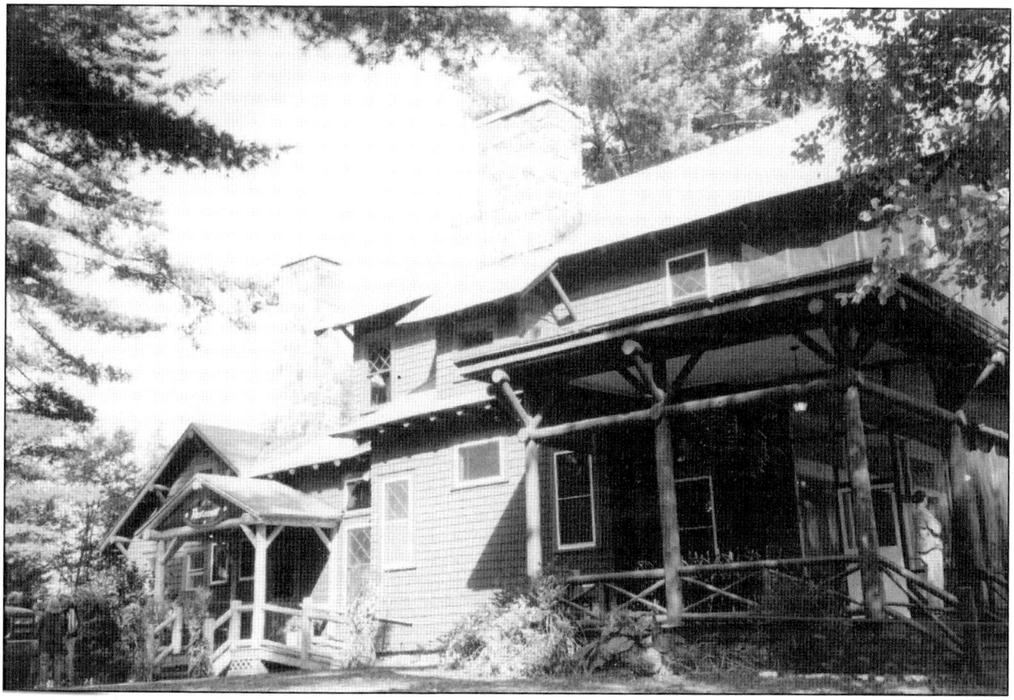

Much of the Adirondacks of yesteryear is being lost to fires and the wrecking ball. Buildings on lakefronts are razed so that new ones can take their place. The fire shown here destroyed an old Adirondack mill, and the log building Wawbeek is no longer standing. The Adirondack Architectural Heritage Association has done much to preserve some of the valuable buildings of the past, but each year it prints a list of endangered buildings, much as there are lists of endangered animals. The author's book *Adirondack Hotel and Inns* is filled with photographs of hostelries that have burned or have been torn down. Publishing the vintage photographs in books is one way to preserve some of the Adirondack heritage.

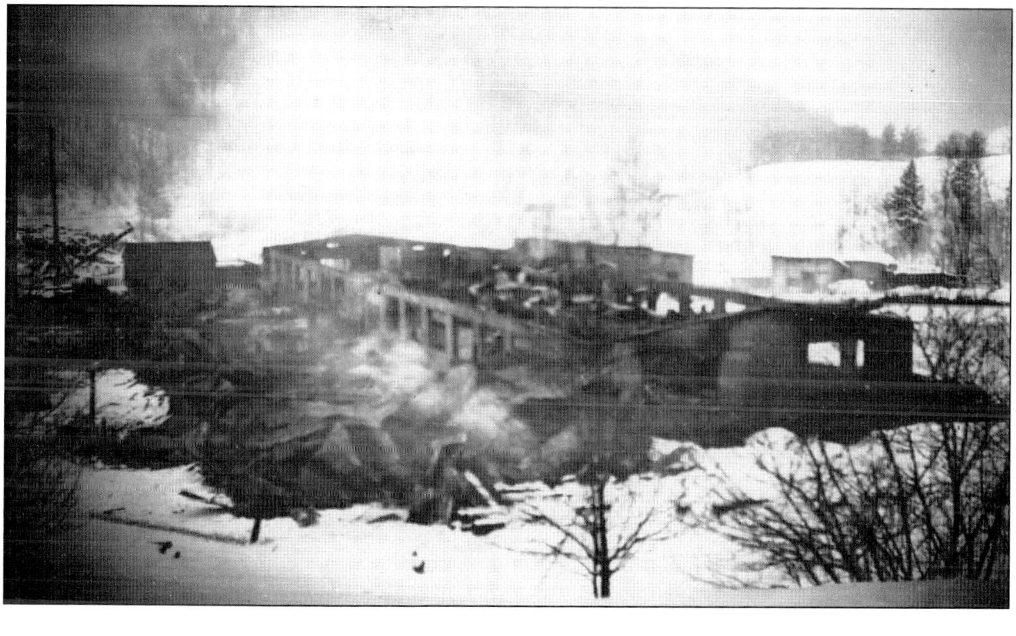

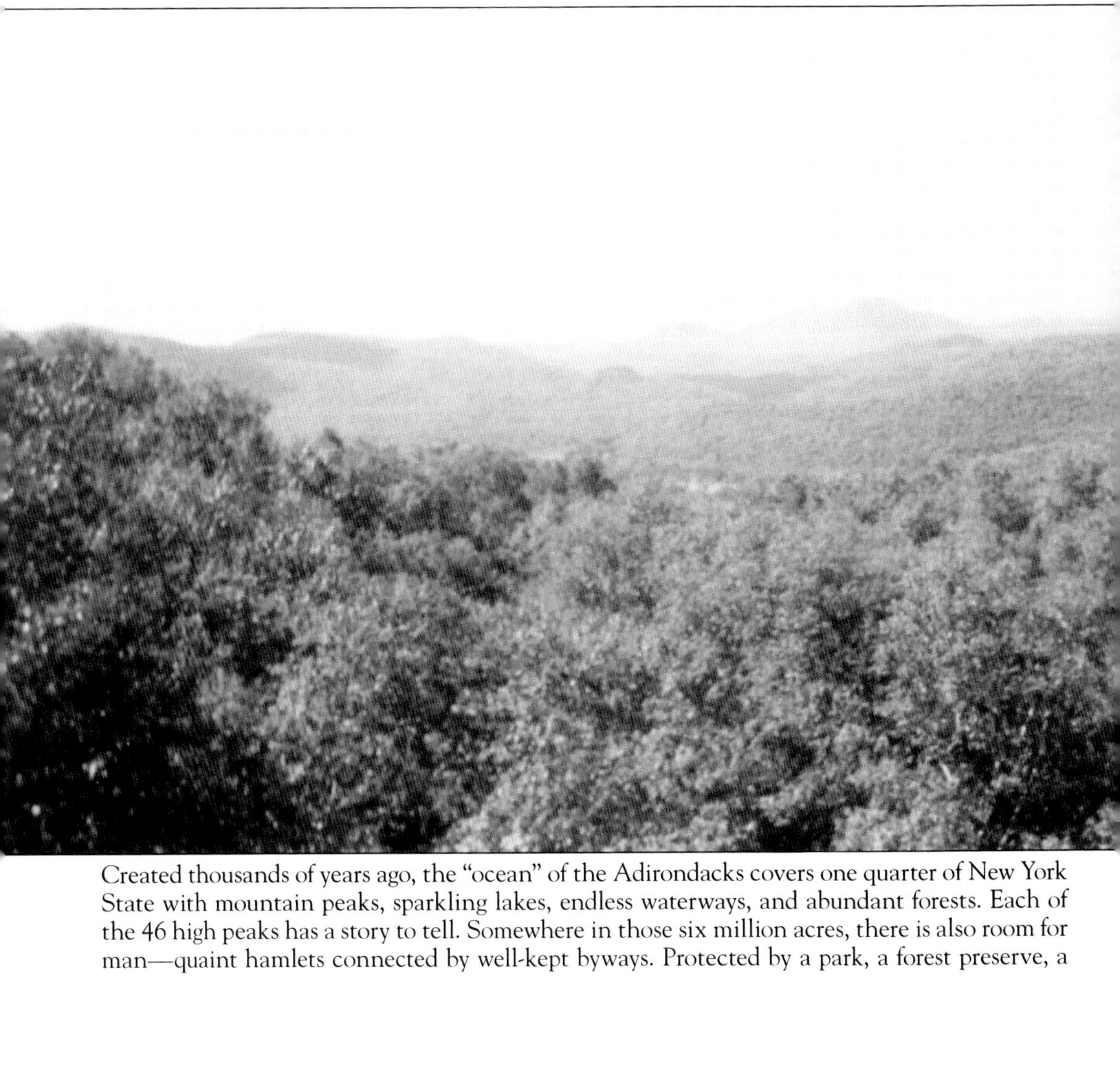

Created thousands of years ago, the "ocean" of the Adirondacks covers one quarter of New York State with mountain peaks, sparkling lakes, endless waterways, and abundant forests. Each of the 46 high peaks has a story to tell. Somewhere in those six million acres, there is also room for man—quaint hamlets connected by well-kept byways. Protected by a park, a forest preserve, a

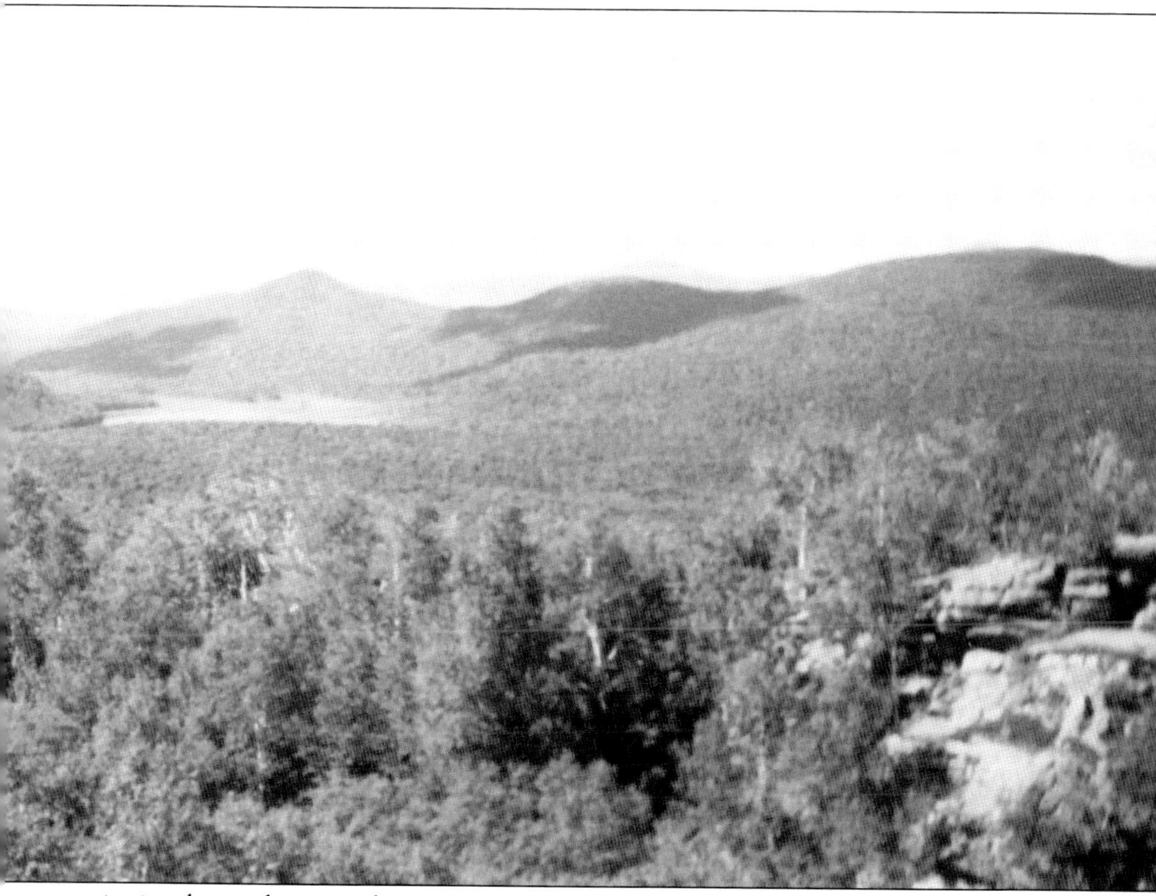

constitutional amendment, and a state agency, the Adirondacks, with the public's best wisdom, should be here for years to come—a home for the fish, birds, and animals, a refuge for mankind from the stress of living in a modern world, and a place where nature can thrive to its fullest.